AESCULAPIUS
Greek God of Medicine

By courtesy of The Wellcome Museum of Medicine

MEDICINAL PLANTS and THEIR HISTORY

EDITH GREY WHEELWRIGHT

Illustrated by photographs,
and sketches by Ethel M. Barlow

'Herbs gladly cure our flesh, because they
 Find their acquaintance there.'

'More servants wait on man
Than he'll take notice of. In every path
He treads down that which doth befriend him
When sickness makes him pale and wan.
O mighty love! Man is one world, and hath
 Another to attend him'
George Herbert

DOVER PUBLICATIONS, INC., NEW YORK

This Dover edition, first published in 1974, is an unabridged and unaltered republication of the work originally published by Houghton Mifflin Company, Boston & New York, in 1935 under the title *The Physick Garden: Medicinal Plants and their History*.

International Standard Book Number: 0-486-23103-8
Library of Congress Catalog Card Number: 74-78815

Manufactured in the United States of America
Dover Publications, Inc.
180 Varick Street
New York, N.Y. 10014

CONTENTS

ILLUSTRATIONS

To 'Beatrix Potter'
in memory of the summer when
I found the Grass of Parnassus
on the mountain side, and we dried
the foxglove leaves in her barn

INTRODUCTION

CARDINAL NEWMAN once asked a question which has often occurred to others. 'Who,' he said, 'first discovered the wild herbs which from ancient times have been our resource in illness?' The question, although in a sense unanswerable, is not an idle one, for we have at least deciphered an ancient and heritable body of tradition existing in all the races of mankind so far as they are known. Travellers at the present day constantly report that primitive people use remedies of traditional value many of which have been adopted by the white man and attested by his science. To form a coherent picture of such remedies and their history may well be deemed an impossible task; so prodigious in fact, that any reader of this book will inevitably be reminded of the saying about the fools who rush in unwarily. For the story of man's healing tradition belongs to history; the cultivation of drug plants to agriculture; the portrayal of them to art, and the written records of that art to literature. In all departments of knowledge to-day we incline to specification, because of the multitude of allied subjects which crowd in upon our view. Perhaps one day the long association between man and his healing plants may be told in one comprehensive whole by a Master. Meanwhile, the present book, as will readily be seen, is no more than a student's excursion into certain aspects of the subject; and only the fascination of the quest can be urged in defence of such temerity.

With the usual kindness of workers in science, several experts have aided me at various stages in the adventure.

Particularly am I indebted to Dr. Charles Singer for his encouragement at the beginning, and for his advice in respect of Chapter v. To Dr. Macgregor Skene of the Botany Department in Bristol University I am also much indebted for his revision of Chapter x; and my thanks are due to M. Em. Perrot, Professor of Materia Medica in the University of Paris, for the literature bearing upon his own work, and for his kindness in reading Chapter VIII.

Mr. H. Stanley Redgrove's kind help in the thorough revision

9

of the parts dealing with classification and pharmacology has been indispensable to the production of the work as a whole.

The literature bearing upon all the interrelated subjects of this quest is voluminous. Sir James Frazer's work, *The Golden Bough* has long been a standard book dealing with primitive magic and ritual. It has not been replaced by any other, though a more modern treatment of the subject of origins will be found in Father Schmidt's book *The Origin and Growth of Religions* and in *Sacraments of Simple Folk* by Dr. Marett, Rector of Exeter College, Oxford. In a small book, *The Dawn of History*, by the late Professor Myres, the early movements of the races across Asia are dealt with in a picturesque narrative, and Dr. Clemow's *Geography of Disease* covers some of the same ground from a different standpoint.

Several modern writers have devoted themselves to the history of medicine as a whole. Among the standard works are those by Dr. Charles Singer, Sir William Osler, and Messrs. Stubbs and Bligh. The Anglo-Saxon period and the early European herbals form the subject of Dr. Singer's fascinating and beautifully illustrated book, *From Magic to Science*. A comprehensive study of English herbal literature has been given us by Miss Eleanour Sinclair Rohde in her book, *The Old English Herbals;* and there is a delightful book[1] on medieval botanists by Dr. Gunther of Magdalen College, Oxford, who has also recently published a translation of Dioscorides.

The history of pharmacy has been told in Wootton's *Chronicles*, and in Lewis' *History of Materia Medica.*

For the early history of the Pharmaceutical Society of Great Britain we may still consult the volume published by Bell and Redwood in 1880 entitled *Historical Sketch of the Progress of Pharmacy in Great Britain.*

The literature of pharmacology is, of course, only for students. The tide of specialization that has overtaken us has carried this subject as well as bio-chemistry beyond the grasp of the ordinary reader. Yet it is now impossible to touch the subject of plant phyisology upon which our pharmacy rests without reference to this department of research, in which work is always sweeping forward with

[1] Early Medical science.

results which, from the botanist's point of view, are enriching the glamour of the world. Some idea of the high specialization attained in these subjects is given by such books as Armstrong's work on *The Glucosides*, and Professor Dixon's *Manual of Pharmacy*. Works on materia medica deal with the drug plant in relation to its remedial use. In this branch again there is a large literature. Still indispensable to the student as older works of reference are Jonathan Periera's text book, and the later one by Flückiger and Hanbury.

Bentley and Trimen's *Medicinal Plants* published in four volumes in 1880 remains a classic and has not been replaced. Other modern works on materia medica are those of Professor Greenish and Dr. Mitchell Bruce.

Henslow's *The Uses of British Plants* makes a useful little manual for general readers, and the *Guides to the Museum of Economic Botany* published by the authorities at Kew contain much useful and up-to-date information.

Many gardeners are interested in the growing and preparation of sweet and medicinal herbs on a small scale. They will find a most able adviser in Mrs. Grieve of Whins Cottage, Chalfont St. Peter, Bucks. Her numerous pamphlets on lavender, dill, etc., are cheap and practical, and her *Modern Herbal*, published by Jonathan Cape in 1929, is a veritable *vade mecum* for all who are studying the subject medically and historically.

Interesting work has been done since the war in cultivation and research on the Continent. Several brochures dealing with this branch of the subject have been issued by the Comité Interministériel des Plantes Medicinales in Paris, and can be obtained from the Office National des Matières Premières at 12, Avenue du Maine, Paris. The story of the French enterprises in this direction is well worth reading.

As to the 'herbs of grace' for many centuries so beloved in our English gardens, they too have a literature of their own. A particularly delightful work is *A Garden of Herbs* by Miss Eleanour Sinclair Rohde in which she deals with the cultivation of the plants, the charm of the gardens, and the fascinating recipes used by our great grandmothers in the seventeenth and eighteenth centuries. Most of these herbs contain the essential oils of commerce and pharmacy; and here again we have a highly specialized subject demanding its special literature. Mr. H. S. Redgrove's books, *Scent and All About It*, and *Spices and Condiments* are indispensable to students of this branch. They show that the volatile oils enter by many avenues into modern life, ministering to health as well as to luxury, while the trade in them is as brisk to-day as it ever was in past ages when the caravans plied to and fro across the desert margin between Egypt and Babylonia.

Nor are the essential oils and spices only used in pharmacy: they are required by soap makers, confectioners, dyers, perfumers and even by artists and colourmen. In fact, the medicinal plant trade is a peculiar one, with unexpected ramifications.

The industry however, was not the theme which, when lecturing up and down the country I always found to be the most certain to evoke the public interest. It is, after all, the 'herb of grace' with its gift of health and healing which speaks to the heart of the English countryside. This homely speech is a link still binding us to mediævalism, for the herbal remedy is largely derived from the women of the Middle Ages — mostly of the landed class in England — who were trained in simple medicine and who had to minister to their wounded knights and husbands in places where no doctor could be found. The literature of the fourteenth century included some treatises for the use of these amateur physicians, and many of the herbs which they used both here and on the Continent have been approved by science.

This is what may be called the picturesque side of the subject, and many will feel that it was worthy of better treatment in the present book. Yet it was felt that there were other more pressing considerations based upon the wonder and interest of the plant itself in its countless reactions. For all civilization is built up upon the relation between man and the plants which enter into every human activity, giving us food, clothing, and fuel: they were the beginning of the progressive life of the world, and remain the background of all human organizations. In our own day vitamins have become

INTRODUCTION

common coin in language and commerce, but the word implies the organic life whose full meaning remains a mystery even while its physical basis is known. Considerations such as these impelled me to include in the book the scientific as well as the historical aspects of man and medicine. I can only hope that this necessarily popularized treatment may be pardoned by the expert, and may yield some points of interest to meet the catholic tastes of the general reader.

E. G. W.

CLEVEDON

ABREVIATIONS

B.P. The British Pharmacopoeia.
B.P. Codex. (The British Pharmaceutical Codex; The companion
   work to the B.P.)
U.S.P. United Stated Pharmacopoeia — Xth Revision.
N.O. In botany the 'Natural Order' which comprises those plants
   which have similar structure.

GLOSSARY OF
TERMS USED IN MEDICAL PRACTICE

Alterative. Altering the course of a disease or correcting an un-
   healthy function. (Mode of action said to be unknown.)
Analgesic. Diminishing pain.
Anthelmintic. A drug which kills the parasites of the intestinal
   tract.
Anti-pyretic. Causing the fall of the body temperature in fever.
Anti-spasmodic. Relieving spasm by the action of the muscular coat
   of the bronchial tubes.
Carminative. Relieving flatulence.
Cathartic. A purge.
Cholagogue. Increasing the flow of bile.
Demulcent. Soothing the skin or mucous membranes.
Diaphoretic. Inducing perspiration. Sudorific.
Hypnotic. Sleep producing without causing cerebral excitement.
Narcotic. Producing diminution of mental activity tending towards
   unconsciousness, and depressing the functions of respira-
   tion and circulation.
Styptic. Arresting bleeding.
Tonic. Increasing muscular tone.
Vermicide. A drug that kills entozoa.
Vermifuge. A drug given later to expel the worm.

GLOSSARY

Vulnerary. For the cure of external wounds.

NOTE. The word 'official' denotes a remedy included in the British Pharmacopoeia or Codex as distinct from those used by herbalists or homoeopaths. 'Officinalis' as a specific name of a plant signifies that it was at some time used in medicine.

PRE-HISTORY
AND EARLY AGRICULTURAL RITES

CLIMATIC INFLUENCES AND
MIGRATIONS

DISEASE AMONG PRIMITIVE RACES

POISONOUS PLANTS

A MEDICINE-MAN OF RHODESIA

From the model in The Wellcome Museum of Medicine, by kind permission of the authorities

No aspect of human development from the age of the mammoth to that of machines is more instructive than the history of medicine. The whole story can never be known ; its origins belong to the prehistoric days when our palæolithic ancestors, like the modern Tasmanian, lighted his fire by a fire-drill, or made it by rubbing together two bits of iron pyrites or even two pieces of oak. Yet such fragmentary relics of pre-history as we possess are by no means without significance. All over the world death has preserved the records of life, whether in dark immemorial caverns, or in perishing earthworks, or in sepulchres and cities long buried under lava or sand.

These records, especially the oldest, when studied in connection with such primitive cultures as still exist, show us how from the beginning the rudiments of the healing art were linked with the contemporary inchoate material of religion. Both were the outcome of collective desires and necessities preyed upon by fear and issuing in an emotion easily convertible into belief. Both in their successive stages were associated with agriculture: the Earth Mother, the Goddess of Fertility and the God of Healing belong to the stratum of primal beliefs. At the back of these, a vista, immeasurably remote, portrays our earliest ancestors as nomads and hunters not yet evolved into the shepherding or agricultural stage. Their rudely worked flints have been found in the plateau gravels and alluvial deposits of the Pleistocene period, contemporaneous with the cave bear, rhinoceros and bison. The pre-history of man, in so far as we have deciphered it in its European origins, begins with the caves. In these converted lairs, we find traces of the successive races of mankind, from the inarticulate and brutish to the advancing types whose drawings showed the emergence of a rudimentary culture.

Both in Europe and in North America we have many such traces of Magdalenian man. In the Dordogne caverns of France, and in those of Pindal in north-west Spain, we find bold drawings in black or red ochre drawn with remarkable accuracy. One can but gaze at them with awe and wonder, seeing that here, at the very threshold of human history, had emerged the first stirrings of the imitative, imaginative faculty which has been man's blessing, or occasionally, his curse. Not that the rudimentary art of the cave men can in itself throw any light upon the origin of medicine, but other remains have been found bearing more directly upon the subject. For instance, we have found at least one clay image of an animal with a dart piercing its breast: it may well be the world's earliest sculpture. We have also from a cave at Antiège a drawing, half man, half animal. In these relics we have the beginnings of a 'cult', the confused origin of the magic which as we shall see, has for ages accompanied the development of medicine, religion and art. Its roots lay in man's powerlessness against the natural phenomena of his unintelligible world, and in his realized necessity for the capture of his food. The clay bison shows us the savage working out upon it the consummation of his desire: in this manner, with such a weapon will he slay his quarry and obtain his meal. Again, the Animal Guardian-spirit idea was linked with these manifestations. The cave dwelling became in a sense a sanctuary, and primitive man was, as many backward races are still, the celebrant in an early totemic ritual.

It is probable that, while our hunting ancestors of the post-glacial age applied themselves to magical ritual in the capture of their food, they may also have originated the corresponding rites which are everywhere associated with primitive medicine and relief from bodily pain. In all native races to-day we find simple remedies combined with, or rather, complicated by, the use of ritual. Tribal magic, as it persists in the present age, is still allied to the gratification of some natural desire and is thus a recapitulation of man's history; but in considering its origin we must always remember the two dominant factors in the lives of our neolithic ancestors: first, the precariousness of his food supply which depended upon the capture of the lower animals, and secondly, his insecurity in the face of terrifying events like flood and earthquake, eclipse or storm.

It is difficult for us in our hardly won security to picture these perilous lives surrounded by natural forces whose origin and meaning were unknown. Anthropologists in the past have no doubt over-estimated the part played by fear in the growth of religion : nevertheless we have a great deal of scattered evidence testifying to its influence in the primitive cults. That the world order should be conceived of as unstable was intelligible enough, and occasionally it might be envisaged as actively hostile. 'Something was here for tears', — much more for distrust. For not only was the earth smitten through unforeseen disasters, but man himself was more grievously smitten by attacks from the lower animals, from the insect world, from accident, and — as relics from times undated lead us to infer — from disease and pestilence. Bewildered references to 'strange diseases of the head' come to us from Chaldea. 'No one knew whence they came or what was their object', but the Chaldeans did know that there was a demon of the south-west wind; that wind that ravaged their country from the Arabian deserts, and who could tell in what other direction his malevolence might work?

The personification of such doubtful agencies was natural to the human mind. A vast Pantheon of such agencies can be collected from all over the world. Survivals of animism persist in various forms at the present day. The godlings of the streams and rivers have lingered on in the underworld of 'the little people' who often exist quite harmlessly and poetically as fairies and elves. Sacred stones, carrying associations both good and evil, have abounded in the history of many an ancient race. Thus, the stones of the Temple of Heaven in Pekin have long guarded the Emperor's fortunes, and superstition still lingers round the Lia Fail or Stone of Destiny upon which Jacob, in the Hebrew story, was said to have slept. The Melanesians bury a stone near their bread-fruit trees to ensure their fruitfulness.

THE MEDICINE MAN

From this motley riot of personification it was not far to the next step in neolithic tribal custom, the idea of placating the Unknown.

It is at this stage that the Medicine Man emerges, and he is a most important and interesting figure, because in him we can trace the origin of a group of ideas which link the uncharted region of prehistory with the succeeding ages. That he belongs to history is clear from the early records of all primitive races, while the masked and terrifying figures shown in the Wellcome Museum of Medicine attest to his survival in modern times. He represents the old magical side in therapeutics, the practical side being the use of simple remedies such as exist in all primitive cultures and are mostly of vegetable origin. Mr. W. E. Roth, the Protector of the Aborigines in Northern Australia, tells us of forty-two herbal remedies that are in use, genuine remedies culled from the native flora; but in cases where the 'popular medicine' fails, the Medicine Man is called in to scare away with ear-splitting noise or incantation the demon of the disease.

He was the product of the tragic community belief that accident or illness came from 'the abyss' and was due to the anger of a shadowy underworld. His business at this stage was not so much to heal the sufferer as to release him from evil influence; and this was done by a sort of flamboyant exaggeration of fury calculated to put the fear of Hades into the demon. There were various ideas about these demonic agencies. A sense of the 'numinous', as it is called, invested the whole unseen world with power and purpose, but it was also thought that dead men might still be lurking somewhere, jealous of the living and inclined to do them damage. The Medicine Man, by a species of magic, undertook to drive away evil in either shape by doing in his own person what he wished some superior force to do. In working out such an idea it was natural that he should have vivified and developed it: from out of the primitive tangle he drew shapes and images, for every cult more or less creates the thing which it set out to worship. Gradually he acquired what the anthropologists call 'mana', that power and prestige by which later on, when ritual was more complicated, he drew into himself the vitality of a bull or other sacred animal. He thus became invested with a halo of veneration which at length endowed him with the priestly role.

It would be unfair, however, to this ancient and picturesque figure to suggest that his function was limited to magical exorcism. At the very beginnings of such primitive leech-craft as we are able to discover, we find that mixture of common sense blended with intuition that has often characterized the therapeusis of an early race. In addition to the use of the medicinal plants of the district, we know that such practices as bleeding, fumigation, poulticing and rubbing are of immense antiquity. So is urtication. The name comes from *Urtica*, a nettle. To the Natural Order, *Urticacae*, our native Stinging Nettle and a good many shrubby plants of the East Indies belong. All have a stinging acrid juice in their glands relatively innocent in our own *Urtica dioica*, Linn., but producing violent effects in some of the foreign species, especially in *Urtica pathulata*, Sm. In cases of palsy or paralysis, the unfortunate patient was switched with a bunch of these nettles; and the custom persisted into the Middle Ages where it was adopted in lighter cases as a counter irritant. Indeed, it exists among the Malayans at the present day.

EARLY AGRICULTURAL RITES

The newer school of 'geographical' historians are stressing the connection between racial movements and climate. We infer that the Magdalenian hunters vanished from Europe together with their quarry when, at the close of the Ice Age, a damp, mild climate more favourable to forests and vegetation spread over the land. We know too that the human race has witnessed vast changes in the relative position of land and water. Man roamed across the plateau heart of Asia Minor when the low lying country round the Aral and Caspian seas formed part of the ocean. The heterogenous cultural conditions which mark the Neolithic age reflect these changes and migrations just as the bone scratchings show us the typical fauna both of the north and south. Again, the nomadic life was one of constant movements conditioned by the grazing animals in their quest for food. Nor did this type of existence give place everywhere to the agricultural type: it lasted on. Professor Ellis Minns has taught us much about the decorative art of the nomads who inhabited the steppes or pasture land between Mongolia and Hungary, showing that their work in gold, electrum, or bronze, bearing traces of Eastern origin, and spreading through Hungary into Europe, had its influence even in the Middle Ages.

As to the early agricultural civilizations in Europe, we find them largely dominated by the cult of the Mother Goddess and her son, this being associated with an ancient ritual based, like the magic of the cave dweller, upon the old tribal emotion connected with food. The tilling of the soil meant a stationary population, and must have led to a stage of social unity in which daily life became more specialized; and yet it was by no means more secure. The story of Man's dependence upon the periodic pulsations of climate is told in a thousand early invocations. He knew that the same sun that ripened his crops in one season scorched them in the next; and that the streams that irrigated his valleys might either withhold their gift of waters or might exceed them in devastating flood. This agricultural stage, depending upon the right relation then beginning to be apprehended between the sun and the earth inaugurated a most important new stage in human evolution. The intense emotion that symbolized the seed, the sun, and the harvest in a cycle of orgiastic ceremonies now drew down the unseen world into the plant rather than the animal. Corn spirits and maize spirits were personified, while the Medicine Man's function, no longer confined to disease and demonic possession, became extended into a further field of magic, the control of thunder and rain.

It may be said that the agricultural rites of early communities have no direct bearing upon the healing art, and therefore have no real place in this inquiry. Nevertheless, they are so essentially a part of our ancestral inheritance that it seems impossible to ignore them in any study, whether of religion, medicine or art, since in the early stages the three were intertwined. World wide was the ritual of the Mother Goddess and her son. Equally wide spread was the idea that the God died each year, passing to the land of death while life ceased upon the earth in his absence. Often he was the Sun God, and appropriately in many cases he became the God of Healing.

Tacitus mentions the Great Mother who was worshipped by the Aryans. The Hittites who so greatly influenced the ancient world had a God of Vegetation as well. The Greeks had Dionysus, and Demeter, one of the many Corn Goddesses. The dramatic ritual that was born out of the earth cycle rose from it by necessity, if we may use the word as Robert Bridges used it in his phrase 'the necessity of poetry', and we can the better understand it because it is functioning still.

In Australia until very recently there have been extraordinary food-producing ceremonies which had all the emotional intensity of primitive magic. In the country which was Transylvania there was also a modernized seasonal festival of life and death which, as Miss Harrison has shown, was directly traceable to the old vegetative rites. In modern Ceylon, the rice sowing and harvesting is still linked up with superstitious ceremonies.

Many other instances abound in the pages of *The Golden Bough*. Sir James Frazer tells us that in Russia, Macedonia, and Swabia food rituals are commonly performed. The peasants will often leap high into the air to encourage their hemp or other crop to grow tall. In the early totemic societies the emphasis was laid on the production and prosperity of the crop. A magical co-operation with the source of the food supply passed through ceremonial into religion which fostered a sacramental conception and a growing sense of gratitude to the beneficent plants themselves. The magical dance and song which were the outcome of these vegetative festivals was seized upon by the genius of the Greeks in the phrase χρορεύει ὁ κόσμος, the universe is rhythmic, or in Professor Gilbert Murray's lovely rendering, 'The universe treads a measure'. In the first millennium, B.C., Euripides immortalized for all time in the Bacchae one of these wild and poignant rites.

Out of the same pervading concern of man with his food and with the ordinary cares and personal desires of daily life, there grew up also an elemental system of divination. On the religious side, the 'numinous' sense produced the Mysteries with their attendant initiations, needing the co-operation of a Priest or Priestess, but the matter of divination could be left to the lower order of sorcerers and soothsayers which, at least in Chaldea, had by 2000 B.C., grown to large proportions. Divinations were generally made from examination of an animal's liver, excellent models of which were fashioned of clay with divination texts inscribed on them. The practice of making an image of an afflicted region such as the eye or ear and offering it to the God of Healing began in this way and lasted for centuries. Indeed, in some Catholic countries to-day, the peasant will dedicate such a model to his patron saint in supplication. The superstition as well as the valour of our ancestors has been settled upon the race.

PRIMITIVE RACES AND DISEASE

The question naturally arises as to the evidence, if any, of special physical ills from which early races suffered. Were they immune from the illnesses that afflict us now, or has disease been present in similar forms all through human history? The question is closely related to the geography of disease, and has been dealt with by Dr. Clemow in the work which bears this title.

Such evidence as we possess leads us to infer that as man was broken in from the nomadic stage to that of settled habitation, he naturally tended to settle where soil and climate combined to favour a quick return for his toil. We know that the yellow race has from times undated inhabited the central part of Eurasia. China attracted population by its fertile plains and rich soil supplied by rivers from the Tibetan plateau. Dravidian India owed its population from immemorial times to the 'water carrier and fertilizer', the river Ganges. The early men whose descendants are said to be traced in the Deccan at the present day had a legend that their sacred river flowed from the feet of the God Vishnu and through Siva's hair. The Nile valley with its seasonal contribution of rich alluvial mud from Abyssinia and Central Africa has always been the scene of important fluctuating civilizations. In the plain of Mesopotamia, 'the happy valley', the earliest Akkadian settlers found an alluvial soil of exceptional fertility where the palm was native, and where two or three crops of wheat could be raised in one year subject to skilled irrigation.

The Minoan culture also grew up in a country of clear air and natural fertility where corn, good pasturage and fruiting trees flourished happily. Yet none of these promising societies were destined to endure; most of them fell through the lust of possession that was the bane of the human race. Hindustan was overrun by Aryan tribes, the Euphrates valley by the Mongol mountaineers and the Assyrians, while the Nile Valley was repeatedly invaded by Hittites, Assyrians and Persians.

Some cultures, however, owed their destruction to climatic changes, for the earth's climate has been subject to pulsations like those of the glacial ages on a large scale, as well as to smaller cycles of variation coincident with the development of man. 'Changes of climate', says Mr. Ellsworth Huntington in his book, *The Pulse of Asia*, 'have been one of the controlling causes of the rise and fall of the great nations . . . With every throb of the climatic pulse which we have felt in Central Asia the centre of civilization has moved this way and that.' And he gives as an example the trekking, after the Ice Age, of the hordes from the North into Europe which was becoming warm and habitable.

The rough picture which we are able to form of the race movements, especially in the third millennium, show us many peaceful agricultural societies broken up by warrior hordes who in the metal age had learnt the arts of war; and war has always given 'the demon of disease' a favourable opportunity. Further, many of the centres of dispersal from which the races overran the surrounding countries lay in those latitudes which have always had a longer list of diseases than the temperate zone, and all through historic times we trace an association of certain virulent diseases with the dark-skinned races. The hot countries have many elements which may be inimical to health. Certainly their disease flora is largely outnumbered by the beneficent species, but some genera like the *Anarcardiaceae* to which the American poison ivy (*Rhus Toxicodendron*) belongs, produce violent erysipelatous inflammations upon people of every colour if they unfortunately come into contact with the leaf. There are also, in all countries, poisonous species which, taken internally, produce severe sickness, delirium, or death; an aspect of the subject which will be dealt with later. The hot countries are to-day as they have probably always been, the centres of many bacterial epidemic diseases as well as the filarial diseases such as elephantiasis, mycetoma, and tropical ulcer due to parasitic blood filariae and nemotode worms. In our own experience we find that ulceration quickly follows any wound or scratch among the African races, such wounds being treated by them with palm oil or poultices made from leaves and roots. Such treatments recall the passage where Homer speaks of Patroclus curing Eurpylus when wounded by an arrow. After washing him, 'he took a bitter root rubbing it between his hands; a root that took pain away, and the wound began to dry, and the blood ceased'.

Modern investigation has shown that the endemic centres of many infectious diseases lie within tropical latitudes. Cholera, so named by Hippocrates in 400 B.C. has a permanent endemic centre in the Far East. Yellow Fever is stated by Dr. Clemow to be endemic only on the tropical coastline of the Atlantic Ocean, but there seem to be several centres for bubonic plague. There are however some other illnesses such as leprosy, syphilis, typhus, and rheumatic fever which, though they are still thought to have originated among the black races, occur all over the world independently of lines of latitude.

It is a matter of common knowledge that undrained, marshy lands are unhealthy to live upon, and that a contaminated water supply will of itself spread cholera, typhoid and dysentery. We know that often in historical times disastrous floods have turned a happy valley into a scene of noisome desolation; and the Babylonian who visualized a dark dragon lurking in the pestilential waters probably knew a good deal about the sickness that followed the retreat of the flood.

From Dravidian India we have some strange legends of the 'Disease Mothers' who were associated with the some of the worst afflictions like smallpox and cholera. Of smallpox there are several records from different countries at an early date. It seems to have originated in Africa, but it was certainly known in Egypt in the second millennium, and, what is more remarkable, there is a legend of its having been treated by 'preventive inoculation'.

PRE-HISTORY

Of the plague a graphic account is given in 2 Samuel xxiv, 15 and there are other references to it from Syria and Libya. It has been found that a disease may become especially virulent if it is transmitted to another country whose natives have not acquired immunity to protect them. The African negro while immune from yellow fever will succumb to smallpox and filarial diseases, just as the white man becomes subject to tropical anaemia on the African coast. Again, smallpox carried to America was said to be more fatal there than in Europe, while leprosy, known as endemic in the Nile valley in 1500 B.C., worked the most devastating havoc when transmitted — it was thought by the Crusades — into Europe.

It has often been debated whether disease manifested itself among the palæolithic races of men; but the researches of Virchow and Bernard Renault have brought a great deal of evidence showing that it existed even earlier. The remains of fishes and mesozoic vertebrates have been found showing arthritic lesions and dental caries. Some of Renault's studies from the Autun in France showed, in fossil vertebrates of the carboniferous age, osseous lacunae with infected areas of bacterial agency. Professor Roy Moodie states that such infected wounds seem to come only from the strata above the Carboniferous; and he considers that the great coal age witnessed the widespread growth of bacteria and fungi, together with a corresponding spread of bacterial disease generally following upon an injury. Such infections and consequent structural deformities no doubt occurred only in aged or weakened animals, and it is most probable — to quote Professor Roy Moodie, that disease remained a minor and unimportant factor for millions of years. Still, it existed, because no living being is or has ever been free from accident. Among human remains Virchow found arthritic deformations in bones of the glacial age, and the Java man found by Dubois in 1891 had a femur showing medial exostoses. Deficiency diseases arising from insufficient or unwholesome food may also have arisen at an early date. Disease therefore in some of its aspects may be said to be older than man. 'The profession of the healing art', wrote Dr. R. M. S. Jackson, 'divine in its origin, grave and grand in its scientific evolution, sacred and sublime in its functions, stands as a necessary part of the order of things, old as humanity and inseparable from its existence upon earth, for when did not man suffer, and when did not his brother try to relieve him?'

A noble sentence, though there is another side to the question seeing that so many of the diseases especially of civilized man have arisen from his imperfect control of his own desire nature. In truth as the Hindu maxim has it, 'we have suffered from ourselves'.

POISONOUS PLANTS AND NATIVE REMEDIES

Just as in health each race came to recognize its dependence upon the seasonal gifts of the great Earth Mother, so too it was natural that in sickness they should go to her to ease their pain. Their experiments in this direction must have led to the gradual building up of a body of approved traditions. Many tropical plants have strongly marked properties, and it is probable that the opium poppy, the hemp, and the kola nut, seed of *Kola accuminata* (Schott and Endl.), were tested and prized by the primitive races. A long tradition lies at the back of the powdered leaf of *Erythroxylum Coca*, a native of Peru, for the plant has long been used as a masticatory and for allaying hunger. The substance called cocaine was derived from this leaf in the nineteenth century.

The poison flora must also have been quickly recognized. The vegetable poisons exist in simple cells undifferentiated from the rest of the tissue except for a different arrangement of the molecules. Dr. Clemow has pointed out that prussic acid is only a union of an atom of nitrogen, with an atom of hydrogen and an atom of carbon! Sometimes the poisonous property is localized in root, leaf, or seed; but sometimes it is contained in the actual leaf hairs. Frequently it affects a whole genus, and is then a valuable basis for classification.

In the *Solanaceae*, the nightshade Order, and in the *Ranunculaceae*, the buttercup Order, poisonous principles exist in numerous species, but are unequally distributed in the various parts of the plant.

For instance, among the former, the potato leaf is unwholesome while the tuber yields an excellent food. In the latter, the common buttercup possesses, to a certain extent, the acrid property; the common celandine is innocent of it, while the monkshood (*Aconitum Napellus*, Linn.) a medicinal plant, has in its leaf and root a powerful poison.

The properties of the tropical flora are generally more marked than in our own, but they also differ in the parts of the plant. Some members even of the poison ivy Order, have edible fruits like the mango and cashew nut, while other species are used in medicine.

The natives of tropical regions had a great deal to learn about all these things, but it is probable that they did learn, and quickly, to separate the sheep from the goats. In one spectacular instance they certainly did so. Common in the hot latitudes were the members of the spurge Order (*Euphorbiaceae*), one of which (*Manihot utilissima*, Pohl.), contains the deadly hydrocyanic acid in its milky juice. Yet the root of this same plant after washing and heating, yields a wholesome meal, and has for centuries been known and used in Central America. It gives us also the tapioca of commerce.

Again the properties of the tropical *Loganiaceae* may have been known at a very early date, for the celebrated arrow poison, the *Wourali* or *Curare* of Guiana comes from the juice of *Strychnos toxifera*, Schomb. The related plant *Strychnos Nux-vomica*, used in nearly every Pharmacopoeia to-day, is indigenous to most parts of India. It was said to have been used by the Arabians of the tenth century, but strychnine was not discovered until 1818 (by Pelletier and Caventon). As a medicine, nux-vomica owes its therapeutic value to the antiseptic alkaloids strychnine and brucine which are yielded by the intensely bitter and poisonous seeds.

The upas tree of Java, *Antiaria toxicaria*, Lesch., (N.O. *Moraceae*) has suffered from many fabulous 'travellers' tales', but it has a strongly poisonous property in its milky juice. Like the allied bread fruit tree, it has no doubt been for ages known to the East Indian native. Altogether it may be said that although there are very few plants injurious to animals by contact, there are many which, taken internally may cause death. Some however, as the early races discovered, are rendered innocuous by cooking.

Dr. Winterbottom in his account of African medicine published in 1803 has some interesting accounts of native remedies. The natives were able to cure ulcerations where European methods had failed. For one of their poultices they used the boiled root of the sweet cassava, *Manihot palmata*, Muell. Arg., just as in New Guinea the natives used the young shoots of *Musa paradisiaca*, Linn., the plantain, with the allied *M. Sapientum*, the banana (N.O. *Musaceae*) for blisters and wounds.

The plantain is much esteemed in India. Among other uses it is applied for snake bite and is called the rattle-snake tree.

Similarly, the Irish have an ancient traditional use in the application of wood sorrel leaves (*Oxalis Acetosella*, Linn., N.O. *Geraniaceae*), for scrofulous ulcers. The leaves contain potassium binoxalate and are said to possess anti-scorbutic properties.

The ways of men with their plants are many and varied: nevertheless we may see in such native cultures as our aggressive cilivization has allowed to survive, the same practices that have existed from the childhood of the world. We cannot trace the origin of pharmacy to those distant ages, because the pharmacist, developing his art on the basis of science, could not arise till many centuries of sophistication had prepared the way. But here, among these unlettered worshippers of the great Earth Mother, is the origin of the simples[1] which have persisted as *remèdes de bonne femme* throughout history. Early man, as we now envisage him, was partly educible and partly instinctive: to many of his healing plants he was doubtless led by that intuition which is among the ultimate and protecting features of conscious life. To learn through pain was inevitable, but it has not been the whole story in Man's relationship with his world.

---

[1] The word 'simple' is used in medical botany for a vegetable remedy that is made up of one plant, used either fresh or dried, and unmixed with any other.

CHAPTER II

MEDICINE AMONG EARLY RACES

DRUG PLANTS OF MESOPOTAMIA, INDIA AND CHINA

THE TEMPLE OF MEDICINE IN TIBET
From *Lhasa and its Mysteries*, by Colonel L. A. Waddell

Photographed (by courtesy of the author and publishers) by Messrs. Fleming

THE MEDICINE OF SOME EARLY RACES

RECENT archaeological work has disclosed the existence of cultural epochs hitherto unknown in pre-dynastic Egypt and the Punjab. Particularly interesting are the accounts of the Indus cities in the third millennium revealing a wonderful civilization which seems to have been without the dynastic ambitions of Egypt or Sumeria. Research is advancing at a high speed, and it may be that we shall soon be in a position to decipher some records from the Indus valley bearing upon medicine. But in the meanwhile, we have in the writings left by the Aryans of India a coherent picture of early medicinal practice which can be deciphered through our knowledge of the language and our access to their sacred books.

. In this literature we find one or two remarkable developments which are absent from all other contemporary records in so far as we know them. It seems that from the earliest known date in India there was a distinction between physician and surgeon, while both flourished side by side with the ubiquitous Medicine Man. From the same sources we also learn of horses (which were used in India as in China at a very early date) being surgically treated when they met with any injury. Again, there is a delightful touch in the description of a doctor's house being surrounded by medicinal herbs in cultivation. This may be the earliest record of a miniature herb farm.

In the Rig-Veda – compiled between 4500 and 1600 B.C. – one of the oldest repositories of human learning, we find references to the medicinal plants in use, and among them to the Sowa plant and its properties. The Ayurveda — a later work supplementary to the great Vedas — treats of the native remedies in more detail, and constitutes the basis of the ancient Indian system of medicine. Hindu medicine and surgery continued to flourish until the time of the Mohammedan invasion after which a decline set in, and the old remedies were either abandoned, or retained in 'popular' practice in a superstitious manner.

The early Aryans were no mean students of chemistry, and in their materia medica minerals were included among the herbs. On the other hand, their list of diseases is a formidable one, for scrofula, phthisis and leprosy seem to have been rife from the earliest times. The operation of trephining — or trepanning — is mentioned, and it is extraordinary how prevalent this practice was and still is among some native races. Interesting accounts of it and pictures of the holed skulls furnished by Mr. Wilson Parry can be seen in the Wellcome Museum of Medicine. The primitive idea was to allow the escape of a demon, but the operation was also done for headache, epilepsy, or infantile convulsions. All sorts of instruments were used. An Inca skull has been found in which the trephining had been done as in China, with a shark's tooth. In modern Melanesia this difficult operation is still said to be practised with an instrument of obsidian. Truly, man is a long suffering creature. In the third millennium B.C. in India there was a distinguished surgeon, Susruta, whose works were edited, like those of Hippocrates, for succeeding centuries. The chapter on chemistry in this work contains descriptions of preparations of sulphates and oxides which place it in advance of any other written in pre-Christian times. Dr. Muthu in his book on Hindu medicine tells us that it also had a chapter on midwifery showing that 'caesarian' section was even then in practice. The Hindus describe in their writings over a hundred surgical instruments used for such major operations as stone in the bladder, rupture, and amputation of the limbs. Boiling pitch and oil were used to stop bleeding, and whether the early practice of the 'soporific sponge' was applied as a form of anaesthesia we cannot be sure. The most remarkable operation described in detail is that of an artificial nose being formed from the skin of the cheek. It has been unkindly suggested that this was done to counter the Indian habit of cutting off an enemy's nose in revenge for an injury.

Modern scientific research has shown that many of the old Hindu remedies were justified. In recent years, an investigation has been carried on in India itself, concerning the use and properties of the ancient drugs. From this inquiry, due to the enthusiasm of Professor Chopra of the School of Tropical Medicine and Hygiene and the Medical College, Calcutta, very interesting results are being obtained. Students interested in Indian medicine should consult Prof. Chopra's book, *Indigenous Drugs of India* (Calcutta, 1933), and Sir George Watt's *The Commercial Products of India* (London, 1908). There is also an older catalogue of Indian drugs by Dr. John Fleming. Many of the plants included to-day in the Indian Pharmacopoeia have been used for centuries, and many more are exported to other countries where they are in constant use. The seeds of *Plantago ovata*, Forsk, are used as a demulcent. The fruits called Myrobalans are the dried, immature capsules of *Terminalia Chebula*, Retz. (N.O. *Combretaeae*), a tree widely distributed in India and Burma. This drug used to be official in the B.P. as a laxative. The native *Acacias* have been valued all through the ages for the highly astringent properties of their bark which made them serviceable both to the tanner and the pharmacist. *Acacia arabica*, Willd. (*Leguminoseae*) yields the Babul bark of commerce, and another strong astringent, black catechu, comes from *Acacia Catechu*, Willd. The variety of *Catechu* known as *Gambier* formerly included in our own B.P. comes from a plant of the N.O *Rubiaceae* (the same order that gives us ipecacuanha and quinine). Its name is *Uncaria Gambier*, Roxb. In pharmacy it is sold in square cakes as 'pale catechu' and is one of the most powerful astringents known.

Other drug plants have been put under cultivation in Bengal and elsewhere in order to meet the demands of commerce. Among these are *Argemone mexicana*, Linn., and *Carica Papaye*, Linn., but neither plant is truly native, and there is a tradition that they were imported by the Portuguese. The former which is one of the *Papaverceae*, is called the Mexican or Prickly Poppy. It grows rapidly, and the oil expressed from the seeds has been used externally for indolent ulcers and herpetic eruptions, and internally as a purgative in dysentery, etc. The *Carica* is one of the *Caricaceae*, the Papaw family. The juice of the unripe fruit and the powdered seeds are claimed to be useful anthelmintics, as well as being valuable in dyspepsia.

The hemp, *Cannabis sativa*, Linn., (*Cannabinaceae*) has a long history, and by reason of its varied uses is a very interesting plant. A native of India and other hot countries, it proves 'temperamental' when transferred to the temperate latitudes where its properties change. The resin from the flower bracts is intoxicating and hallucinating. Under its Indian name of 'charas', 'the laughter mover' or 'exciter of desire', it is held responsible for many of the feats of the fakirs. The Saracens were said to have made use of it as a stimulant before their military exploits, and the Arabian hashish is made from its flowering tops. The European and Indian plants are not, as is often assumed, different species, although the resinous variety of hot latitudes is named *Cannabis indica*; flat gunjah locally. The hemp fibres are the source of our toughest ropes, cordage and sacking, the strength of the fibre varying with the climate; the product of cold climates, and especially of Russia proving the best. Hemp is an easy and accommodating crop to grow. Herodotus found the Scythians cultivating it for their linen, and it is grown in many widely different countries at the present day. In Lewin's interesting book *Phantastica; Narcotic and Stimulating Drugs* (London, 1931), there is a full account of the action of hemp, opium, and other drug plants used for euphoric purposes.

Another notable Indian native is *Holarrhena dysenterica* which according to Indian fable originated from the drops of water which fell from the bodies of Rama's monkeys which were restored to life by the God Indra. It has often been confused with *Wrightia tinctoria*, R.Br., also belonging to the N.O. *Apocynaceae*. The latter was the source of a blue dye, but it was found medicinally worthless. The Indian *Hollarrhena* contains the alkaloids conessine, kurchine, and kurchicine, and has been proved of use in the treatment of amoebic infections of the intestines which are common in the East.

The drug plants of the Indian Pharmacopoeia are so numerous, and comprise so many species of universal benefit that we have placed a selection of them in a special section at the end of the book.

In 327 B.C. Alexander the Great invaded and conquered northern India, but the conquest was barren and temporary. By 250 B.C. the garrisons that he had left behind were driven out, and the country was practically united under the rule of the really 'great' Buddhist king, Asoka. In his reign hospitals were built; medicine was well organized, and it is said that medicinal trees and plants were planted in many parts of the country. There was a state pharmacy which dispensed medicines, not only for men, but in accordance with the gracious Buddhist rule, for the lower animals also. Learning became more disseminated, and the monks travelled about with medical manuscripts which discouraged surgery but laid stress upon vegetable remedies. 'Go forth,' they were commanded, 'and intermingle, and bring them to the righteousness which passeth knowledge. Go forth among the terrible and powerful, both here and in foreign countries, in kindred ties both of brotherhood and sisterhood, everywhere.' Such missions of men illumined by an ideal of moral beauty brought religion and medicine into a natural fellowship in the purview of humanity and they took place at a time when the western world was slowly struggling out of barbarism. There is no doubt that the reign of Asoka was one of the high water marks of civilization, and that the Greeks before the Christian era and the Arabs after it owed much to the knowledge that had been garnered by the Aryans of India.

CHINESE ORIGINS

Our knowledge of ancient China does not begin much earlier than 1000 B.C., for no excavations have ever been attempted in the land. We only know that at that time, the country consisted of a number of vassal states ruled by 'The Son of Heaven', and that there was some knowledge of medicine, and a literature written upon strips of bamboo. At the same time, there is a large body of legend upon which some have built up a picture of an earlier civilization with approximate dates. This tradition gives us the first God of Healing in Shen Nung, as well as the earliest herbal which according to some authorities was compiled by one of the ancient Emperors, Chin Nong, who ruled in 2699 B.C. This herbal which is said to be still in use, was largely devoted to poisons. Then there are traditional records purporting to date from the Chow dynasty of about 1122 B.C. Some of these refer to medicine, and they mention the examination of medical practitioners, but we are left to conjecture the motive which may have been either a sense of responsibility or a fear of the unholy practices which were so often allied to a specialization in drugs. The medicine men of the earlier dynasties seem to have been very drastic in method, for we read of 'divining youths stripped to the waist, dancing frantically and pricking blood from the arm to expel a demon of disease'. In the popular religion however, medicine was held in high reverence, for 29 out of the 72 Buddhas were associated with the knowledge of the healing art. The Chinese were the first people to use goose grease which is still employed for its penetrating powers. They are credited with the ancient practice afterwards known as polypharmacy, of mixing up dozens of different ingredients in one prescription. They depended largely upon talismans. The Taoist religion especially abounded in charms which could be used indifferently in mental or physical distress.

Trephining was common, and for the old reason, to allow a demon or confined spirit to escape.

A very interesting fact concerning their science is their pre-occupation with the quest for gold to be extracted from the baser metals. This quest which engaged so many inquiring minds down to Newton and was extended by the Arabian alchemists, is thought to have originated among the Chinese from whom the Arabians may have learnt it. Nor was the search confined to gold, for they were intent upon finding a panacea for all diseases, a universal cure-all and an elixir of immortality. In fact, in their medical practice they treated most of the hundred and twenty remedies which they used as panaceas. Many were directed against the effects of poison, and they had a strange belief in the power of a cup made from rhinoceros horn to render its contents harmless. Although like the Hindus they used minerals like arsenic and mercury, and some animal products such as powdered tortoiseshell, most of their remedies were of vegetable origin. The Chinese had an important herbal written by Le She chin in the sixteenth century A.D., and called Pun Tsaou Kang müh. The fact that this has only once been revised testifies to the innate conservatism of the race. Indeed an even earlier one dating from about A.D. 220 and bearing the name of Su Wen is still extant in Chinese literature, while the compilation of Chin Nong above mentioned is as we have said, still revered.

Mr. Daniel Hanbury has left us a valuable study of the Chinese materia medica. It included the medicinal rhubarb which was also known to the Egyptians and Greeks. Rhubarb is a plant of the N.O. *Polygonaceae* whose plants are marked by the presence of malic or oxalic acid. *Rheum rhaponticum*, Linn., is a native of Siberia. This and *R. undulatum* are believed to be the plants from which the varieties of rhubarb cultivated for culinary purposes in various parts of the world have originated. They all contain oxalic acid in their leaves and to a less extent in their stems.

Medicinal rhubarb is the dried rhizome of *R. palmaticum*, Linn., (and possibly of other species cultivated in China and Thibet) deprived of most of its bark. The activity of the drug as a purgative is not due as is sometimes thought, to oxalic acid, but to a substance which it contains of a resinous character and complex constitution.

In ancient China many things were done, especially in agriculture, which later science has ratified and explained. The following instance in their medical practice is particularly interesting. For five thousand years, the Chinese have used a plant known to them as 'Ma Huang' in the treatment of hay fever. This is *Ephedra* (N.O. *Gnetaceae*), of which there are two important Chinese species, *E. sinacea*, Stapf., and *E. euisetana*, Bunge, as well as numerous other species growing in both the Old and the New Worlds. The plants are known to us as 'Shrubby Horsetails', and are peculiar on account of their green, slender, jointed branches. In recent years the *Ephedras* have received the attention of European scientists, and have been found to contain a medicinally valuable alkaloid, *ephedrine*, the hydrochloride of which is now official in the B.P., and is used in the treatment of asthma. Moreover the Chinese always held the idea that Ma Huang should be collected in the autumn. This practice has been justified by chemical analyses which show that the ephedrine content rises, by as much as nearly two hundred per cent, from spring to autumn. In veterinary work they used remedies for cattle disease which may be considered modern ; they fumigated when there was a murrain, and they used salines in bathing the eyes and skin. On the other hand, they retain in their materia medica such outworn remedies as powdered jade, and their practice to-day seems to be a blend of modern science mingled with superstition. They may have been the first to use herbal anaesthesia or the 'soporific sponge', giving inhalations of henbane, hashish, and other narcotics to produce temporary relief in pain or before an operation. It is a curious thing that with all the commerce between the nations in the Christian era, this practice which is said to have obtained in Europe in the twelfth century should have been allowed to die out in the Middle Ages. The plant known as the Chinese panacea, the Ginseng, from *Aralia quinquefolia*, Decne, and Planch., (*Araliaceae*), a native of the Korea and Mongolia, is still much esteemed in China though not elsewhere. The Chinese also import it from America, though giving preference to the native product which is really a variety of the plant, called var. Ginseng. A remarkable account of the drug is given in Lockhart's *Medical Mission in China*.

Other medicinal plants retained in modern use are the following :

Thea sinensis, Linn. (*Camellia Thea*, Link, *Theaceae*), tea, possibly originating in Cochin China, cultivated in China, India, Ceylon, etc. Source of the alkaloid, caffeine, official in B.P.

Glycine Soja, Sieb. and Zucc. (*Leguminosae*). The soy bean constitutes an important item of food in China and Japan. Used to make soy sauce. Also employed medicinally in China, where the black variety of the bean is supposed to give strength and to form an antidote to vegetable poisons.

Amomum spp. (*Zingiberaceae*). A number of species grow in China and Indo-China, and yield various sorts of cardamoms. The genus is highly critical. *See* Burkill in Kew Bull. Misc. Inf. No. 1. 1930.

Smilax China, Linn. (*Liliaceae*). China root, used in the East for rheumatic and syphilitic complaints. Replaced in European medicine by *Smilax ornata*, Hook F., *Sarsaparilla* (Costa Rica) though to-day the latter is not considered to be of much use save as a vehicle for administration of mercury and potassium iodide.

Cordyceps sinensis or vegetable caterpillar is a fungus which grows from the head of living caterpillars. The growth finally kills the caterpillar when the insects are collected and dried, the combination of insect and fungus being so peculiar that it is considered to possess great medicinal virtue in the treatment of jaundice, phthisis, etc.

In the British Museum Handbook of the larger British Fungi, p. 192 there is the following note: —

'*Cordyceps sinensis* is a celebrated drug in the Chinese Pharmacopoeia (summer plant, winter insect). It is brought to Canton in bundles of a dozen or so tied up with silk thread. According to some authorities it is sold as food, but the usual statement is that the fungus is so rare, being found in Tibet and outlying parts of the Empire, that it is only used by the Emperor's physicians. Black, old and rotten specimens are said to be worth four times their weight in silver.'

The Chinese name for the 'Plant Worm' is Hia Tsao Tchong.

Allium sativum, Linn., the garlic is much used by the Chinese as a medicine.

Zanthoxylum alatum, Roxb. (*Rutaceae*) is the Chinese wild pepper, considered in China to possess carminative, astringent anthelmintic and astringent properties. Rarely seen to-day in European commerce.

Diospyros Kaki, Linn., F. (*Ebenaceae*) is Japanese persimmon, one of the most important fruits of China and Japan. The bark, wood and roots are used medicinally in China.

Sesamum indicum, Linn. (*Pedalalinaceae*) is sesame, gingelly, or tael. It is grown extensively in China, also in India and Asia Minor. The expressed oil is official in the B.P. and is used for the administration of iodine. The seeds are employed in China for numerous medicinal purposes.

Gymnocladus chinensis, Baill. (*Leguminosae*). Soap seeds. Used in China as a substitute for soap, also in medicine in treatment of rheumatism, dysentry and skin diseases.

The green putchuh of the Chinese is considered by Dr. Hance to be *Aristolochia recurvifolia*. Other authorities identify it with *Costus* an Eastern composite (*See* p. 46).

THE PHYSICK GARDEN

Several plants of the Prickly Ash Order, *Zanthoxylaceae*, are and always have been used by the Chinese and Japanese, especially the fruit of *Xanthoxylum piperitum*, esteemed as an antidote against poison. The root of *X. nitidum* is used as a stimulant and febrifuge. From *Pilocarpus microphyllus* we get the alkaloid pilocarpine used in modern pharmacy in Bright's disease. The product of this plant, often called *jaborandi*, is the most powerful diaphoretic drug that we possess. It is employed in many hair washes as a tonic to increase the growth.

CHALDEAN AND ASSYRIAN RECORDS

The labours of Mr. Woolley, Dr. Langdon, and other workers have greatly enlarged our knowledge of the ancient civilizations of Mesopotamia. Medical records have been derived from the Kuyunjik collection in the British Museum (translated by Bezoid and King) showing the sources of Babylonian and Assyrian medicine, such information having been preserved by the admirable habit of the priestly caste of making records upon tablets of baked clay with the point of a graver. Dates are still conjectural, nor is it yet certain whether the theory that the Mesopotamian cultures were derived from pre-dynastic Egypt is the correct one. For our purpose however, it is sufficiently interesting that several ancient sites have yielded tablets bearing upon medicinal remedies, while the first God of Healing known to us through statuary is the Chaldean Ea whose statue is to be seen bearing its approximate date of 5000 B.C. in the Wellcome Museum of Medicine.

The God had various names; alternatively he was Lord of the Deep and the Benevolent Spirit of the Earth. At the same time, the popular religion swarmed with evil spirits: in fact, the earliest Deity connected with poisons is Gula, the Sumerian Goddess of sorcery whose name appears on one of the tablets. Ea however was consistently addressed with hope and fervour as having power over disease. The 'magic texts' taken from inscriptions upon the cylinders have preserved some of the incantations to the Healing God. One runs as follows.

The disease of the head hath issued from the abyss:
Impart to a bucket of water Thy exalted, magic power.

The magic of the Mesopotamians was not however confined to food or water: healing herbs were gathered and prepared with incantations and ceremonies. While the Ministrant prayed that the wrath of Ea might fall 'on the worm that causeth the toothache', he applied at the same time a poultice which may have been made of henbane as we know that this valuable narcotic was known to several early peoples. Fumigations consisting of resinous plants and trees such as the *Coniferae* were also frequent; and Dr. Campbell Thompson in his book on the Devils and Evil Spirits of Babylon translates one of the cylinder texts in a couplet that might have been written by one of our Saxon ancestors.

Flea-bane on the lintel of the door I have hung:
St. John's wort, caper, and wheat ears.

In recent times Mr. Woolley has made the interesting suggestion that the bodies in the death pits of the Sumerians had the appearance of a peaceful end induced by a soporific drug.

Some knowledge of anatomy is shown by the Chaldean statues, and from their inscriptions we learn of operations such as trephining, cupping, and circumcision. There are even references to operations upon oxen with a bronze lancet, probably after an injury.

Talismans seem to have been widely used, and had the power of acting at a distance, whereas a charm against wild animals or disease had to be worn on the person to make it effective. One particular talisman, a plaque hung up in the room of a pregnant woman, is of especial interest, as there is an odd survival of it at the present day among the Jews who hang up a stone over the bed 'to ward off Lilith and her gang'. It is possible that the holed stone and the thyroid talismans may also be traceable to this source. These holed stones have always exercised a strange fascination. Sailors still wear them as a protection against drowning, and many a soldier wore one in 1915.

THE PHYSICK GARDEN

DRUG PLANTS OF MESOPOTAMIA

The code of Hammurabi engraved in about 2100 B.C. on a black diorite pillar, has taught us a great deal about the medical practice of his day. This great ruler who described himself as 'risen for the illumination of the land' made the united Amorites and Akkadians the 'schoolmasters of the ancient world', and his great city, Babylon, was said to be the best administered of all ancient empires. The code shows that the medical profession was organized with an elaborate set of rules and some terrifying penalties for malpractice. Surgery was evidently more esteemed than medicine, and neither under the Akkadian nor the Chaldean rule did the physician take the same place as in the adventurous schools of Egypt. The medicine plants used by the various Semitic races who followed each other into the 'fertile valley' were no doubt mostly those of the native flora, and the genera inscribed upon the clay tablets may be taken as typical. We are fortunate to possess these records seeing how many libraries were in later days destroyed. Some of the drug plants which have been deciphered are those which are still in constant use. We will consider some of the best known.

Cassia. This is an unfortunate name, which, like others in botany has been applied to plants that differ not only in their structure but also in affinities. There is more confusion over it in the popular mind than over any other medicinal plant, and those who wish for a lucid description of the *Cassias* of commerce and cinnamon should consult Redgrove's *Spices and Condiments* (London, 1933).

In the Bible, the word qinnamon which occurs in Exod. xxx, 23, Prov. vii, 17, and Canticles iv, 14, has, very naturally, been translated 'cinnamon', whereas the words qiddah (Exod. xxx, 24, and Ezek. xxvii, 19) and qetzioth (Psalms xlv, 8) are both translated 'cassia'. Mr. Redgrove considers it open to question as to whether any of these translations are correct. It has been suggested that both the cinnamon and cassia of the ancients were different grades of cassia, or that the passages refer to other aromatic products. Costus, the root of *Saussurea Lappa*, Clarke, N.O. *Compositae* (a Kashmir plant), may have been meant, or, as others with less plausibility have suggested, orris root.

Our commercial cinnamon is to-day the prepared inner bark of *Cinnamomum zeylanicum*, Nees, (N.O. *Lauraceae*) grown in Ceylon. The spice is exclusively a Singhalese product, but there is a Chinese product called cassia obtained from *Cinnamomum Cassia*, Blume. In the U.S.A. the word 'cinnamon' is used as identical with cassia. Cinnamon oil has proved of value in influenza and colds.

The cassia buds which are used medicinally, are the unripe fruits of *C. Cassia*, and are imported from China. In the east some other species with aromatic fruits are used for flavouring. The buds contain a volatile oil, the most important ingredient of which is cinnamic acid, a substance having antiseptic properties.

The camphor tree of China and Formosa is an important member of the *Lauraceae*. Botanically it is *Cinnamomum Camphora*, Nees. The stearoptene or crude camphor is obtained by boiling pieces of the root and branches and straining the liquor which is afterwards 'refined' by lime. Camphor is much used as a carminative and stimulant, but is poisonous in large quantities. 'Camphorated oil' is a simple solution of camphor in olive oil.

The word *kofer* translated 'camphire' in the Authorised Version of our Bible almost certainly referred to henna (*Lawsonia inermis L. N.O. Lythraceae*) a point which is recognized in the R.V.

There is still another cassia which should be mentioned although it has nothing to do with oil of *Cassia* or the Laurel family for it is the source of the senna so frequently used. Alexandrian senna (*C. acutifolia*, Del.) is a native of Nubia and the Sudan. Tinnevelly senna (*C. angustifolia*, Vahl.) comes from South Arabia, India, etc. The dried leaves and fruits — or 'pods' — of both are official in our B.P., those of the former species being more highly esteemed.

Anise and dill recall familiar associations with plants which we have known from childhood. Parsley, carrot, parsnip, fennel, and caraway all belong to the great Natural Order, *Umbelliferae*, clearly marked for the field botanist by their flower heads or umbels and hollow stems. In properties they are very variable. Carrot and parsnip have edible roots; fennel and parsley edible leaves, while the fruits, commonly called 'seeds' of many members of the family contain volatile oils which are usually carminative and stimulant. Others like the hemlock and water dropwort are poisonous with an acrid juice. The aniseed of the pharmacist is the fruit of *Pimpinella Anisum*, though little of the oil is used in modern practice, its place having been taken by star-anise oil, distilled from the fruits of a small, evergreen plant, *Illicium verum*, Hk. f. (N.O. *Winteraceae*), which does not appear to be known in a wild state. The little tree is only cultivated in two relatively small areas in China and Tonkin, from whence the world's supply is obtained.

The essential oil of star-anise is very similar to, though not identical with, genuine anise oil, in odour, flavour and chemical constitution. Both oils contain anethole as their chief constituent. For medical use, the B.P. recognizes them both, and draws no distinction between them.

The true *Pimpinella Anisum*, Linn., is a native of Egypt and the Mediterranean, and was a favourite ingredient in the Roman cuisine. The Roman epicures ate aniseed cakes to promote digestion, and the drug was much praised by Pliny. In the Middle Ages its cultivation spread to Central Europe and thence to England, but to succeed, the crop should be grown in a warm country. The fruits are very small, and it takes about 30 to 50 pounds of fruit to produce one pound of the essential oil by distillation. Aniseed was known to Hippocrates and has been used ever since as a mild expectorant. It is a common ingredient in dentifices and liqueurs. In cultivation to-day, the Russian crops are the most productive, but the flavour of the Spanish plants is preferred.

The plant mentioned in Matthew xxiii, 23, as 'anise' should be translated 'dill'. The two plants are of course allied, but their volatile oils are totally different in chemical composition and flavour. The dill, *Anethum graveolens*, Linn., is carminative, and often used for flatulence in children.

With the jasmine and oleander of the clay tablets we are back in the tropical flora; and at the outset we are met by one of those confusions which the botanist has prepared for the layman. For this jasmine has nothing whatever to do with the delicious shrubby species, white or yellow, of our English gardens. They belong to the jasmine order, *Jasminaceae*, but this Chaldean 'jasmine' must have been some other plant. The name is misleadingly given to the North American *Gelsemium sempervirens*, Sit., which belongs to the poisonous *Loganiaceae*. This plant is a dangerous poison, but its alkaloid, gelsemine acts as a febrifuge and sedative.

The Mesopotamians seem to have discovered the properties of the virulent Order to which the oleander belongs. The beautiful plant of our greenhouses is *Nerium Oleander*, Linn., of the N.O. *Apocynaceae*. It contains in its leaf a highly poisonous glucoside allied to the glucosides in the foxglove. In his *Flowers of the Field*, Johns tells the story of twelve soldiers of the French troops who were in Spain in 1807 cutting down some oleander branches and using them for skewers when they roasted their meat. All the twelve were desperately ill, and seven died.

The equally lovely *Allamanda cathartica*, Linn., is another member of this baneful family whose leaves are violently cathertic. It is a native of Brazil. The only two English plants of this Order are the pretty periwinkles, *Vinca major*, Linn., and *Vinca minor*, Linn., whose leaves are astringent and are used in herbal medicine in diabetes. Many other of the foreign species are extremely poisonous. The Madagascar poison-nut, *Gerbera Tanghuin*, Hook, has no doubt often been put to nefarious uses. The bark of *Alstonia scholaris*, R. Brown, is however, a popular remedy for dysentery and malaria in the East Indies.

The names of the mints, henbane, and liquorice are among the clay tablet inscriptions, and these plants will be met with in the course of our history again and again. The chief difficulty in deciphering these early records is the lack of scientific grouping, and it is quite likely that the names of many remedies are still undeciphered. One fact, however, does emerge from our investigation of all primitive medicinal records, and that is the predominance of the plant remedies over the mineral. Probably the picture of neolithic man at the chase and the woman gathering herbs is not far from the truth, for at every stage in civilization, in forest, on hillsides, and in pastures the plant was there for the asking, the common green of the world, fruitful and serviceable. In Mesopotamia, as in Syria or Egypt, the people occasionally fell back upon the primitive practice of mixing unsavoury animal substances with their drug plants; the use of such things as insect remains, excrements or powdered gem stones probably representing some inheritance of superstition. It was a practice which lasted on through many centuries, for though the Greeks abandoned it, the European races revived it in the Middle Ages. In England, the herbalist Culpeper who died in 1654 used 'ashes of a cat's head' with crab's claws, etc., in his prescriptions. It was the last remnant of the old idea that when you consumed a bit of a creature's body, you obtained what virtue strength, cunning, or speed it had formerly possessed.

Some very interesting records of medicinal plant remedies have been left to us by the followers of the desert God Ashur who had Nineveh as their centre, the ruthless, plundering Assyrians, who left the carved sculptures now familiar to us in museums, and whose capital city fell to the Chaldeans in 606 B.C. These records which have been arranged by Dr. Campbell Thompson in his monograph of Assyrian vegetable drugs show that about 30 per cent of crude drugs were known at that time. 'The Assyrian botanist,' writes Dr. Thompson, 'had a very fair capacity for dividing his herbal into classes according to his needs, though it was not systematic botany in our sense.' Out of the 660 tablets examined, the vegetable species enumerated amount to 250. Another 120 remedies were stones or minerals, and the rest alcohols, fats, wax and oils. Among the plant genera, *Abies* and *Pinus* are mentioned as the sources of Kukru or turpentine. Bitumen was known and alum is mentioned among the non-vegetable remedies. The manna of the Assyrians was probably the exudation from *Tamarix mannifera*, Rhrenb. & Bunge, the tamarisk of Mount Sinai, also used by the Hebrews. Another kind of manna came from a Persian plant, *Alhagi maurorum*, madic, and the substance which is still included in modern pharmacy is the dried saccharine juice from *Fraxinus Ornus*, Linn., our ash tree which is cultivated for the purpose in Sicily.

Among the genera identified by Dr. Campbell Thompson are the following: *Calendula, Styrax, Sinapis, Hyoscymus, Myrrha, Liquid-*

ambar, Asafoetida, Mentha, Lupinus, Solanum, Ricinus, Ferula, Foeniculum, Anthemis, Papaver, Glycyrrhiza, Rhus, Mandragora, Nerium, Opopanax, Rhamnus, Artemesia, Cannabis, Conium, Juniperus, Crocus, Thymus, Urtica, Oenanthe, Ruta, Citrus, Allium, Anacyclus, Cumin, Anemone and *Origanum.*

In many cases, naturally, the species are impossible to identify. But in the case of the *Origanum* (the genus to which our pretty English marjoram belongs), it has been suggested that it might be *O. Maru,* Linn., a native of Syria and Arabia. As to the anemones, several of them have been used in medicine from early times, and two are native to Palestine, *A. coronaria,* in variety, and *A. blanda,* Schott and Ky. The Mesopotamians described the anemones well as some other species in poetic manner as 'silver sheen' or 'waving in the wind'. *A. coronaria,* Linn., and *A. pulsatilla,* Linn., have been used for various purposes in many countries. From the former a drink was made in Palestine, and the latter was prescribed for ulcers in England as late as the sixteenth century.

The Assyrians compounded many of their prescriptions in what was called 'beer'. In most cases the proportions were carefully noted, and it seems that the doctors and chemists of the time had attained a high level of efficiency. Probably they were the most civilized element in the brutal and bellicose society which existed mainly for warfare until by its own weapons it fell and passed away. Only sixty years after Assyria had been merged into Chaldea, Mesopotamia was finally conquered by the Aryan peoples when in 539 B.C. the Persians entered Babylon.

EGYPTIAN RECORDS

GREEK MEDICINE

HIPPOCRATES

HIPPOCRATES
the Father of Medicine

Photograph by Messrs. Fleming, from the British Museum

WITH Egyptian history an interesting chapter opens in the development of medicine, for in it we have the first great physician who became a god. Both Imhotep, the Egyptian, and the Greek Aesculapius were historical figures; men, it was said, of versatile attainments who were surrounded by some mysterious legends in their lives. Death finally translated them to divine honours.

Their later reputation naturally represented them as being incredibly distinguished in the art of healing. It is not suggested that this art rested upon personal contact or any mesmeric gifts: they both practised the art of medicine. All through this and the succeeding centuries we find the herb given its place as an agent of healing. 'Virtuous herbs' are mentioned upon the papyri as they were upon the Chaldean cylinders from time to time; and when, later on, in the Minoan civilization and in that of Greece, the serpent became a sacred emblem, it was said to have had a knowledge of herbs. The well known statue of Aesculapius depicts the sacred symbol with a herb in its mouth.

Imhotep, the priest, vizier and physician who designed the first pyramid, lived in about 2900 B.C. He was a kindly, popular figure who healed men living, and was said to care for them after death.

Recent excavators claim to have discovered his tomb near the Sakkarah pyramid. For a long time after his passing, the offices of priest and physician were inseparable.

To the inquirer in any branch of archaeology, the history of Egypt is of the first importance, for among the many pre-Christian civilizations it was unique in its stability, its social and religious life remaining unchanged through thousands of years. As physicians and pharmacists, the Egyptians have left us records of imperishable interest. On the other hand, medical records of their contemporaries and indeed of many of the races that succeeded them are extremely scanty, so that the history of medicine has many gaps. Of the Hittites whose military empire in about 2000 B.C. had land routes from Ionia to the Euphrates and whose script has only lately been deciphered at Hattosas, now the Turkish village of Boghaz-Keui, we know little except that they were bee-keepers and cultivators of the vine. Excavations however, are being carried out at Ras Shamra on the north coast of Syria where it appears that there was a cosmopolitan port with an Achaean colony whose tombs show affinities with Cretan types. A library of inscribed cuneiform tablets representing eight languages is said to have been found there, together with dictionaries for the use of the scribes. These tablets may eventually throw some light upon the medical practice of the Hittites and Achaeans.

Nor at present have we any records of the civic life of the seafaring and bartering Phœnicians who possessed a lovely strip of fertile land in the Mediterranean area with colonies in Africa and Spain; while as to the Etruscans whose strange script has baffled philologists for generations, their doings are equally shrouded in obscurity. True, they left sculptures of a vivid realism, and their agricultural rites are said to have included the oft told story of magical dance and song. Yet in their Pantheon of Gods there was none equal to Ceres, nor has any Healing Figure emerged from their record of a thousand years. A forthcoming book by Professor Pironti may perhaps throw some light upon this mysterious but beguiling gap in European history.

Again, there were the nomad Scythians who wandered over the Central Asian steppes at an early period. They have left us those realistic reliefs in metal called 'the animal style', together with bronze and gold ornaments, and we know that they cultivated flax; but of their medicine we have no traces.

It is otherwise with Persia, because the great Persian empire absorbed so many pre-existing and contemporary cultures. In his *Materia Medica*, Dr. Periera says regarding Persian medicine 'records are lacking', but that many of their remedies were indirectly known through the Greeks and Hebrews. Herodotus, it would seem, had no great opinion of them, for he states that under the Persian rule

Babylonian medicine finally became degenerate, and that there were no doctors to tend the sick who were simply exposed in the streets to beg for charity. The truth no doubt was that these vigorous highlanders from the north, at first so frugal and self-respecting in their settled agricultural life, became degenerate through internal luxury and corruption, so that when in 331 B.C. the empire fell to Alexander, its fall had been prepared from within.

The high table lands of Persia support a rather scanty vegetation with many thorn bushes, tamarisks and acacias, though the valleys are clothed with oak and other forest trees. It is possible that many of their most important drug plants were those of the N.O. *Umbelliferae*, many of which yield gum resins. We know that *Dorema Ammoniacum*, D. Don., has been collected for its resin (gum ammoniacum) from early times in Persia. This gum-resin exudes from the stem in masses which harden into 'tears' on exposure to the air. It was much used in fumigation. The Assyrians as we have seen, knew the camel thorn or manna bearing tree, *Alhagi maurorum*, Madic, native in Persia, whose product was also used in the same way.

The *Asafoetida* of modern pharmacy is an oleo resin derived from *Ferula foetida*, Regel., which grows in East Persia and Afghanistan. As a medicine and condiment it is still esteemed in Persia and is official in our B.P. Another umbelliferous Persian plant is *Ferula galbaniflua*, Boiss and Hohse, from which gum galbanum is obtained. An identical resin is however collected from allied species, one of them according to the B.P. being *Ferula rubricaulis*. Another possible source of the gum is *Ferula Schair*, Horze, which grows in the Syr-Daria desert on the confines of Siberia and Turkestan. The so-called 'Persian berries' of commerce are the product of a species of *Rhamnus* or buckthorn.

Other civilizations of which we hope to learn more and which have in fact already captured the modern imagination are those of the Indus valley of the third millennium and the Minoan civilization built up by the trading, maritime people of Crete. When we have deciphered their forbidding, inscrutable script we may glean something bearing upon our question, for we know that for about twenty centuries they went questing about the Aegean in those eight-oared galleys that look as if they must have capsized in a gale. By 2500 B.C., they were established with a strong government and a capital city, Cnossos, on the north coast. They carried on an energetic trade with Egypt, and are thought to have established the important colony of Mycenae on the mainland of Europe. They made some of the loveliest pottery — with the exception of the Chinese — that the world has ever seen, and they adorned the walls of their palaces with frescoes. Many of these frescoes resemble those on the walls of Akhenaton's palace at Tel-el-Amarna, showing a naturalistic treatment of vegetable forms, mostly lilies and other flowers, with birds, animals and marine shells and seaweeds. None of them apparently, represent medicinal plants.

Excavation has shown that the Minoans were in advance of many later races in their architecture and knowledge of sanitary principles. Some day, when the key has been found to the inscriptions on their terra cotta tablets, we may know more of their origin, social life, and contacts with the hoary old civilization of the Nile valley. In the meantime, we only know for certain that the Dorian Greeks absorbed their culture, and that between 1500 and 1400 B.C., the Minoan civilization passed into other hands. Yet Egypt remained. For another thousand years she endured, resisting all invaders, as immutable as her own Sphinx. Modern archaeology, in revealing many of her secrets, has brought to light several things that relate to our inquiry: therefore to Egypt we must return.

MEDICINE IN ANCIENT EGYPT

The Egyptian papyrus or hieratic script was a scroll 22 yards long, written on the paper made from *Papyrus antiquorum*, the bulrush of the Nile. It has proved wonderfully enduring, and we now have five main papyri which reveal the mind of ancient Egypt to the modern world. The Edwin Smith papyrus translated by Professor Breasted dated from c. 1600, and the Ebers papyrus translated by Cyril Bryan from c. 1500. The Kahun papyrus dealing with veterinary practice bears the older date of 2000 B.C., and there is also a London medical papyrus of the first millennium.

Perhaps the Ebers translation is the most familiar from its inexpensive modern translation. It is said to be one of the missing books of Hermes Trismagistus, Father of Alchemy. The papyrus originally compiled by a priest, contains 700 prescriptions, some of which have thirty or more ingredients. The blood of the ibis was frequently given, and we are told a great deal about the therapeutic value of precious stones. At the same time, the prescriptions testify to a developed knowledge of pharmacy, showing that a considerable number of our crude vegetable extracts, used to-day, were known in Egypt. On the other hand, some horrible animal ingredients were prescribed, accompanied by the usual incantations. The mineral remedies included a solution of ammonium hydroxide with the sulphates, carbonates, and oxides of several metals. Salts of copper may have been prescribed for the ophthalmia which was always prevalent in their hot and sandy country. Sodium chloride, iron sulphate, and the oxides and carbonates of lead are all mentioned though not in such exact detail as by the Indian Susruta. The vegetable remedies include onion, caraway, mint, aloes, myrrh, colchicum, saffron and cedar. There are prescriptions for deafness, nervous troubles and incipient baldness, many of the remedies ending with the comforting assurance that 'this has proved most efficacious'. This cheerful custom has its parallel in the leechdoms of our Anglo-Saxon ancestors who used to end their prescriptions with the suggestion that 'it would soon be well' with the patient.

The Egyptian doctor was expected not only to cure his clients but to prevent snakes from entering their houses and to drive all vermin away. His reputation was one of the things which most impressed Herodotus when he visited Egypt in about 450 B.C. He compared it with the comparative lack of physicians in Babylonia. 'Every disease,' he said, 'has his physician, whereof it cometh that every corner of Egypt is full of them, many for the teeth, not a few for the stomach and inwards.' Indeed the papyri show that between the eighteenth and the thirty-first dynasties a vigorous medical practice coincided with a high though painfully one sided standard of living, for the excavations at Thebes and elsewhere have shown us spacious, sunlit dwellings prepared for a leisured class with doctors and dentists at their doors. Homer in the *Odyssey* speaks of the Egyptians as 'sons of Paean all', Paean being the physician of the Olympian Gods, the name afterwards conferred upon Apollo. The prophet Jeremiah also spoke of the country as 'the land of many medicines'.

Yet disease must have been all too common. Dysentery, scurvy and stomach derangements afflicted the dwellers in the Nile valley where asthma was also a scourge, and dental disease prevalent. There is no record however of some other diseases, such as rickets or syphilis.

The Egyptian practice of embalming involved some knowledge of anatomy and also of the various gum-resins and balsams employed in the work. An examination of many skeletons found in recent years shows a fracture of the ulna near the wrist to have been especially common in women. The ingenious explanation has been advanced that the accident was caused in a play like the old English quarter staff, where the left arm was frequently raised and often injured. The fractures, so far as we can see, mended well, but there is one uncomfortable picture in the Ebers papyrus where a compound fracture of the arm was wrapped in a rough splint of palm fibre, with disastrous consequences. Nevertheless, we can tell that in the second millennium these people were advancing towards the higher standard of practice which they displayed when Herodotus went touring. By that time they had attained considerable skill in manipulation; they made suppositories, gargles, inhalations and plasters; they left some careful clinical notes upon various cases, and they even appear to have known that the heart distributed the blood through the arteries, thus anticipating Harvey's 'discovery' of the heart's true function. Above all, they paid great attention to personal hygiene in their dwelling houses, and formulated a dietary suitable to their climate. They even organized the profession itself, making it into a sort of corporation after the fashion of the mediæval guilds.

But to all this there is a sinister background. Egypt abounded with sorcerers and magicians whose performances were generally no more than conjuring tricks deliberately aimed at deceiving the people.

Many of them were carried out by the Priesthood and were described by Heron, a Greek mathematician of the second century B.C. It has been said that both their religion and science were spoilt by magic just as their civilization was spoilt by the usual background of slavery. The extensive examination of skeletons carried out more especially in the Nile valley by such investigators as Ruffer, Derry, le Baron, Ricetti, and Jones have brought to light the astonishing prevalence of deformities caused by arthritic lesions and *spondylitis deformans*. Ruffer thinks that the standard of living must have been extremely low and that the average age probably did not exceed fifty. Messrs. Stubbs and Bligh, in their interesting book, *Sixty Centuries of Health and Disease*, also mention these Egyptian skeletons as testifying to hardship and malnutrition. Some of the lesions have been thought to be tubercular, and one clear instance of Pott's disease in the spinal column has been found in a mummy of the XXI dynasty in Thebes. But a very large majority show degenerative changes in the joints similar to those found in the humanoid stocks and early vertebrates by Virchow. It has been suggested that in Egypt the bulk of the deformed bones belong to the class of the *corvée* who sweated to satisfy that extraordinary craving for continued life which possessed the Egyptian rulers.

The process of embalming was a similar attempt to secure some kind of physical immortality, and it will always be associated with Egypt. It was an expensive business and might cost £700, though a poor man might conceivably be turned into a mummy for about ten pounds, being merely washed in myrrh and salted for seventy days. Myrrh is derived from *Commiphera Myrrha*, Eng., and probably from other allied species of the *Burseraceae*. Other fragrant resins and gums in constant use were the gum *olibanum* and the 'Balm of Gilead'. *Gum olibanum*, the frankincense of the Bible, came from *Boswellia*, Carteri, Birdw., and from allied species. A gum is a substance soluble in water but not in alcohol. A resin on the other hand is soluble in alcohol but not in water. An oleo-resin is a substance midway between a resin — that is a vitreous solid — and an oil. Balm of Gilead is an oleo-resin derived from *Commiphora opobalsamum*, Engl., and this is thought to be the plant mentioned by

Josephus in his *Antiquities of the Jews*, Book VIII, Ch. vi, and Book XIV, Ch. iv. Some think that the Balm of Gilead mentioned in the Bible may have been mastic, the resinous exudation from *Pistacia Lentiscus*, L., N.O. *Anarcardiaceae*. *Commiphora* and *Boswellia* now belong to the N.O. *Burseraceae*.

To the pea and bean family, the *Leguminoseae*, belong the *Acacias*, *Mimosas*, and *Cassias* which are characteristic of the Nile valley. The Egyptians, like the Hindus, made use of the gum arabic produced by *Acacia arabica*, Willd., and its relatives. In the last century one heard of travellers in caravans who subsisted upon this gum for days when food was scarce, and also found it effective against insect bites. The bark of many of these lovely trees is commercially employed in tanning.

Garlic, aloes, and fig were included in the Egyptian materia medica as in that of the Hebrews. The fig, *Ficus Carica*, L., *Moraceae*, was valued by most of the nations of antiquity. In Sparta it was part of the daily menu, and both Greeks and Romans thought that it conferred bodily strength upon the consumers.[1] The first fig poultice upon record is that of King Hezekiah, but the fruit has been frequently given in the East for dysentery as well as outwardly for glandular swellings. In modern pharmacy, syrup of figs is a common aperient. The pulp of the fruit is also used in popular medicine for a pectoral emollient.

Linen woven from the fibres of *Linum usitatissimum*, the flax plant, *Linaceae*, has been used from antiquity, and has been found upon the Egyptian mummies. The plant is one of the most useful in the service of man. The scrapings of the linen form the surgical lint, and the short fibres of the flax are utilized as tow. The toughness of the fibre is equalled by the mucilaginous content of the seeds. Linseed oil is obtained from them by expression, and the cake left over is the oil cake used for cattle food, or powdered for linseed meal. The demulcent and emollient properties of the poultice are well known. In herbal practice, an infusion of the seeds is prescribed for catarrh.

---

[1] A species of Fig, *Ficus religiosa*, has been found depicted on a seal – probably of the first millennium, with animal heads issuing from the stem.

Garlic, *Allium sativum*, Linn., of the Order *Liliaceae*, is praised by many old writers for its virtues as a medicine, though its principal use in Egypt seems to have been for food. Herodotus states that the builders of the great Pyramid were largely fed upon the bulb, and Pliny says that garlic and onion were held in reverence at the ceremonies in Egyptian temples. The fastidious Greeks, however, detested it, and no one who had eaten it was allowed in Cybele's Temple. Oil of garlic has long been used as a diaphoretic and stomachic, and Galen extolled it as the rustic's cure-all. Syrup of garlic is often prescribed in disorders of the lungs, and, during the war, the oil was used in considerable quantities for its antiseptic value.

As a condiment it is extensively used on the Continent, and the Bulgarians claim that their longevity is related to their consumption of the bulb as a food. Diallyl bisulphide and diallyl trisulphide are the chief constituents of the oil.

HEBREW MEDICINE

Such records as we possess show that there was much in common between the materia medica of the Hebrews and that of the Egyptians. Both made extensive use of the resinous and aromatic species of plants, and both used olive oil for the hair and skin as well as occasionally in religious ceremonies. One of the most interesting plants often mentioned in the Jewish Scriptures is called 'Saffron' or to give it its Hebrew name, *Kharkum*. (It has, however, been suggested that the word *Kharkum* may refer to *Carthamus tinctorius*, L., or to *turmeric*.)

Saffron is the substance yielded by the saffron crocus, *Crocus sativus*, Linn., N.O. *Iridaceae*, whose dried stigmas, pressed into a mass, were for many centuries used in Europe as a remedy in nervous complaints. It was also sedative, and its volatile oil was given as an anti-spasmodic. The crocus has been persistently cultivated by many races and in various countries. In the sixteenth century it was under cultivation in Europe, but of late it has been imported mainly from Spain. In the Middle Ages it was held to be a specific against consumption. Its yellow dye has also given it a secondary commercial value. The finest saffron consists of the dried stigmas with portions of the styles attached, in loose masses. Cake saffron consists of safflower florets mixed with a little of the real saffron and honey. These florets come from *Carthamus tinctorius* which is used — mostly in Cornwall and the West of England — for flavouring and colouring cakes. On the Continent it figures in the dish called *bouillabaisse;* but its use, both in cooking and pharmacy, is diminishing.

Allusions to the spice herbs are frequent in the Scriptures. Dill was evidently used in condiments; and cumin, *Cuminum Cyminum,* Linn., another of the *Umbelliferae,* was probably taken, as Pliny took it, with bread, to promote digestion. The plant was cultivated in India, Arabia, and Egypt. In modern medicine it has been replaced by its relative caraway. The hyssop used by the Priesthood in sprinkling was probably a species of *Origanum* allied to our marjoram, but it is possible that the real hyssop, *Hyssopus officinalis,* Linn., may have been in use also, for in the time of Dioscorides it was spoken of as a holy herb. Both plants contain — as do most of the *Labiatae* — volatile oils. The holy, anointing oil (Exodus xxx, 23—25) is said to be compounded of myrrh, sweet cinnamon (possibly cassia), sweet calamus (probably not *Acorus Calamus,* Linn., but a scented grass of the genus *Cymbopogon*); cassia, (or costus) and olive oil. There is no mention of cloves which do not appear to have been known to the ancient Hebrews.

Hyssop in our own day has almost gone out of use, though its essential oil is retained in the manufacture of flavouring essences, and, to a small extent, in perfumery.

The curious reference to the 'dove's dung' sold for 'five pieces of silver' in 2 Kings vi, 25, is thought to mean the bulb of *Ornithogalum, umbellatum,* Linn., the Star of Bethlehem. This species which may be a native of our own country, covers the plains of Palestine with white flowers, and has edible bulbs which in the East are cooked like chestnuts and were formerly stored at Damascus for the use of travellers. Gerard, who enumerated six species of the genus calls one 'the great Arabische Star-floure'. The bulbs were prized as an article of food in many Eastern countries.

The Hebrews made more extensive use of fragrant gum-resins than perhaps any other people. It has been suggested that after the captivity in Egypt the habit of employing holy oils increased, and the substance which they used for anointing the sacred utensils of the Temple was made up of many fragrant materials such as costus, cassia, myrrh, etc. In the Canticles there is a full description of the aromatics which they burnt in the Temple services; and others may have been used in the houses in Eastern fashion, or medicinally, and as fumigants. That they traded in such drug plants is shown by several references to 'the powders of the merchant'. and to the 'precious drugs and ladanum resin' which the Ishmaelites carried about on sale. The *Bdellium* mentioned in Genesis was most probably a gum-resin derived from one of the trees of the myrrh and frankincense family, i.e. N.O. *Burseraceae.* Frankincense itself or Lebonah, was afterwards renamed *Olibanum* by the Romans; but 'ladanum resin' was quite a different thing. The word 'lot' translated myrrh in Genesis xxxvii, 25 and lxiii, 11 is taken to refer to this gum-resin which is exuded from several shrubs of the Rockrose Order, the *Cistaceae* of Southern Europe and North Africa. The beautiful *Cistus ladaniferus*, Linn., is one source of this oleo-resin, but commercially a good deal is obtained from the Cretan plant, *C. villosus*, Linn., var. *Creticus*, Boiss. The oleo-resin which is present even in the plant hairs has a heavy fragrance somewhat allied to that of ambergris, and this scent, together with its fixative properties, gives it its present day value in perfumes of an oriental type. Mr. Redgrove in the *Gardener's Chronicle* for November 19th, 1932, tells us that Cyprus was from early times an important centre for the production of labdanum, and the word 'Chypre' (the name of the perfume for making which labdanum was so much employed), is, of course, the French for 'Cyprus'. In the island, labdanum producing plants are so abundant that the fleeces of sheep and beards of goats become covered with the sticky exudation while pasturing, and the shepherds remove the oleo-resin from the animals by means of combs.

The labdanum of commerce occurs in the form of dark brown cakes, hard in cold weather, or in that of a soft resinous-like mass. Mr. Redgrove adds that the substance contains four to eight per cent of ether-soluble resin, two per cent of essential oil, and o.8 per cent of a crystalline substance which has been named 'ladaniol'.

One of the constituents of the essential oil is acetophenone; and this was known as a synthetic substance before it was discovered in labdanum oil. It is a fragrant body, and is utilized in Hawthorn perfume.

Since the analysis of the labdanum oil, this acetophenone has been also found in the essential oil of *Stirluigia latifolia*, Steud; a member of the *Proteaceae*.

The Spikenard of the Bible (used in early times by the Hindus) was a product of *Nardostachys Jatamansi*, Dc., one of the *Valerianaceae*. It is interesting to read that the ancient races used the plant in epilepsy and nervous diseases, as it is a near relative of our own wild Valerian, long employed as a nervous stimulant. The odour of spikenard — which has been described as a mixture of musk, patchouli and valerian has long been prized in India as a perfume.

The Hebrews resembled the Egyptians in their strict dietary and in their detailed personal hygiene though they carried this much farther and gave it a more ceremonial aspect than any other ancient race. For the rest, we know how they surpassed others in the splendour of their poetic imagination united to their unswerving ideal of righteousness. It was that ideal rather than any scientific achievements which was their gift to the world, though in the tenth century A.D. we shall find them uniting with another Semitic race to influence the course of medicine.

In 332 B.C. Egypt that had enslaved them and had in turn been conquered, was finally merged into the Empire of Alexander who wiped out the glories of Thebes and enslaved the inhabitants. Only the ruins and the Nile valley itself remained as it had been for long ages, presenting to the conquerors the old inescapable problems of the sun, the river, and the desert sand. Each race that succeeded to the Egyptian civilization — and none of them remained there long — had to put up much the same defences against Nature and against

EGYPTIAN AND GREEK MEDICINE

invading foes. But the new city, Alexandria, was to become the
intellectual centre of the Roman Empire for 300 years, and in her
museums and libraries arose that blend of Hellenic and Asiatic
learning which influenced Europe from the time of the Ptolemies
down to the Middle Ages.

GREEK MEDICINE

Herodotus among his many activities drew up a map which survived and was afterwards known as *Orbis Terrarum ad mentem
Herodoti.* Following the vague ideas of his time he was fain to make
Asia a great sprawling region as large as Europe, but what he meant
by Asia was in reality Asia Minor. He resisted however, the tempta-
tion to which later map makers, notably in Columbus' time, suc-
cumbed, adding 'where unknown, there place Terrors'.

It might almost be said that prophetically, Herodotus in his
emphasis of Asia Minor was wiser than he knew, for the story of
that region was to have far reaching influence upon the modern
European world in regard to literature, science and medicine. The
Cretans as we know, first blazed the trail of culture along the Mediterranean shores, until the Dorian Greeks, 'men from the north',
dispossessed them, and introduced into the land a new order of
Indo-European traditions and institutions. It was a fateful fusion
in Mediterranean history, but there was another brought about by
that *nation boutiquière,* the Phœnicians, who were likewise coasting
about those shores bringing a contact between East and West,
bartering goods from Tyre to exchange for wool and timber; from
them it is believed that the Greeks learnt an alphabet and the science
of navigation.

The Dorian Greeks settled on the peninsula of Cnidus and the
little island of Cos, while the Ionians colonized along the western
shores of the Mediterranean, and in their prosperous cities began
to lay the foundation of the most amazing civilization of the ancient
world. The Grecian system of medicine grew out of their early
activities and genius for colonizing, for wherever they went, they

67

founded other schools and made them centres of education. Their colonies in Southern Italy were destined to play a large part in the development of medicine later on.

Aesculapius, the Greek God of Medicine, was, like Imhotep, an actual person about whom there had grown up a curious legend.

In the forests of Thessaly there were said to be a savage race of men called Centaurs. Legend made great play with these strange beings and depicted the Centaur as half man, half horse. One of them, named Cheiron, came to be celebrated for his knowledge of medicine and especially of herbs. He obtained it, we are told, — the story is mythical — from Apollo himself, the Solar God of Healing. To this Cheiron, the boy Aesculapius was brought, and was instructed in the healing art with such effect that his skill grew to be almost miraculous. He had two sons who fought in the Greek army, but history has nothing more to record of them.[1] The fame of the good Centaur was enduring for we find his form engraved on healing rings of early Grecian workmanship. Also Pliny spoke of him as 'the first herbalist and apothecary', while the lovely English Centaury, *Erythraea Centaurium*, Linn., (or *Centaurium umbellatum*, Gil.) still commemorates his fame. (Mixed with Barberry leaves it is used by herbalists to-day for jaundice.)[2]

The story is not an idle one, for it shows that at a very early date knowledge of herbs was in the forefront of European medical tradition. Another legend concerning Apollo points the same way. He had a favourite pupil named Iapis, to whom in his great Olympian way he offered the gift of supreme skill in any art that he might desire. But the boy simply craved 'the knowledge of herbs and power of healing.' The story is given in the seventh Aeneid, 391. '*Scire potestates herborum usumque medendum maluit.*' It is also reported of Iapis that he first used the herb Dittany in his practice. This was probably an European species of *Origanum* allied to our Marjoram.

The Olympian God of Healing has his place in modern pharmacy, for the Apothecaries show him holding a bow and a serpent in the coat of arms over the door of their Hall. Similarly a phrase from his

---

[1] The legendary Panacea and Hygeia were also said to be his children.
[2] See p. 179.

ovation to Daphne is enshrined in their motto, '*Opifer que per orbem dicor*'.

By the eighth century B.C. Aesculapius had become deified, and gradually his cult spread from beyond Epidaurus in Southern Greece far into Asia Minor. In his honour innumerable temples were founded with priests called Asclepiadac. These temples were for centuries the repositories of medical teaching and practice, and the priests were looked upon as the descendants of the God, and transmitted medical knowledge from father to son. A great many later physicians also bore the name of Asclepiadac, or adopted it.[1]

The temple resorts were, in effect, like sanatoria, and were generally built in beautiful and healthy surroundings, and near healing springs. The temple of Epidaurus where the God was principally worshipped was the most famous. It was surrounded with an extensive grove, and Pausanius mentions the tame serpents which were kept in the Temple sanctuary. In his book *The Evolution of Modern Medicine*, Sir William Osler has an impressive diagram of the Hieron or Sanatorium at Epidaurus, with its extensive and hygienic accommodation for invalids, its gymnasia, baths and treatment rooms. The cult of this God, 'most loving to men', lasted for a thousand years, for in early Christian times the beautiful temple of Aesculapius was built at Rome, and sick slaves and gladiators were treated there. In the old hierons the control still rested in the hands of the priesthood, the practice being a blend of rational and simple methods combined with a healthy element of suggestion. The votive tablets recording the cures of grateful patients at Epidaurus mention such complaints as gastric ulcer, ophthalmia, and the common results of external injury.

In his book, *Marius the Epicurean*, Walter Pater drew a pleasant picture of one of those temple resorts (which were later called Asclepions and under that name finally suppressed by Constantine as of pagan origin). The 'incubation sleep' was instituted by a priest who made a sleeping patient the recipient of healing suggestions. The practice, of course, to some extent forestalled the hypnotic treatments at Nancy and elsewhere; but the treatment recorded of

---

[1] Asclepiades Bithynus (*c.* 124 B.C.) was one of the most celebrated.

these old institutions at their best (for like most human organizations they sometimes degenerated), was an embodiment of principles which were consonant with the wisdom and intelligence of the Greeks. The tag of the *mens sana in corpore sano* came to us through Rome, but it must surely have been Greek in origin.

Before passing from the ages in which religion and medicine were linked, albeit in some strange forms, one interesting survival should be mentioned. It is the Temple of Medicine in Tibet where the priests are the only doctors. The building perched on its precipitous rock has been photographed by travellers as the accompanying illustration will show.

HIPPOCRATES

By the fourth century B.C., the Ionian Greeks had spread their language and ideas along the Mediterranean shore and adjacent islands, founding their colonies at the end of immemorial trade routes; and in Asia Minor several of their greatest men were born. One legend gave Symrna as Homer's birthplace. At Miletus, Thales was born, and on the island of Cos, Hippocrates; while Pythagoras was born at Samos, and Theophrastus in Lesbos in 370 B.C. His works on the history and parts of plants have come down to us together with the other treatises which were designed to supplement the work of Aristotle.

Pythagoras who discovered that the pitch of sound depended upon the length of a vibrating chord was primarily a philosopher, but he was greatly interested in medicine, and paid frequent visits to a famous hieron in Crotona, one of the Greek colonies in Southern Italy.

Crotona was the home of great wrestlers. From early days the Greeks had brought the practice of physical exercise to a cult, believing that through exercise and massage the blood could be changed and the tissues vivified. It was at Crotona that Hippocrates, son of Heraclides of Cos, studied as a pupil of the gymnasts. This great man, born in about 460 B.C., initiated the classical period of Greek medicine. He lived in those amazing years when Athens was at her zenith, the home of a galaxy of men of genius in every branch of science and art.

When he left the Aesculapian temple he travelled and studied, and it was he who gave the impress known as the Hippocratic tradition which medicine retained for 800 years. His influence was twofold. First, he led people away from spells and magic, teaching them to observe the natural laws of the human body and its inherent trend towards self-healing. Secondly, he instituted the lofty ethical principles which defined the ideal of a great physician as modest, incorruptible, and humane. Morally, he infused into medicine a spirit of selfless and devoted purpose; and practically, he made use of methods which science has consistently ratified. For the first time, detailed notes were taken of the cases in his care. Many of his observations such as those upon diphtheria, curvature of the spine and dislocations, were well in advance of his age. Indeed Dr. Francis Adams (1796 — 1861) expressed the opinion that up to the middle of the nineteenth century no writer on surgery had given so complete a description of the dislocations of the hip joint as Hippocrates.

In other matters such as the insistence upon clean hands and boiled water in the treatment of wounds, he anticipated the reforms of the nineteenth century in aseptic surgery. Rest, quiet and dietetics were the methods upon which he most relied, but he used baths and massage as well as the gymnasium practice of his time. Bleeding, too, was almost as commonly resorted to in these early centuries as it was in the Middle Ages. Many of his aphorisms are marked by a quiet characteristic wisdom. For instance, 'the more we nourish unhealthy bodies the more we injure them'; and again, 'Complete abstinence often acts well if the strength of the patient can in any way sustain it'. One of his most memorable precepts is the following: 'Where the love of man is, there is also love of the (healing) art.'

The celebrated Oath of the Asclepiads, representing the ethics of Hippocrates is worthy of reproduction. Here is an abridged version of it.

'I will look on him who shall have taught me this art even as one of my own parents. I will share my substance with him and will supply his necessities if he be in need. I will regard his offspring as my own brother, and will teach them this art if they would learn it without fee or covenant. The regimen I adopt shall be for the benefit of the patient according to my ability and judgement, and not for their hurt or for any wrong. I will give no deadly drug to any, nor aid a woman to procure abortion. Whatsoever things I hear concerning the life of men in my attendance on the sick or even apart therefrom which ought not to be noised abroad I will keep silence thereon . . . Pure and holy will I keep my life and my art.'

The drug plants which Hippocrates used were few in comparison with the Indian or Egyptian practice, and the noxious animal compounds were entirely absent. Leclerc has collected 400 samples from the collection, of which the following genera are familiar to all students of ancient medicine.

Absinthe, Anise, Anthemis, Aristolochia, Asphodel, Atriplex, Polygonum, Bryonia, Lappa, Carduus benedictus, Dancus, Centaurium, Chenopodium, Cinnamon, Cinquefoil, Clove, Coriander, Cyclamen, Dictamnus, Cytisus, Erica, Euphorbia, Cassia, Allium, Helleborus, Teucrium, Hyoscyamus, Conium, Isatis, Cinnamomum, Malva, Melilotus, Mentha Artemesia, Olea, Parthenium, Phaseolus, Potentilla, Ruta, Ranunculus, Paeonia, Ricinus, Rhus, Crithmum, Solanum, Scilla, Thymus, Rosemarinus, Viola.

He insisted strongly upon a suitable dietary in each case, and approved the use of barley water and lime water.

It was characteristic of the old 'magical' strain which he abandoned but which came back again through Rome that later physicians like Dioscorides could not use their herbs without investing them with some ritual or symbolism. For instance, the little Cinquefoil (*Potentilla*) of our waysides was one of the simplest remedies which Hippocrates gave for the ague which for so many centuries afflicted the fever victims in undrained swamps. In later practice Dioscorides could not use this plant merely as a 'simple', but prescribed 'three leaves' for a tertian fever and four for a quartan, the leaves in both cases to be mixed with an amulet of three spiders!

In Hippocrates' day — and before it — malaria was the scourge of Greece. It was not until recent times that Sir Ronald Ross and Sir Patrick Manson confirmed its association with the mosquito (*Ano-*

pheles) with the result that under the auspices of the British Government many infected areas have been cleared. The consequences of this dreaded disease was said to be worse than typhoid, especially with regard to its evil moral influences and its attacks upon children. An interesting suggestion has been made that the extraordinary deterioration of character and morale which was manifest among the Greeks in the last centuries before the Christian era was attributable, at least in part, to malaria. Hippocrates, who studied its symptoms very closely, noticed the decline in mental and moral strength left by its ravages together with a recurrent melancholy.

At the present day there are still in many places in Greece malarious conditions similar to those in Africa and India, but the Greek anti-malarial league started in 1905 is doing good work, and it is said that the modern peasant values his quinine, when he can get it, as he values bread.

The gift of the Father of Medicine to his generation may justly be said to have been the scientific method. In his *Greek Thinkers*, Gomperz says, 'the Hippocratic treatises were a product of the Greek intellect not merely incomparable but no less unique'. After his death the writings and notes that he left were edited with additions by his pupils. This annotation went on for centuries till it was issued in the twenty volumes known as the Hippocratic Collection. All through the succeeding ages, physicians copied from it and trans-lated — or occasionally mis-translated — it into other tongues, notably into Arabic when the Saracen schools arose in the tenth century. As late as 1840 a copious edition was issued in Paris by M. Littré, and the Loeb Classical Library re-issued the *Aphorisms of Hippocrates* only a year or two ago. His influence in the ancient world extended wherever the Hellenized culture spread; and after the absorption of the Persian Empire into Macedon in 330 B.C. and the conquest of Asia Minor, the Hellenization of Western Asia went on without further check. New cities were founded; while Egypt under the Ptolemies became as Greek in language and culture as the Mediterranean colonies. In North India also the Punjab had become Hellenized; and even after the Scythians expelled the Greeks, the Grecian tradition remained. The Greco-Buddhist school in art in the first century A.D. showed how penetrating their influence had become.

It has been said that 'save the blind forces of Nature nothing lives or moves that is not Greek in origin'. This is of course a challenging over-statement when we consider that their great age only sprang into being some 2300 years ago. At the same, time the fact of their lasting supremacy in art and literature is beyond dispute, while their greatest physician stands for a type of their ethical philosophy. The Greeks of the 'great age' showed us the world being measured without fear or prejudice by one of its inquiring creatures, seeking without prepossessions for the truth; though central to their thinking was the ideal of an ultimate harmony to which the mind and conduct of man should conform. In social life they were the first to grasp the privilege of leisure as a means to self development, although it is true that the labour of the Helots existed to make this possible. Greece fell like all her neighbours from war, jealousy and aggression, but we have only to consider the astute saying of Herodotus that individual men were not stupid but that together they invariably acted as if they were, or the piercing sincerity of Themistocles in denouncing the capture of Melos, or the teaching of Hippocrates to realize that these men of Ionia were often startlingly in advance of their time. The world waited for its Father of rational medicine until Hippocrates was born.

CHAPTER IV

THE EARLY CHRISTIAN ERA
MEDICINE IN ROME
THE RISE OF THE SARACENS

(1) THE TEMPLE HOSPITAL OF SAN BARTHOLOMMAO AT ROME
Photographed, by permission of Messrs. Black, from Besant's *London*
Photo by Ben Marks, Clevedon

(2) IRIS FROM THE WALLS OF KARNAC
(by permission of Professor Capart, author of *Thèbes*)
Photo by Miss L. M. Bonar, of University College, London

THE GRAECO-ROMAN PERIOD

THE two men who directly followed Hippocrates and whose influence was enduring were Theophrastus and the great philosopher, Aristotle. From the latter we get the foundation of Natural Science and morphology. He kept a druggist's shop in Athens, but though he was a naturalist of genuis, and wrote among other things a treatise upon plants, his greater interest was in morphology relating to the evolution of organic species whose structural plan he already glimpsed. We often fail to realize how much has been done for our thinking by these Fathers of the race to whom the green world beckoned, mysterious and alluring, without chart or guide. His successor, Theophrastus, made the first line of division for practical purposes between flowering and non-flowering plants; he also recognized the annual rings of the tree, and went so far as to anticipate Goethe's work on metamorphosis by an acute observation that petals were only leaves altered in shape and colour. To each plant moreover he assigned such 'virtues' and properties as were then known; and it was this consideration of the healing attributes which was to influence the later development of the Herbal.

It has been pointed out by students botanically minded that primitive man who drew his animals so graphically, as a rule ignored his plants. Clearly, the latter were of lesser moment, since they were only to be sought and gathered instead of being hunted or magically wooed. From early cultures however, one or two fine specimens of pictorial art have come down to us, such as the garden plants on the frescoes of Knossos in Crete, and the representation — which has a medical significance — of other plants from Thebes.

On the walls of Karnac we find the imprint of bygone pictures of gourds, irises and cereals which we can recognize. This first floral exhibition dates from the time of Thothmes III (*c.* 1500 B.C.), and we are told that it was made after an expedition into Syria and Palestine. The account of this earliest of 'botanic gardens' is given in Professor Caparts' book on Thebes from which the following is an extract:

Dans les appartements de Thoutmes III au fond du grand temple de Karnak, il y a une salle facile à retrouver grâce aux quatre colonnes papyri formes qui se dressent encore intactes.

Tout le haut des murs a été enlevé, nous faisant perdre ainsi, sans aucun doubte de précieux documents. Ce qui subsiste, la décoration de la partie inférieure des murailles, a fait donner à cette salle le nom de jardin botanique.

On y voit 'les plantes que Sa Majesté avait trouvée dans le pays de Retenon (Syria); toutes les plantes qui poussent, toutes les fleurs qui sont dans le terre des dieux et que Sa Majesté y a découverte lorsqu'elle est allée pour subjuguer toutes les contrées d'apres les commandements de son père Amon qui les mise sous ses sandales'.

Schweinfurth, the great German naturalist, in speaking of these pictures, observes that in some cases the artist has drawn upon his imagination, but that the *Arum Italicum*, the Iris and the Pomgranate are clearly recognizable.

When we come to the early Greeks, we immediately find that close association of the plant with the medicinal uses assigned to it which marks the beginning of botany and of the herbal. These illustrated works began in the fourth century before Christ, if not earlier. Diocles, an Athenian physician of that century, is mentioned as the author of one of the earliest of these herbal texts. The work was a compilation, accompanied by comments and illustrations, of the plants at that time used in the materia medica.

When we consider the tediousness of such a task carried out with exquisite precision in the script of the age, we marvel at the amount of time that was given to these works both in the ancient and the Christian centuries. Of course they always reflected some body of tradition. There is no doubt that folk-lore as well as 'popular' medicine has in every country been derived from age-long sources of knowledge which were often wrapped up in voluminous charms and incantations.

Even in Greece, where in the classical age people were much less concerned with talismans than were the Chaldeans, there was a class of men called rhizomatists, or root gatherers, who applied themselves to ceremonial and ritual gathering such as that of coltsfoot taken at sunrise or henbane at the waxing of the moon. Theophrastus had a great deal to say about these practices.

Poisonous species as we might expect, seem to have been well known. The *Alexipharmica*, a loosely compiled herbal written by Nicander in the second century B.C., confines itself to a list of such poisons and their antidotes, among the former, hemlock, wolf's bane and opium. The title came from the Greek words, *alexo*, I ward off, and *pharmakon*, poison. Nicander however recognized that small doses were often remedial. He mentions 'water distilled from roses', which points to some existing knowledge of distillation. He was followed by the herbalist Crateuas who was often mentioned by Galen and Pliny. He is looked upon as the real Father of the herbal which after his time increased in importance as an illustrated manual of drug plants and their application. His own herbal perished, but from reproductions we can identify many of his plants such as the Comfrey, *Symphytum officinale*, Linn., (*Boraginaceae*), still valued by herbalists for bronchial trouble, and the *Aristolochia Clematitis*, Linn., or Birthwort, which had been used by Hippocrates and continued to be a 'wort' in Anglo-Saxon England. It belongs to the N.O. *Aristolochiaceae*. Several species were long in use, but have been mostly superseded. *A. indica*, Linn., is retained as a bitter tonic in the Indian materia medica.

In about A.D. 77, Pliny's *Natural History*, a work of prodigious learning, appeared, seven of its 37 volumes being devoted to medical botany. They were treatises more than herbals, and as such, led up to the equally discursive literature of Dioscorides and Galen in the next century. All these Roman authors kept up the ritual of herb gathering, perhaps as a concession to popular beliefs. They also began to dry and preserve their plants for purposes of reference, thus laying the foundation of the *hortus siccus* or dried collection.

It was in Pliny's treatise that we find the theriac mentioned as an antidote to poison. This was the Roman name given in Trajan's time to the antidote of Mithridates Eupator, the King of Pontus, who was defeated by Pompey. This monarch was the most celebrated pioneer of toxicology, experimenting — if we may believe the records — with poison and antidote in his own person with the spectacular result that when he desired to end his life no poison would act on his hardened system. His prescription was known as the Mithridate all through the succeeding centuries, and was one of the four so-called 'officinal capitals' or highly esteemed medicines. The others were Venice treacle, invented by Nero's doctor; the Philonium of Philo of Tarsus, and the Diascordium, invented by Jerome Frascata to ward off plague.

The Mithridate was of inordinate length containing about sixty ingredients, one of them being the viper's flesh which was esteemed for centuries. This old Mithridate, in spite of several *theriaca* which were thought to supersede it, was actually in use until the nineteenth century, and was included in the Pharmacopoeia of 1882. It was one of the most remarkable instances of polypharmacy, the multiplication of ingredients in a single draught.

Other monarchs dabbled in the poisonous elements of medicine. Attalus III who was the last King of Pergamos, and who died in 134 B.C., was reputed to have made use of henbane, hemlock, and hellebore for the removal of his 'friends'. The Emperor Hadrian was also interested in the subject.

It was probably in Roman society that the professional poisoner first made his appearance. In the pages of Livy and Tacitus we find references to many mysterious deaths, in which crimes women were often implicated. Some of the most notorious cases were followed by a public inquiry which was the precursor of our inquest. These early excursions into toxicology may have been useful to the amiable Borgias who brought poisoning to a fine art in the Middle Ages.

In Alexander's new kingdom, after the city of his name had been spaciously rebuilt, another galaxy of men of Grecian origin foregathered, attaining scientific eminence. Euclid was among them, and Archimedes, and many another attracted by the patronage of Ptolemy

Sotor and his successors. A large medical school with clinics and laboratories was founded, and progressive work was done both in anatomy and surgery. When in A.D. 30, Alexandria was finally absorbed into the Roman Empire, it ceased to be a centre of intellectual activity, and from that time to the birth of Galen a hundred years later, there was nothing in European history to record bearing upon the history of the plant in medicine.

THE ROMAN CONTRIBUTION

Rome was the world's great organizer, and the Romans applied their practical, organizing genius to the healing art in much the same spirit as they undertook their drainage, or the wonderful water supply that brought 300,000 gallons of water daily into Rome. Medical social services were instituted. The *valetudinaria* which followed the Hospital of Aesculapius on the Tiber were the precursors of our hospital system, but with the exception of Celsus in the first century, and of Pliny whom we have already mentioned, there were no Latin speaking doctors of any note till two men, both of Greek origin, were born. Dioscorides, a soldier who wrote in Greek, was what we should call a good field botanist, if somewhat loose in his detail. He wrote a book describing about 500 plants used in medicine, and this elaborate treatise achieved such fame that it remained in use for six centuries.

The plants themselves are full of interest botanically, as many belonged to the Greek Flora, and as such, were identified by Dr. Sibthorpe of Oxford when he travelled in Greece to get material for a collection. (His book was brought out later by Dr. Lindley.) Among the plants were gentians, thought to be named after Gentius, a King of Illyria, who, like so many typical Greeks, whether of Olympus or Thessaly, 'had a knowledge of herbs'.

Dioscorides made a sort of confection with the celebrated Viper's flesh so long used as a poison antidote. He called it *Sal Viperum*. The snake was roasted with figs, salt, and honey and spikenard. This materialized version of the ancient snake symbol had a long popularity, for it was afterwards made into a sort of wine and later again into a soup which is still esteemed on the Continent. The Viper's flesh (together with the Mithridate and some later theriacs), was retained in the *London Pharmacopoeia* of the seventeenth century. Dioscorides used his herbs much as Hippocrates had done, but with some interesting additions. For instance, he prescribed male fern extract which is still in use as a vermifuge, and horehound which is in the modern herbalist's collection. He also used some weeds which we are apt to treat with derision, such as yarrow, cleavers and colts-foot. Yet this yarrow, *Achillea millefolium*, Linn. (*Compositae*), was retained as late as 1820 in the Edinburgh Pharmacopoeia, and is still esteemed as a tonic in the U.S.A. The Greeks had valued it for internal haemorrhage.

The cleavers, *Galium Aparine*, Linn. (*Rubiaceae*), a familiar 'follower' in our country lanes, looks a disreputable subject for pharmacy, yet it has remained in use as an anti-scorbutic for 2000 years. The use of coltsfoot (*Tussilago farfara, Compositae*) is not so startling because one often sees its name at the present day upon bottles of cough mixture. The leaves which contain tannin and a trace of a bitter glucoside were put by Dioscorides into a pipe for smoking. He made great use of a cabbage cultivated by the Romans, and he knew the emollient properties of some species of elm bark, especially of the 'Slippery Elm', *Ulmus fulva (Michaux)*, which is extensively used in the United States as well as in herbal ·medicine at the present day.

Another European plant known to the Roman doctor was *Aconitum napellus*, Linn., the Monkshood, N.O. *Ranunculaceae*. The alkaloids of this plant are among the most deadly poisons of the world. Plutarch gives an account of Mark Antony's army being in want of food, grubbing up some of these roots which they devoured with the result that every man died in a paroxysm. The root used to be called 'Kill panther', and the sorceress Hecate was said to have discovered it and passed on the knowledge to her daughters, Circe and Medea. Hence the reference made by Sydney Smith: 'After partaking of Circe's cup I am now eating the herb Moly (garlic)'. The idea that Circe's poisons which included mandrake, could be rendered harm-

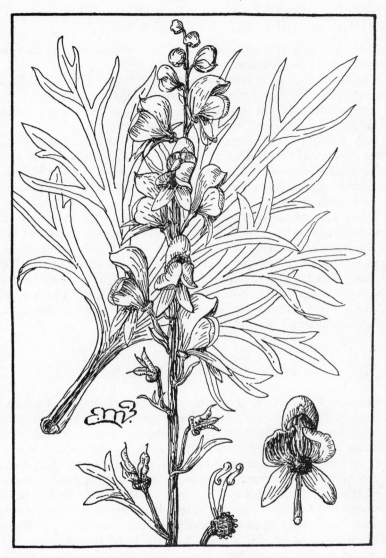

ACONITUM NAPELLUS
Monkshood

less by garlic is a very old one, said to have originated with Hermes who taught it to Odysseus.

The dried root of *Aconitum napellus*, still official in the B.P., is imported here from Germany, the Swiss Alps and the Tyrol, but is not greatly used. It is employed mainly for making a liniment as an anodyne in chronic rheumatism and neuralgia.

It is difficult to know whether chamomile was used in Rome, for there are several Composites outwardly similar, but the true chamomile, *Anthemis nobilis*, Linn., was named 'Roman' by the German scholar Joachim Camerarius, who found it growing near Rome in the sixteenth century.

Many legends in after years gathered about the name of the popular Dioscorides. There is a delightful symbolic picture of him in the Juliana Anicia Codex of the fifth century A.D. in which the nymph 'Discovery' is depicted giving him the mandrake about which so many legends are circulated. (This plant will be mentioned in Chapter vii among its related members of the Order *Solanaceae*). There is also a recently published English translation of the herbal by Dr. Gunther of Magdalen College, Oxford.

THE GREEK PHYSICIAN, GALEN

Claudius Galenus, commonly called Galen, was born at Pergamos in Asia Minor in A.D. 131. In his early years we hear as usual of his travels, for nothing is more remarkable than the way that these Romans travelled both by sea and land routes, although they were not naturally navigators and colonists as the Greeks had been. Galen, who became surgeon in Rome, is reckoned the greatest anatomist of antiquity, but his own statement that he went in fear of his life because he thought that his jealous confrères would poison him, throws a lurid light upon the prevailing medical morality. Anyhow, he survived to adorn the post of physician to Marcus Aurelius, and later, he applied his exuberant energies to the writing of the 83 treatises which are still extant. In fact, an edition of his works was published in Paris as late as 1679. He had a shop where he sold

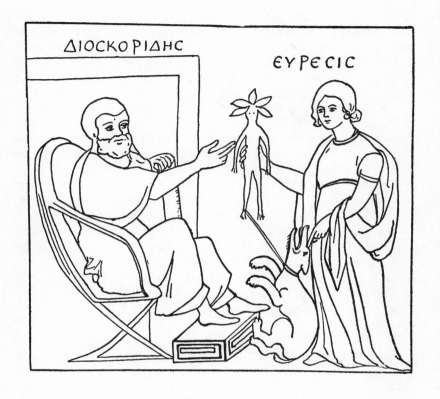

THE NYMPH DISCOVERY PRESENTS A MANDRAKE TO DIOSCORIDES
from Dr. Charles Singer's book, *From Magic to Science*

Photographed by Messrs. Heming

drugs from many countries — no one minded keeping a shop in those days — and his materia medica showed an advance upon that of Dioscorides, including many well attested remedies. Our word 'galenical' is derived from his name, and he is thought of in our day as the first experimental physiologist, for among other things he discovered the difference between pneumonia and pleurisy, while he also left some sound observations upon tuberculosis. He was not above the popular traffic in charms and talismans, but he was emphatically a man of the world, and put himself at the patient's point of view in prescribing a charm as well as a potion, unless indeed he was so psychologically minded as to recognize that the power of suggestion linked with one or the other might be a powerful asset in the cure. Nor was he without his own prejudices. He clung to the original Mithridate in the full belief that for one whole day it would give immunity from poison. Theriacs were at that time largely used, and often mixed with precious stones, a relic of the Egyptian belief in their efficacy.

Some medicinal compounds had come to Rome by way of Egypt and Greece, apparently unaltered. Many such mixtures were called *Hiera Picra*, literally, sacred bitters. They had the reputation of a cure-all.

According to Wootton (*Chron. Pharm.*), the original *Hiera Picra* of Galen was composed of Soccotrine aloes, cinnamon, spikenard, mastic, *Asarum*, *Xylobalsumum*, saffron and honey. This prescription lasted on for centuries, occasionally undergoing some revision, except in the case of the aloes which remained constant. At last, in 1746, the formula became finally watered down to aloes and wild cinnamon, the bark of *Canella alba*, Gaertn. (N.O. *Canellaceae*). These sacred bitters were in fact, the beginning of patent or secret medicines for which, as we shall see later on, enormous sums were often paid.

Galen, of course, dispensed his own medicines, for in those days, physician and chemist were one. The Latin word for drug was *medicina*, and although the office of the apothecary was not yet formulated, the word *apotheca* came into use for the warehouse in which drug plants were stored. In his book *Four Thousand Years of Pharmacy*, Dr. La Wall gives the recipe said to have been used by

Galen, and called *Unguentum refrigerans*, or cold cream, an emulsion of water in almond oil made with white wax and scented with roses. A simple extract made from poppy heads was called *meconion*, from *mekon*, a poppy.

ROME IN DECLINE

The first centuries of the Christian era always seem one of the most dramatic periods in history. Imperial Rome was in Virgil's phrase working 'to impose the fashion of peace' within her far-flung boundaries and had indeed by the *Pax Augusta* proclaimed the ideal of a self-governing community. But the peace imposed by force was inevitably broken up by elements of slightly mitigated barbarism; and when the Empire fell to Odoacer, Europe was in the melting pot once more. The new order that rose from the ruins, an order whose central authority was to be Papal and ecclesiastical, had far reaching effects on the history of medicine. All this time Christianity had been under a cloud: in Nero's reign the symbol of Jupiter (2+) which is still preserved on our prescriptions, came into use among physicians to show that they were the right sort of people and had no connection with the Christians who might not practise medicine. Yet despite three centuries of persecution, the gallant little band whom the spirit of their Founder had inspired to simple but heroic living preserved a joyous belief in the wholeness of body and mind. But when the persecution ended, and the religion was absorbed into the State, it became subjected to a welter of materialistic influences. Worn down perhaps by repression and disappointment, the early vision of the Christian votaries had begun to fade, and a change in thought had an unfortunate influence upon the life and habits of the people. They gradually broke away from the *mens sana in corpore sano*, and in the age of the creed spinners, when life was hard, insecure and perplexing, their religious practice became darkened by disputes. Meanwhile, Constantine had closed the Temple hospitals, and new institutions rose in their place. The object — a zealous one — was the displacement of a pagan by a Christian organization, and the lavish Romans did it in a royal style. Yet from the medical point of view it seems to have been of little worth. The medical practice of the Asclepions was not very advanced, but the hygiene and physical culture based on the teachings of Hippocrates were, at least, remedial, whereas the new institutions were mainly philanthropic, and seem to have been lacking in skilled attendance. Moreover, as religion deteriorated into the repressions and negations of mediævalism, hygiene and physical exercises were discouraged. The body came to be looked upon as partly 'vile' and partly unimportant: holy people neglected to wash. Gradually, everything to do with the body became anathema, and the world was conceived as ordered for each one's particular treadmill. The excesses of the Christian anchorite resembled those of the Eastern fakir in that both tried to pass from the animal to the angel without pausing upon man.

Through the turbulent ages that followed the fall of Rome, we hear of constant outbreaks of pestilence. A pathetic little procession set out in Rome on April 25th, A.D. 590, headed by Pope Gregory, chanting hymns of intercession against the plague. Surgery had passed into the hands of the Priesthood, but in the year 660 the Hôtel-Dieu was built in Paris for the relief of the sick poor, and this foundation is still the largest hospital in the city. The materia medica of the period consisted of the eternal copying of the books of Pliny and Dioscorides often mingled with folk-lore. It was a custom which might have inspired the phrase of Laurence Binyon:

> Break the word and free the thought;
> Break the thought and free the thing;

but it dominated the evolution of medicine for many centuries.

THE SARACENS

The years from 500 to 1000, formerly called the Dark Ages, are being more gently treated by the modern historian who realizes that some civilizing influences were still at work, some of them coming from the East into Europe, and some like the fine educative work of Saint Boniface in the seventh century emanating from the Church. The ideal of Otto in the Holy Roman Empire remained an ideal; but inasmuch as it did aim at a Commonwealth of the human race, it looked to the future. Still, the fact remained that the ideal was too limited and the general barbarism too widespread to stop the devastating warfare in which, for two hundred years, one land after another was blackened by fire, and spoilt by men who were too busy destroying life to give much thought to its amelioration.

Meanwhile, a new force was taking shape, a contact between East and West at least as fateful as that in the earlier story of Asia Minor; and, once again, Mesopotamia was in part its background.

The Arabs for many centuries had been merely a wandering or pastoral people, but after the death of Mohammed and their absorption into the Saracen empire, the deserts of Arabia suddenly blossomed out into men organized with astonishing rapidity for conquest. As early as A.D. 638, during the Caliphate of Omar, Palestine and Asia Minor were overrun, and the gigantic foundations of the Saracen power were established by ruthless fanaticism, until, by the eighth century, Persia, Tartary and Northern Africa were added to the empire. The Saracens then invaded Europe and established the Caliphate of Cordova in Spain. It seemed as if a tangent had glanced against the circle of the world, leaving a new and permanent division. From the Oxus and Indus to the Atlantic Ocean the followers of Mohammed were supreme until two circumstances checked them. In 718 their repeated attempts upon Constantinople were frustrated by Leo III, and in 732 Charles Martel routed them at Tours, after which their power began to decline.

The Arabian learning seemed to be a phenomenon to which the Saracen alliance gave its opportunity. Something in the mental attitude of the Saracen Caliphs was favourable to scientific skill; and wherever they ruled, schools and colleges were founded. The cities of Bassora and Baghdad became centres of learning where Hindu mathematicians were made as welcome as Syrian or Greek. Copies of Greek and Sanscrit MSS. were sought for and copied, the Arabians especially being the most ardent scholars and pioneers.

A curious trend of events had opened the way some centuries

earlier for this revival. A Christian sect called Nestorians, from Nestorius, Patriarch of Constantinople, had broken off from the orthodox church on account of heresy, and had been driven forth into Persia. From thence they began to spread: in fact, the peaceful penetration of these 'modernists' is one of the oddest stories in history. They found their way into India, into Mesopotamia and Asia Minor. In several places they were persecuted, but they held their ground, and colonies of them still exist in Persia at the present day.

In Mesopotamia they came in contact with the intellectual Saracen element which then included some learned Jews who were working at medicine. Together, Nestorian and Jew founded a hospital at Dschondisabour; an interesting example of men who could 'compose their differences' in the fervour of a common aim.

This alliance of Saracen, Christian and Jew was destined to influence the course of medicine through the Middle Ages. The mantle of the Greek now fell upon the Arab.

ARABIAN MEDICINE

In the eighth century the Arabs discovered the heel and toe of Italy together with the island of Sicily where Greeek was spoken and which had remained comparatively free from invasion. Sicily they annexed; and settling there, absorbed all the extant Greek tradition. Salerno, thirty miles south of Naples, had long been a Greek colony, with a central medical school. Hither now came the Arabs; and thus, the city grew into a meeting place for Saracen and Italian students. Later the Normans were attracted thither, and under the enterprising rule of Robert the Norman, Salerno became a flourishing home of medicine. A Moor, named Constantine the African, translated the Greek and Arabic scripts into Latin, and Nicholas Salernitas brought in a standard for pharmacy which lasted for centuries and was the basis of our measures, the scruple, the grain and the drachm. The well equipped hospital received many unwholesome hordes of crusaders as patients, and remained until it was abolished by Napoleon. There was a tradition that the University of Salerno was founded by four Masters, Greek, Latin, Arabian and Jewish; and certainly it became one of the most famous medical colonies in Europe. Readers of Chaucer will remember his allusion to the tremendous physician who came from Salerne. They will also remember the allusions in the Prologue to the *Canterbury Tales* to the English physicians, Gilbert, Bernard, and John of Gaddesden. The delightful description of the Doctour of Phisik runs thus:

> Ne was ther noon hym lik
> To speke of phisik and of surgerye,
> For he was grounded in astronomye . . .
> He knew the cause of every maladye
> Were it of hoot or cold or moyste or drye,
> And where engendred and of what humour.
> He was a verray parfit prakisour.

In the same Prologue, Chaucer mentions the Arabian physicians, 'Razis and Avycen' as well as their predecessors, 'Galyen and olde Hippocras'. But he ends with an unkind thrust at the profession, which shows an evident lack of respect, in the lines

> For gold in phisik is a cordial
> Therefor he lovede gold in special.

The allusion to the 'causes' of a malady is based upon the 'humoral' theory which obtained in pathology from Hippocrates to Sydenham, and which taught that the body was composed of four humours or liquids, blood, phlegm, yellow bile and black bile, the four mystically corresponding to the four elements and setting up disease whenever their proportions were disturbed. It was only a theory, but as there was no true knowledge to contradict it, it lasted until the physicians of the seventeenth century swept it away.

The doctors of this age were partly Arabian, partly Jewish, several of them attaining a high celebrity. In fact, the head of Avicenna who, born in 980, was called 'The Prince of Doctors', adorns the Diploma of the Pharmaceutical Society to-day. A beautiful ideal, framed by Maimonides, pupil of Averroes (*c.* 1135), deserves to rank with that of Hippocrates. 'I desire to sustain and help the rich and poor, good and bad, enemy and friend; and let me ever behold in the afflicted and suffering only the human body.'

The example set by these Fathers of the medical profession no doubt influenced the later ages: witness the promise made by the French apothecaries, and the ideal set before our own medical schools at the present day.

A great revival of medical practice issued from the union of Arab and Jew in Salerno. Hospitals were founded in Europe with Nestorian Jews as teachers. One of the most famous doctors was Rhazes, of whom it was said that he treated his gastric patients with barley water while for melancholy he recommended chess! In the application of their knowledge and in social service the Saracens notably outstripped the Christian world. They paved and lighted their cities at a time when London was an undrained area with houses without chimneys. They were teaching geography from globes while the Church was insisting that the earth was flat: they were practising chemistry and distillation which they introduced into Spain. While showing a remarkable aptitude for the exact sciences they were keenly interested in the alchemy which is always associated with their name. Perhaps they were influenced by the Nestorian group which had adopted some of the Chaldean ideas; in any case they evolved some theories which brought back the old belief in planetary influences. Their alchemists apparently accepted the old Aristotelean theory of the four elements, air, earth, fire and water. Arising from these elements they claimed two principles in all things, namely sulphur and mercury. Later they added salt. Their philosophy gave to every particle of matter an animating spirit, and therefore they judged that all volatile products of distillation were of the nature of spirit. Upon this idea their alchemy with its quintessences and transmutations was largely based, and in a sense it has been justified by modern discovery.

The earliest directions for the distillation of roses are, according to Gildemeister and Hoffmann (*Die Aetherischen oele*), found in the writings of Ibn Chaldun. Simple retorts of glass and earthenware were used which could be heated over an open fire while the oils were received in a condenser. They also employed the screw and wedge presses which lasted till the hydraulic press came into use in about 1800. The primitive Arabian stills are said to be used to-day in Europe, but they have mostly given place to the various methods of steam distillation which were greatly improved towards the end of the nineteenth century.

Cinnamon oil was one of the first subjects of distillation, and it figured largely in the commerce between Arabia and Africa where the spice was produced, and the European countries to which it was exported. During the Middle Ages great cargoes of spices and drugs were shipped to Venice. Later, the Portuguese valued the island of Ceylon chiefly because cinnamon was found there; and when the Dutch took over the island, the cultivation of the tree was begun.

Another oil which became extremely popular, more especially in Persia in the Middle Ages was otto of rose, used for its fragrance. It may have been distilled at an early date, but Mr. Redgrove tells us that the first authentic record of the oil occurs in the almanac of Harib for the year A.D. 961.

Some unexpected results came from the Arabian laboratories, for though the Chinese had found gunpowder before them and the Hindus the strong acids, the Saracens had a way of stumbling upon new substances by accident. Thus, Achild Bechil, in distilling an extract of urine, lime and charcoal, obtained something that 'shone in the dark like a good moon'. The substance was found to be phosphorus. And Rhazes, while distilling spirit of wine with quicklime unexpectedly found alcohol.

The practice of alchemy also had its effect in the training of its votaries, and some great men followed each other from the alchemists' schools. One, Basil Valentine, became the teacher of Paracelsus von Hohenheim who in his turn influenced Jean Baptiste van Helmont, one of the first chemists to get a glimpse of the action of enzymes in fermentation. It was probably owing to his training in alchemy that Paracelsus in the fifteenth century abandoned so many of Galen's vegetable prescriptions and preferred mineral remedies such as zinc and antimony. But he led men back to the original quest of alchemy which was, as he insisted, to make medicines and not to make gold or silver. His search for a panacea or elixir which should be a universal remedy against disease came from the Saracens, but they sometimes abandoned it in their enthusiasm for gold which they conceived of as capable of being extracted from the baser metals. They failed, as the chemistry of their age was bound to fail; but they pointed forward to the marvels, so long unsuspected, of radio-activity.

In agriculture they brought into cultivation some important crops such as sugar, rice, and the fruiting trees. In Spain especially, under the Moorish domination, agriculture flourished as never before. They also improved the manufacture of the textiles and of steel.

In medical practice they made use of about 50 per cent of crude, vegetable drugs, while supplementing them with such mineral remedies as arsenic and zinc. Many of them were keen botanists; and pharmacists like Avenzoar travelled about in other countries studying plants. They made lists of their collections, though no herbal is connected with their research. It seems that they spent much time in studying and annotating the medical texts of the Nestorians, and, on the whole, they must be considered followers of tradition as far as materia medica was concerned. They employed the same *Hiera Picra* that had been used by the Romans, but they gave prominence to one of myrrh and aloes which they called *pil. Rufi.* because it had been prescribed by Rufus of Ephesus. Like the Hebrews, they made extensive use of scents and aromatics, many of the products of the Spice Islands, India and China being brought to Europe by Arabian merchants. They took their perfumes into Spain, and are credited with a luxurious use of cosmetics as well as medicines. It was an ancient saying among them that Adam when turned out of Paradise, took a grain of wheat, a sprig of myrtle, and the date which they esteemed as the king of all fruits. Nearly every part of the date palm was utilized by them for some useful purpose, and the fruit was often their principal food.

They imported and used the clove, *Eugenia caryophyllata*, Thb., the fragrant plant of the Myrtle Order native in the Molucca Islands. It had been known from the time of the Chinese, and is still employed as a carminative.

One of their remedies has quite fallen into disuse, the juice of the bulb of the wild daffodil, *Narcissus Pseudo-Narcissus*, Linn. They used it for baldness, but it had been in use among the Greeks probably as a narcotic, for Socrates mentions it in connection with 'The Chaplet of the Infernal Gods'. Its juice was said to produce numbness and paralysis.

The modern custom in Arabia of sprinkling a guest with rose water and burning a fragrant wood (often said to be 'Aloes wood'), in token of friendliness had descended from ancient times. This aloes wood may be identical with that used in the East for incense, a resinous substance found in the interior of *Aquilaria Agallocha*, Roxb. (N.O. *Thymelaceae*). It is unfortunate that this wood should be called aloes wood, for it has nothing to do with the medicinal aloes of the *Hiera Picra* and of modern medicine. The latter consists of the liquid exudation, evaporated to dryness, of various species of aloes belonging to the N.O. *Liliaceae*.

Salep, commonly used in the Middle Ages, was included in the Arabian pharmacy. The European salep was mainly derived from three species of orchis, *O. Mascula*, Linn., *O. Masculata*, Linn., and *O. latifolia*, Linn., all of which are native orchids. Persian salep is believed to be furnished by *O. latifolia* and *O. laxifolia*, Lam., while the so-called Royal Salep of Afghanistan is said to come from a species of *Allium* (*Liliaceae*).

Salep is still highly esteemed in the East. It was formerly sold in London as a beverage before coffee was known, and is still taken for a morning drink in Smyrna whence the supplies mainly come, but there is little demand for the product in modern Europe.

Several plants of the *Convolvulaceae* furnished medicines in the Arabian materia medica. One was *Ipomoea Nil*, Roth. (called Habb ul nil), whose seeds are still sold in the Indian bazaars as Kala-dana — or black seed. *Convolvulus Scammonia* is a closely related plant, with the cathartic properties common to the whole Order. This used to be cultivated in England in Gerard's day.

The word jalap comes from the Spanish *xalapa*, and refers to the resinous product of the Mexican plant *Ipomoea purga*, Hayne, formerly classified as *Exogonium purga*, Benth. This jalap was included among the strong purgatives in many countries until — perhaps mercifully — the supply dwindled so that another plant came to be substituted for it. It has however, been put under cultivation in the Nilgerries in India.

One of the best known of all medicinal plants, most beneficial but unhappily most abused, is the Opium poppy, *Papaver somniferum*, Linn. It shall be mentioned here because the Arabs introduced it into Persia. For a detailed account of the 'sleep-bearing poppy', the reader may be referred to Mr. Redgrove's *Spices and Condiments*, but the author has kindly made the following notes upon the plant and its cultivation:

'It is only when *Papaver somniferum* is grown in a warm and sunny clime that it is capable of yielding latex in sufficient amount to make it worth cultivating for opium; and this fact rather than cheap oriental labour has been the main factor in limiting the cultivation of the poppy in Europe. The plant however, is not cultivated only for opium. The capsules or heads as they are commonly called, are mildly sedative, in virtue of the small percentage of the active constituents of opium they contain. They are used in the preparations of fomentations for bruises and external wounds, and for dental and other abscesses. The seeds which contain no morphine or other narcotic substances are of gastronomic value, and are much appreciated in Eastern Europe. The oil expressed from them is also put to various uses, e.g. in making artists' colours, and as a salad oil, etc. The refined oil is however hardly cheap enough to figure prominently as an adulterant of olive oil.'

Papaver somniferum is grown on a commercial scale for the production of opium in Persia, India and China. The production and the trade in the drug has now been brought to a great extent under the League of Nations.

Morphine, the chief alkaloid of opium was known to the Parisian, Charles Derosne (1780 — 1846), whose work was extended by Sertümer. It was actually isolated by Seguin in 1804, but he did not recognize its basic character. His paper, read before the Institute of France in which he described the experiments, was not published before 1814, and in the meantime, Sertümer had obtained both morphine and meconic acid, realizing the basic character of the former, describing it as the first of a new series of substances, 'the plant alkalies'.

It was not until Guy Lussac drew attention to it in 1817, that morphine began to take its important place in medicine. In opium it is very variable. The B.P. recognizes only those grades which contain at least 9.5 per cent. Two other important alkaloids are codeine and narcotine.

The juice which is inspissated by the action of the air comes only from the unripe cells of the fruit. There is always a steady demand for the larger capsules, 'poppy heads', sold for infusions. Opium is an ingredient in the popular medicine, paragoric; and mixed with milk, sugar and ipecacuanha, is also contained in Dover's powder. In herbal practice a poultice is often made from the crushed heads mixed with chamomile flowers, and 'syrup of poppies' is still made in the Arabian manner and given for catarrh.

Morphine manufacturers are now giving preference to Indian opium, the chief areas for its cultivation being Benares and Behar; the output controlled by the Government. The medical opium of commerce is usually sold in 2lb. cakes wrapped in oil paper. It is subjected before packing to a careful laboratory test for impurities.

In small doses and in external application the drug is, of course, of the greatest utility and is the most valuable narcotic in materia medica. This makes it the more tragic that its abuse should have led to such disastrous consequences after its introduction into China in or about the ninth century. It was not however until 1790 that a depot of opium vessels was established by the East India Company in the ports of China under the Treaty of Nankin, and it was not till later still that the vice of opium smoking began and spread like a plague through the country. Sir Alexander Hosie in *The Trail of the Opium Poppy* tells the whole unhappy story from the time when the British Government set out in an ineffectual effort to destroy the poppy fields in the Yang Tsze river valley.

The cultivation of the plant dates from early times, for Dioscorides mentions the collection of it in Asia Minor. As a medicine it was used by the Roman physicians of the second century A.D.

In 1918, Russia extended her cultivation of the poppy in the Ukraine both for morphine extraction and for the seeds and capsules. The French also put some ground under cultivation, but the European trade belongs principally to Jugo-Slavia where it has been cultivated for centuries on a considerable scale.

With *Papaver somniferum* we may take leave of the Arabian pharmacy. After Granada was captured in 1492, the Moslem ascendancy was broken in Spain where for two hundred years there had been a perpetual warfare between the two races and creeds both of which were disfigured by the bigotry which animated their religion. The antagonism between Aryan and Semite at a time when they might have been united in a common quest for knowledge was one of those 'wilful missings' by which racial prejudices have destroyed the comity of nations and blocked the path of progress. The Arabian translations of the Greek authors into Latin was nevertheless one of their contributions to the intellectual life of the age; and the books influenced the students in the newly-formed universities which were a feature of mediævalism. After the Moors disappeared from Spain, the racial pendulum gave another powerful swing, and Europe once again became the stage for a further development of the Aryan peoples.

CHAPTER V

EUROPEAN HERBALS

THE ORGANIZATION OF MEDICINE
FROM THE ANGLO-SAXON LEECHDOM
TO THE BRITISH PHARMACOPOEIA

ANGLO-SAXON MEDICINE

AND what about Britain all this time? The records of Anglo-Saxon medicine fall within the Dark Ages, and have much in common with those of contemporary Europe, but the record is scanty and has not yet been deciphered with special regard to the development of medicine. Most MSS. of the age are of monkish origin, but there is a considerable body of evidence to show that there was a literate medical fraternity outside monastic or clerical circles in England. In one respect, England was unique in that she had a line of several able and resolute kings. Alfred (849 — 901), the noblest of them, by the purity of his life, by his intellectual foresight and his encouragement of the English tongue set his mark upon the land for all time. In the book of Anglo-Saxon leechdoms edited by the Rev. O. Cockayne, we read of a correspondence that took place between the King and Helias, Patriarch of Jerusalen. The latter seems to have been learned in pharmacy, and as Alfred's health was poor, the friendly patriarch sent over certain drugs to benefit him. They were said to be aloes, balsam, scammony, tragacanth and galbanum. We note that the resinous plants of the East predominated in this interesting consignment which also included a 'theriac' and a stone charm. What use the King made of them is not recorded.

By the tenth century the British School at Glastonbury — the finest expression of the church's influence — had become a focus for those civilizing forces which emanated from the community at Iona whose tender and heroic lives had recaptured the lost radiance of Christianity.

In many of the religious institutions there was considerable literary activity, while within their gates the sick were tended and sanctuary given to the outlaw. The churches which were built all over the country became the nucleus of villages where studious men might live quiet lives in fellowship and comparative security. For doubtless, then as now, security was the chief concern of laymen in an undisciplined and fear-ridden world; and as usual, the real progress of art or science was impeded by the lower instincts and ambitions of society. Hence it is not surprising that all through Anglo-Saxon times medicine remained at a low level. The high water mark of civilization was in Ireland whose missionaries went out overseas to found centres of learning in Gaul, Italy, or Germany. At one of the Irish settlements (St. Gall in Switzerland, named after Gallus, a follower of St. Columban), there is a tradition of a physick garden and hospital as early as the ninth century, but we know of nothing comparable in England at this date. Anyone who wanted to study medicine went abroad to Italy.

As in all other countries, the popular religion, built up from many sources, pagan and Christian alike, and commonly expressed through ceremonial and ritual, influenced the practice of the healing art. Pilgrimages to holy wells and shrines were frequent in Saxon England. The Church had adopted many of the old pagan wells, and the names of the saints were substituted for or blended with those of the older Teutonic deities, for Woden and Thor had been the Protectors of well and springs. Some of these, as for instance St. Madron, St. Kenelm, Winchcombe and St. Cleer still remain, although they degenerated into 'Wishing Wells' in the Middle Ages. At Tessingham the picturesque ceremony of 'Well Flowering Day' is retained with other old English customs. Leeches were apparently rare; and in illness priests were called in as often as physicians. Medical treatment was frequently accompanied by a Paternoster, or occasionally by a ceremony of exorcism. As late as 1559, a ceremony of this kind testified to the still prevailing demonic beliefs. The patient was made to sit in a chair which the priest had blessed. Then, after he had drunk a pint of sack and salad oil, burning brimstone was held to his nose till his face was blackened, the priest meanwhile conjuring the demon to depart. 'The rest is silence.' Exorcism still finds a place in Roman Catholic ritual.

Charms were varied, and many which have been preserved in

association with medical manuscripts are of exceptional interest. In his interesting book, *From Magic to Science*, Dr. Charles Singer gives an account of the best known MSS. some of which were of the nature of charms. Of these 'The Lorica of Gildas the Briton' is perhaps the most remarkable. The root idea was that of a lorica or coat of mail which would protect the wearer. Hence, the charm became a protection, and took the form of a text or prayer worn by the suppliant who enumerated in his petition the various parts of the body which he wished defended from harm. The lorica of Gildas is written in the curious 'Hisperic' Latin of the sixth and seventh centuries. One text is preserved in the Harleian collection in the British Museum, and others are to be found in various British and foreign libraries.

The Leech Book of Bald and the Lacnunga are two other Saxon MSS. which have a bearing upon the healing art.

From the Lacnunga we get that wonderful old fragment, 'The lay of the nine healing herbs' which was written in the Wessex dialect and has been translated in many different ways. Here we have a survival of the primitive Teutonic magic with its doctrine of the 'nines', the doctrine of the 'flying venom', and the introduction of Woden who was identified by the Romans with Mercury. The enemy to be overcome by Woden's magic was the 'worm' which recalls the Chaldean symbolism of a thousand years before. Another tenth century manuscript of a charm which invokes the aid of Woden is in substance similar to one in the Atharva-Veda, which was the section of the Hindu Vedas devoted to charms accompanying the ritual exercises of religion.

Miss Rohde in her interesting chapter upon this period (in her *Old English Herbals*) enumerates the herbs which were given when certain charms were used, as for instance, when the patient was attacked by the 'water elf disease'. They were lupin, yew berries, helenium, marsh-mallow, dock, elder, wormwood and strawberry leaves. She adds that nightmare and mischief wrought by goblins was treated in a similar manner. The good old wood betony of our countryside which we shall hear of all through the ensuing centuries was held in high repute for 'monstrous nocturnal visions'.

One stanza of the lay of the nine healing herbs runs as follows:

These nine healing herbs march on
'Gainst nine ugly poisons —
A worm sneaking came
To slay and to slaughter.
Then took up Woden nine wondrous twigs
He smote the worm till it flew in nine bits.

Among the herbs enumerated were fennel, mugwort, plantain (Way-broad), chamomile (whose equally delightful name was Maythen), nettle (or wergulu), crab-apple and chervil. It is not surprising to find the plantain in the list, for the common species, *Plantago major*, had been used in the time of Pliny and perhaps earlier for broken skin and wounds. References to its use occur in later English litera-ture. 'Your plantain skin is excellent for that,' said Romeo. The plant is known to have been used as a medicine among the Bretons as early as the ninth century. It was also thought to be a 'soveraigne counterpoison', and was included in many compounds. The same astringent properties are present in *Plantago media*, the persistent invader of our lawns. The seeds of both species abound in mucilage which makes them palatable to birds, and they have been used as a substitute for linseed.

As to the Maythen of our ancestors we do not know for certain whether or not it was the true chamomile, *Anthemis nobilis*, L., *Compositae*. It may have been *Pyrethrum inodorum*, Sm., called feverfew from its use as a febrifuge, or *Matricaria Chamomilla*, L., a similar plant of waste lands, formerly largely cultivated in Belgium. The flowers of the cultivated *Anthemis* are official in the B.P., and yield one per cent of a volatile oil, a fatty oil, and a glucoside, the properties being tonic and stomachic. William Turner in his herbal spoke of it as being 'plenteous on Richmon Greene', but in no country to-day is the wild chamomile plentiful enough for the demand.

The Anglo-Saxons were said to have a wider knowledge of their native flora than any other race, and they used most of their wild plants in medicine. Pliny had previously noted a similar knowledge among the British, accompanied by an elaborate ritual in the gathering of the herbs. This ritual was doubtless absorbed by the Saxons and incorporated with their own. The words leech-craft and wort bring us to the Anglo-Saxon pharmacy, but here we have to confess that though they may have been alert and observant botanists in the field — for they recorded about 500 plants, their medical practice was lamentably degenerate. The lore of Dioscorides which had filtered through to them with that of Pliny, had deteriorated on the way: many of the prescriptions contained elements such as animal excreta, even more repellent than those of early Egypt, while they all suffered from the polypharmacy of which the old Mithridate had been so conspicuous an example, and which included haphazard ingredients that might well neutralize each other. A book of Anglo-Saxon leechdoms makes sorry reading. One typical prescription counsels the use of paeony seeds made into a sort of poultice to lay on a man for lunacy after which he might be expected 'to upheave himself whole'. These seeds are surprisingly said to 'shine as a light fat or lamp', and herdsmen were to go out at night and gather them. One wonders where. Was our only native species, the rare *Paeonia corallina*, now confined to the one habitat on the Steep Holm island beyond Weston-super-Mare, really common in those days? And has it disappeared through drainage, or through the assiduous plucking of the 'herdsmen' who had 'lunacy' in their midst?

Another leechdom with commoner ingredients runs as follows: Seed of fennel and parsley, dill and rue. Celandine and fever-few. Garden and horse mint. Seed of betony, of Alexanders, sage and wormwood. Savory, bishopswort, elecampane, henbane, agrimony, stonecrop, horehound, nepeta, and carline thistle. Take equal parts of all these worts. Then to these worts add anise, cummin, pepper, ginger, and gum mastich worked to a very small dust. Make a drink to take at night, after fasting, for giddiness, fever or spasm.'

In what age, one wonders, did the proverb originate about the remedy being worse than the disease?

In a prescription for styes the patient is told to mix barley meal with honey, 'a leechcraft tested by many'. Here we have the old 'electuary' mentioned in an earlier chapter as characteristic of the practice of the Arabians and Jews. Many powdered substances came to be mixed in this way with either syrup or honey.

Another remedy much revered — and indeed looked upon as sacred by the Druids — was the Club-moss, *Lycopodium Selago*.

In most of their ceremonies, the old racial conception of the Earth-mother was still retained. The following is a beautiful prayer from a twelfth century herbal:

> 'Whatsoever herb thy power dost produce, give, I pray with good will to all nations to save them, and grant me this my medicine. Those who rightly receive these herbs from me, do thou make them whole.'

'When the Anglo-Saxon peasant went to gather his healing herb,' says Miss Rohde, 'he may have used church prayers and ceremonies, but he did not forget the Goddess of the Dawn.' Nor have centuries of sophistication entirely separated the people of rural England from the old worship of Nature, for among the Romany folk and some of the peasantry there are echoes of it at the present day.

THE ANGLO-SAXON AND EUROPEAN HERBALS

The Odyssey of the herbal began with Theophrastus in Ionian Greece; was continued in new forms in mediæval Europe, and became one of the sources of the English herbals of the sixteenth century. Like all human enterprises it had its periods of splendour and decline. The inescapable tradition handed down by Pliny and Dioscorides, and disseminated by translation into many languages both of Europe and Asia, ran all through the centuries like a lengthening chain. The whole history is a most curious commentary upon the paralysing force of tradition. Century after century the old manuscripts were copied, and their only interest for us is when we find an artist who added something to the received form and enriched it with a new idea. Occasionally a man had the gift to work within the old convention and yet to make it as fresh as if it had come down from heaven.

Others unfortunately did what has been done in every sphere of craftsmanship: they copied the originals without intelligence, and in so doing debased them till the primal freshness was destroyed. The only thing that can be said of this great multitude of slavish imitators is that had they been idle in the lawless world outside of them they would probably have wrought mischief in it. As it was, they lived withdrawn from the social stresses and conflicts of their age, for although some of them were doubtless laymen, the majority were monks. And apart from the work itself, sometimes good and often bad, this at least must be remembered of the Anglo-Saxon medical manuscripts, that they helped to make the vernacular into literature at a time when the language was emerging from dialect.

Many of the mediæval European herbals are things of rare and costly beauty which the great libraries of the world have preserved. One splendid copy of Dioscorides in Greek was given on her wedding day to Juliana Alicia, daughter of Anicius Olybrius, the Eastern Emperor, in A.D. 472. Notable illustrations were, 1, a Cranesbill (*Geranium molle*); 2, the Castor oil plant; and 3, the famous picture of Dioscorides and the nymph mentioned in the last chapter. This was one of the high water marks in botanical illustration, but others appeared from time to time. A well-known MS. taken from an earlier Greek source is the Latin herbal of Apuleius treasured in the Leyden library and dating from *c.* A.D. 600. From this work innumerable copies were taken, thereby perpetuating a system of plant synonyms that were unhappily becoming meaningless as the mediæval languages were taking shape. This herbal was one of the first to be issued from the printing press in the sixteenth century.

Two other early medical works were the Johnson papyrus written in Greek in the early fifth century, a portion of which is preserved in the Wellcome Museum of Medicine, and the '*Antidotarium*' of Nicholaus Praepositus, a physician of the Salernian school. This was printed several times in later centuries.

When we come to the Anglo-Saxon herbals, we find that with few exceptions they took their medicine as they took their illustrations, from traditional sources, but Dr. Singer tells us of one herbal written in Latin at Bury St. Edmunds in about 1120 in which the monk used his own initiative and copied in place of the illustration an actual plant which may have been growing in his monastery garden. In one case, for instance, he substituted a Southern European *Teucrium* (*T. chamaedrys*) for the allied species, the '*Camedrum*' of the original text from which he was working. This labiate may still occasionally be found on a ruined wall recalling for the botanist the story of its introduction centuries ago and its subsequent use as a wort. Perhaps it came over marked with the approval of the European herbalists, for Déscaine and Le Maout say that 'the Germander group to which it belongs contain gallic acid with a bitter principle very serviceable as a tonic'. The flowers of this rare species are purple, whereas the only *Teucrium* common in England is the green flowered Wood Sage, *T. Scorodonia*.

In another instance the Bury St. Edmund's monk substituted a plant which he knew for the one in the European tradition, for he gave us the portrait of a thistle, *Carduus Marianus*, a European species which may have been cultivated in his day, but is now extremely rare in Britain. The 'blessed thistle', *C. benedictus*, is also a European species, and has been used for centuries in dyspepsia.

This dependence of the Anglo-Saxons upon continental traditions is referred to in a chance paragraph in Sharon Turner's old history of the period, where he states that a Saxon wrote to St. Boniface asking for medical books, and complaining that the drawings in those which he had were of plants unknown to his countrymen.

Through the later Middle Ages the peaks of achievements in floral illustration were reached by several of the Flemish artists, and by others of the Italian and German schools. A Salernian monk in the eleventh century named Constantine the African, was the author of a popular herbal. The botanical treatise of Albertus Magnus, 'the Christianized Aristotle' in the thirteenth century was also a famous work; but it was two hundred years later that the art of the herbal reached its zenith with Jean de Bourdichon, Leonard Fuchs of Bavaria, and Otto von Brünfels. These later illustrators were more than scribes with an accomplished pen: they must have valued the plant for its colour and form as well as for the source of medicine; and in their work, done with a sure touch and delicate observation they expressed the natural habit of the plant in noble and memorable forms. In one of the most famous illuminated manuscripts of the early sixteenth century, the 'Book of Hours of Queen Anne of Brittany', by Jean de Bourdichon, we have for the first time, pictures of the plants together with some of the insects which frequented them. When printing became popularized in Europe, the old Gothic script gradually altered, but the illustrations took on an ever increasing beauty. In 1530 the herbal of Otto von Brünfels came out in Strasburg. The writer was contemporary with the celebrated Dutch physician Rambert Dodoens whose Latin herbal was written when he was Professor of Medicine at Leyden. This work was translated by Charles Clusius who held the Chair of Botany in the same university at about the same time, and it finally appeared in an altered form in Gerard's herbal. The splendid herbal of Leonard Fuchs who was a well-known physician, came out in 1542 under the name of *De historia stirpium*.

Of this herbal Dr. Singer says, 'The woodcuts that illustrate the work are of extraordinary beauty and truth, and are based on a first-hand study of the habits and structure of plants. These figures established a tradition and standard of plant illustration which is clearly traceable down to the middle of the following century, and is perceptible to this day'.

The English group of herbals of the late sixteenth century were the expression of influences peculiar to their time, and must be considered later.

All the ancient herbals on the medical side were of course dominated by the monkish tradition, and they are only treasured to-day as choice specimens of the art of illumination. We may say that among this great company of copyists none was greater than another: they went on copying from inexhaustible material the shapes and images of beauty and natural form without ever, as far as we know, searching for those subtle elements behind beauty and form which occupied the mighty mind of Leonardo da Vinci. Sons and heirs of monotony, in the austere regimen of their sheltered nests, they followed tradition without any disquieting reflections as to its permanent worth. Yet it is well that so many of their manuscripts have been preserved to us, for though their actual value was as evanescent as the flowers themselves, they are among the pleasantest memorials of a quiet life that the modern world has inherited.

FOUNDATIONS OF THE TWELFTH CENTURY

The Middle Ages bequeathed to us many problems, that of authority above all; but they also shaped many of the organizations which achieved permanent results in art, education and trade. During the twelfth century, schools grew up in all parts of Europe, and these schools were the *Studia Generalia* or recognized places of study afterwards called universities. They were of two types, student universities and magisterial universities, the first one of which we have an authentic trace according to Dr. Rashdall, being that of Theobaldus Stampensis, about the year 1110. He adds amusingly that many of the universities owed their origin to schisms and quarrels, as these set up migrations of the revolting scholars to another place. Oxford for instance was formed by a migration from Paris in about 1167. The Oxford Franciscans who early entered the university and worked among the poor were led through that work to study medicine: otherwise, the earliest curricula only included lectures in arts and theology. It was not until the fifteenth century that medicine took its place as a profitable and humane bread study.

In many other directions, as we know, the amazing energy of the mediæval mind overflowered into organization. Its curious learning, its splendours of art and architecture were only equalled by its vigorous social life and commercialism. The scourges which beset society, famine, spoliation and pestilence were largely due to ignorance and to war. Epidemics were severe and frequent; and it was to cope with them that the hospital system in England and the Continent arose. Although such institutions lie outside our subject, a few words ought to be devoted to the interesting origin of our first great English hospital. The story has been often told, but will bear repeating.

At the court of Henry I of England there was a priest named Rahere in whom the gift of humour, executive skill, and sincerity of purpose must have been remarkably blended. That he 'could walk with kings nor lose the common touch' was evident from the fact that he was jester as well as priest. In 1123 this versatile genius went in accordance with his religious duties on a pilgrimage to Rome where he fell a victim to the ever prevailing malaria. While he was weakened by illness, he had a vision of a glorious, angelic figure who announced himself as Saint Bartholomew come for his succour and also with an important behest. There was work to be done, and Rahere was appointed to do it. 'In my name,' said the apostle, 'thou shalt found a church at Smithfield in London . . . Direct, build, and I shall show my Lordship.'

It was in truth no easy work laid upon Rahere's shoulders, but with indomitable energy he carried it through. The undrained marsh of Smithfield, 'dank and fenny', was the property of the king, and at Rahere's petition, it was given as the required site. The chronicler gives a vivid description of the priest as organizer: 'necessities flowed unto his hand'. All Londoners know how 'Barts' grew out of the priory founded by Rahere, and how the original work is preserved in some of the present structure of St. Bartholomew the Great. On the saint's yearly festival the Prince of Wales presides at a banquet where the old hospital students in assembly drink to the memory of Rahere. The fortunes of the hospital reflected the course of English history. In its original form with a hospitaller and a few nursing sisters, it lasted until the destruction of the monasteries by Henry VIII, after which the whole hospital system, such as it was, suffered eclipse. Meanwhile, the shocking state of London, filthy and unlighted, augmented the prevalence of disease, for in hygiene, the English towns were far behind those of the Graeco-Roman civilization. In 1544 St. Bartholomew's was reopened upon a petition to the King from the citizens on account of the 'many miserable creatures daily dyeing in the stretes'. This reopening on secular lines, was symbolic of the change which under the Tudors was to affect the whole organization of the State, and was part of the gradual separation between State religion and medical practice.

St. Bartholomew's was followed by the foundation of four other hospitals; St. Thomas', Bridewell, Bethelehem (Bedlam), and Christ's.

The history of Bedlam presents us with one of those tragic retrogressions which are so discouraging in human affairs. For it seemed that in its early practice this asylum was remarkably enlightened, the patients being generally looked upon as curable, and allowed to leave if and when they recovered. And yet, five hundred years later, a commission was appointed to inquire into the state of this institution which had by then become a place of horror with beatings, manacles, and dark and filthy cells. It is however good to know that the reproach is for ever removed, as the new Bethelehem now situated in the country, has become a haven of help for the mentally unbalanced in our own time.

Other diseases like leprosy were a constant source of trouble through the Middle Ages. This dread disease (which was not traced to its origin, until in the nineteenth century, Hanson isolated the germ, *Bacillus Leprae*) was endemic in the Nile valley in 1500 B.C., and was probably known at a much earlier date to the Hindus. There are some primitive accounts of its treatment by arsenic and pepper. It was also said to have an endemic centre in the West Indies where the natives used the since famous remedy the Chaulmoogra oil. The disease (*Elephantiasis Grecorum*), is apparently one of the scourges that came to Europe from the home of the black races. Some thought that it was introduced by the Crusaders, just as syphilis was believed to have made its appearance in Europe during the seige of Naples by the French in 1495. Whatever its origin, it certainly flourished exceedingly on European soil. An increase in this disease was, by the way, said to be one of the hideous by-products of the late war.

In England, 'Good Queen Maud', wife of King Henry I, who had inherited a sympathetic outlook from her mother, Margaret of Scotland, founded the first, or nearly the first, hospital (Lazar house) for lepers, and it was even said that she would tend the cases herself without fear. Other isolation houses, 'honourable buildings of pity', they were called, were afterwards founded, and it must be put to the credit of mediævalism that by the sixteenth century owing to isolation and the building of about 2000 hospitals the disease had been largely checked. As early as A.D. 583 an edict of Lyons had been issued to restrict the movements of lepers, but in Europe at least, no other remedy had been devised than the flesh of vipers used by Galen. The ancient remedy from the Chaulmoogra oil known to the Hindus and now generally adopted in medical practice will be described in Chapter ix.

MEDICAL ORGANIZATION IN THE MIDDLE AGES

The organization of the drug trade by the State was practically begun by the enterprising Emperor of the West, Frederic II, who founded the universities of Naples and Vienna. By his edict, pharmacies were to be supervised, and their profits regulated. In Germany the apothecaries' shops belonged to the reigning monarch or the principality. The earliest one on record was that of Wexlar in 1223.

In all European capitals there was a Court physician. An indenture of John of Gaunt, 'roy de Castille' in 1373 grants the sum of forty marks for yearly pension with board and other advantages to William of Appleton, physician and surgeon. John of Gaddesden was the Court doctor under Edward III, and a great authority in his day. He was the first to practise incision for dropsy, and his action in wrapping the king (or some say the Black Prince) in scarlet cloth to heal the scars of small pox has been cited as an anticipation of the modern treatment by red rays. In his book *Rosa Anglica*, we find directions for cookery and dietetics as well as some unexpected prescriptions. He cured a patient of stone by a concoction of the head and wings of crickets immersed in oil. For the spleen he manufactured a remedy from seven heads of fat bats, but his remarkable treatments seemed to prosper. The Court physicians were apparently expensive people, for we read of the sum of £159 11s. 10d. being paid for certain drugs sent from London to Carlisle for King Edward I.

The sale of drugs was controlled by such guilds as the Grocers, Pepperers and Spicers, though the latter company was drained to such an extent for the king's wars that eventually it had to close down.

Later, the centre of the trade passed to Bucklersbury in the City of London where it remained for centuries.

Abroad, its prosperity coincided with the growth and expansion of many of the mediæval towns, notably of Venice which, by the fifteenth century, had become the greatest trading centre of Europe, greater even than Genoa which received so much of the North African trade. There was still no city of Europe which could compare with the famous Chinese city, Kinsai or Hangehow, built with great waterways and large warehouses from which merchandise went out to the whole Eastern world; organized too, by guilds which superintended every branch of art and culture. But in Europe, Venice was easily the most flourishing, partly owing to her monopoly of the salt trade, so that by the end of the fourteenth century the Venetians who numbered two hundred thousand were founding colonies in Egypt and Asia Minor. We read of the consignments of drugs which they sent for export in their ships and in guarded trains across the Alps; and as their maritime power increased, they traded with distant ports for the crude vegetable materials which became more and more expensive. Aloes, cloves, rhubarb, and camphor were among the commonest drugs imported, but sugar was at that time included in the materia medica.

All through the fifteenth century, theriacs remained in constant request. There was one called Venice Turpentine consisting of a large number of ingredients: it was of ancient origin, and was still manufactured by the Italian apothecaries who were as skilful in compounding as those of any other race. Unfortunately, the fame of it spread to England and created a scandal, because certain English apothecaries of the baser sort made a spurious imitation of it in Queen Elizabeth's reign and were convicted of selling 'a false and naughty kind of mithridate to the great hurt of her Majesty's subjects'. Apparently the unhappy people were poisoned twice.

Trade in the Middle Ages became more and more the source of national wealth, but the trade centres naturally shifted as newly discovered countries opened up new markets. Venice declined; and the Mediterranean countries gave place in the commercial world to Holland and Portugal. In about 1500 the Portuguese established themselves near Canton and sent over several Eastern drug plants, new to the western world. Incidentally also they imported the orange, *Citrus aurantium*, Risso. After the discovery of America, England began to share in the impetus given to the various trades, the drug trade among them, through the importation of new remedies.

MEDIÆVAL PHYSICIANS

Several interesting passages marked the final stage in the alliance between State religion and medicine. In 1204, Pope Innocent III built the hospital of San Spirito in Rome, an act which gave an impetus to the foundation of many other institutions which after this date sprang up all over Europe. Several of the Popes took an interest in medicine. Pope Sixtus IV authorized anatomical dissections, and went himself to study at Bologna. Pope John XXII had been a Professor of Surgery, and was the author of a book on cataract. An important influence of the age was that of the Benedictine Order which then had a tolerant and enlightened outlook. This Order, founded by St. Benedict in the fifth century, had from the first favoured education, and what was more remarkable, without distinction of sex. The history of other nations not being our strong point, it was probably not realized by the prejudiced opponents of women doctors in the nineteenth century that such a phenomenon had ever existed, but as a matter of fact, there were occasionally women who practised medicine in the fourteenth century, though the claims of some historians in respect to the women doctors of Salerno are no longer credited. It has been suggested that Paris from the first discouraged them, and as Oxford was closely connected with Paris, this may have led to the prejudice against professional women which was for so long rife in our own country.

As to the male practitioners, their appearance, judging from old pictures, looked more picturesque than practical. Lacroix in his book, *Science in the Middle Ages*, gives a sketch of them gracefully conferring in their long robes, while other pictures such as the well-known one of Chaucer's 'doctour' in the Ellesmere MS. show the physician in similar garments riding on horseback and carrying a crucible. The organization in England seems to have been particularly futile, and it led to incessant bickerings between the three medical Orders, the physicians, the apothecaries and a *tertium quid* called a barber surgeon who was merely a barber who undertook minor surgery such as blood letting in addition to his natural calling. A relic of this business survived in the barber's pole which used to be seen outside a hairdresser's shop painted in spiral bands of colour, black for the staff, red for the blood, and white for the bandage. It must have been an uncommonly good trade, since bleeding, ordained in the Rules of Health of the School of Salerno (*c.* 1100), was resorted to upon all occasions. Many of the monasteries had bleeding rooms, and the unhappy monks of Croyland were bled regularly five times a year.

The barber surgeons became in the end a strong and fully recognized body; and by 1461 they had obtained a charter from Parliament which gave them as recognized a status as the physicians.

One of them, who lived in the horrible time of the religious wars, was the Huguenot, Ambroise Paré, who achieved lasting fame by his practice and his character. He brought in methods of his own which were at that time original, and was surgeon to three of the French kings. His remark upon the case of a wounded soldier whom he successfully tended has come down to us: 'I drest him even to the end of his cure, and God cured him.'

Paré was especially noted for his successful treatment of gunshot wounds, and one of the fomentations which he used is interesting from the herbalist's point of view. It contained sage, rosemary, thyme, lavender, chamomile, melilot flowers and rose leaves (petals), all boiled in white wine with a lye made of oak ashes. Another upon which he relied for healing wounds contained plantain, St. John's wort and centaury.

Outside of the recognized orders, all through the thirteenth and fourteenth centuries, the herbalist also practised up and down the land, selling his tonics and ointments on the village green, promising panaceas for every illness, and affording much entertainment for the comic stage. Rutebeuf in one of his thirteenth-century poems left an immortal picture of one of these itinerant quacks. 'Good people,' said he, 'I am not one of those poor herbalists who stand in front of churches with their miserable ill sewn cloak; who carry boxes and sachets and spread out a carpet, but I belong to a lady whose name is Madame Trote of Salerno, who makes a kerchief of her ears, and whose eyebrows hang down in silver chains behind her shoulders: know that she is the wisest lady that is in all the four parts of the world. . . . Look at my herbs which my lady sends into this land and country; and because she wishes the poor as well as the rich to have access thereto, she told me that I should make pennyworths of them, for a man may have a penny in his purse who has not five pounds. . . '

He then counsels his clients to put the herbs into wine and take them for thirteen days when they would be cured of their various maladies.

From time to time, severe decrees were issued against such quacks for the illegal practice of medicine. In 1311, for instance, the French King, Philip the Fair, legislated against their ignorant and often harmful ministrations. In England in 1421, King Henry V issued an Ordinance against the meddlers with physick and surgery. Henceforth, it said, there would be severe punishments for all practitioners who had not been properly approved. Meanwhile, the Pope, urged by the same scandal of illegal practices, had issued a decree ordaining that all physicians must have seven years' training at one of the medical schools. This led to the physicians having a higher status than their rivals, and ultimately to the formation of a Faculty of Medicine at the various universities. The quack however, was of course, always in evidence, and he remains to this day.

It was not until 1518 that the medical profession in England possessed its own centres of training, an advance which was largely due to the exertions of the Oxford humanist, Thomas Linacre and to a group of leading physicians at Merton College. Before this time Roger Bacon, Bishop Grosstète, Gilbert the Englishman, and John of Gaddesden had more or less devoted themselves to medical studies, but none had founded a school. Linacre himself took his medical training and degree at Padua. When he returned to Oxford, he became the leading physician of his day as well as the friend of

Colet, Erasmus and Latimer; and he founded three lectureships, two of which bear his name at Oxford and one at Cambridge. He was contemporary with John Chambre, another medical graduate of Padua who was physician to Henry VIII, and both he and Linacre are mentioned in the Letters Patent of the king for the foundation of the Royal College of Physicians in 1518. A few years later, the king also approved the appointment of John Warner, Warden of All Souls to be the first of a long line of distinguished Regius Professors of Physick. His duties were those of an examiner; for, in the language of the time, 'many students, raw and inexpert, betook themselves to physick to the utter undoing of many'.

This was written in 1535, but a clause in the 1518 Charter had contained a phrase which was severely directed at the then prevalent scandal of the quack practitioner. 'There are,' it said, 'common artificers such as smiths, weavers, and women who take on great cures to the high displeasure of God, great infamy of the Faculty, and destruction of many of the king's liege people.'

Women, it seemed, were particularly incorrigible, for they 'partly used sorcery and witch-crafte'. The statute ended with the truly human observation that many of the king's liege people were therefore 'unable to descerne the uncunnynge from the cunnynge'.

The travelling quacks seem to have plied their most successful trade out of doors. One set up in All Hallow's Churchyard, Oxford, and another by St. Mary's. Anthony Wood has a great deal to tell us about their practices, especially the shady ones. They advertised such 'stupendous cures' that the credulous students forsook their lawful advisers. 'They flocked to these men and left the Universitie physician.' One particularly notorious person took the money beforehand and ran away with it.

All the same it should be added that the orthodox fell into as grave disrepute as the charlatan. The recognized doctors seem to have poisoned as many people as the quacks, and of them also it came to be said that 'they mynded oonlie theyre owne lucres'.

William Turner, the author of the famous herbal, spoke his mind on the subject with the severity proper to a Dean. He felt it, he said, incumbent upon him to write his herbal in English, for the simple reason that he did not think that either physicians or apothecaries knew any Latin. The physicians, he went on, relied on the apothecaries, and these in turn, on the 'old wives'; the latter being as it has always been in England, a term of derision for an illiterate person, in no way the equal of the Gallic *bonne femme*. Turner ends with the damaging assertion that physicians were never present when prescriptions were made up; and that owing to all these laxities, 'many a good man was put in jeopardy of his life, or good medicine was marred to the dishonesty both of the physician and of God's worthy creature'.

This indictment, written as one feels, more in sorrow than in anger, was endorsed by another statute of Henry VIII dealing with this matter in which it was admitted that 'the moste of the persones of the said crafte of surgeons have small cunnynge'.

William Clowes who later became doctor to Queen Elizabeth, put the case in more trenchant terms. 'Medicine,' he said, 'was in the hands of tinkers, horse gelders, rogues, rat-catchers, idiots, bawds, witches, sow-gelders, and proctors of spittle houses.'

Which reminds one of Dr. Bernard Dawson's gentle comment upon Versalius' treatment of Galen 'in language which, though usual then, might now be considered virulent and offensive'.

And all this time the overlapping between the barbers and the apothecaries continued, not only in England but also abroad where the French, for example, had hit upon the expedient of putting one into a long robe and the other into a short one. It seemed however, that nothing under Heaven would preserve the peace.

Finally, the barbers and the surgeons were united in one Corporation. Moreover, a solemn Act was passed decreeing that every practitioner must be examined before the Bishop of London or the Dean of St. Paul's, the ecclesiastics to be reinforced by four doctors of physick.

Trouble meanwhile had arisen in the guilds. Drugs were sold by the Grocers; *grossarii*, they were called, or sellers in gross; and although this guild was a very prosperous one, it was alleged that they were not above fraudulent practice. The drugs were sold in open booths; and from the beautiful models in the Wellcome Museum of Medicine, one can recapture something of their picturesque and alluring atmosphere with their signs like the three little cloves of the Grocers, and their decorative pharmacy jars. Some of the latter have lately been exhumed from the site of the old Physick School 'in the street of Catts in the Parish of St. Mary' in Oxford. Many were made after the thirteenth-century pattern of Arabian workmanship made at Faenza (Ravenna), glazed with a waterproof glaze of tin dioxide. The booths also contained copper vessels, and many different mortars, made of glass or stone for syrups, red marble for precious stones, or silver 'for men of high degree'. One can imagine poor Paolo entering such a place for his love philtre, or the Court physician prescribing in that aromatic atmosphere some leechcraft that had been approved by Galen.

Not even the beauty of luxury jars or the silver mortars for the medicines of the Court however, could guarantee the soundness of the drugs themselves; and by 1617 the uncomfortable insinuations that had been noised abroad led to an investigation, and finally to the edict framed by King James I which separated the Grocers from the Apothecaries with the remark that 'Grocers were merchants, but the Apothecary's trade was a mystery'. This word is here used in its older meaning as an art or craft. At the same time, an Act of Parliament gave the Faculty of Medicine power to enter the booths and to destroy the compounds when necessary.

Obviously, it has proved as difficult to rid society of poisonous remedies as of poisonous doctrine. During the Middle Ages moreover, poisoning with murderous intent became a widespread practice. We have seen how the subject of poisonous substances and their antidotes engaged speculative minds, but in mediæval Europe, especially in Italy, murderous desires became allied to a powerful, new weapon.

Most of the poisons used were of vegetable origin, for vegetable alkaloids such as aconite, nicotine or belladonna are the deadliest substances known. In Rome and Venice, schools of poisons were instituted, and from the fourteenth to the sixteenth centuries they supplied teachers in the art. The Council of Ten formally recognized poisoning as a form of murder, a regular fee being made to the executioner. In fact, the practice remained a lucrative one all through the sixteenth century and later. At Palermo, in 1650, one particular lady named Toffana was said to have killed 600 people with a cosmetic containing arsenic in hog's fat. Later, a favourite preparation was known as *Aqua Toffana*, containing belladonna, opium and stramonium, which was no doubt, infallible. The name *belladonna*, beautiful lady, had previously been given to the Deadly Nightshade by the Italians who prized it for its effect upon the eyes.

Wootton's *Chronicles of Pharmacy* contains many extraordinary accounts of poisoning cases, one of the most spectacular being that of the Marquise de Brinvilliers who poisoned many prominent people in France. In England, too, there were many convenient removals of unpopular figures in the social world. One wonders whether these scandals may have influenced the retention of the theriacs in the first printed editions of the British Pharmacopoeia.

THE PRINTING PRESS AND THE PHARMACOPOEIA

As early as the sixth century A.D. the Chinese had written books such as the maxims of Confucius upon wooden blocks from which they issued printed type. After A.D. 1000 they used moveable types in wood and copper. It has therefore been suggested that the first printing press set up in Europe fathered by Coster of Haarlem and Gutenberg of Maintz was derived from Chinese sources. In any case, it superseded the old Gothic script which had lasted since 1200 in every part of Europe. The first printed books were no more than exact reproductions of Gothic MSS. and for a long time, the monks continued to copy Arabic texts from the Greek sources in their consistent, angular hand. In bringing the art to perfection, Italy took the lead; and in Venice, books began to be turned out in considerable numbers in the Roman type which we are using to-day. But up to the time of the Renaissance, mediæval thinkers were theologians with a permanent and inelastic creed which was inimical to originality. Copying was therefore the chief business of literature, and a list extant of the books in the library of Da Grado at

Pisa in the fifteenth century shows hardly an original work among them.

It was not until the latter half of the sixteenth century that printing began to influence medicine, but it brought into sight both the English herbals and the Pharmacopoeia, a volume of prescriptions and directions for the preparation of drugs. The first one to be issued under government auspices was produced in Nuremberg in 1542. This was the first recognition of pharmacy as a science applied to the compounding of medicines according to the written instructions of a physician. Early in the following century, similar publications were brought out in London, Dublin and Edinburgh. These compilations were of a conservative type. It was said that in the first London issue in 1618, about half the prescriptions were based upon Arabian formulae. There were 1028 'simples', and 932 preparations or compounds. It also included a theriac that had been invented by Sir Walter Raleigh, and was a mixture of seeds, barks, and leaves macerated in alcohol and then combined with mineral and animal ingredients. Some of the older theriacs also figured in these pages, so that obviously the effects of poison, accidental or malicious, were still under consideration, and were being hopefully treated in the traditional way. All belief in these antidotes vanished in the nineteenth century when they finally disappeared from the Pharmacopoeia. Speaking of their probable effects, Dr. La Wall in his *Four Thousand Years of Pharmacy* says, 'they may have been antiseptic, but they had no antidotal value in medicine'.

The new editions of the *London Pharmacopoeia* that appeared at long intervals generally included some new preparation, and from them we can often trace the approximate date of a new importation from America or the East. In 1650 syrup of buckthorn appeared for the first time. In the next issue, Sir Hans Sloane made a gallant effort to sweep away some of the animal ingredients, and only the wood lice and the crab's eyes were retained: apparently they had secured a hold upon the imagination. In 1778 there was a real advance in chemistry, and some of the theriacs were dropped out together with the 'compound' prescriptions that had been in force so long. In 1809, the measures were revised, and the minim substituted for the drop. In 1836 some of the more modern drugs like ergot, bromine and iodine were included.

The year 1850 brought the most racial and enduring changes, for it led to the unification of the three British Pharmacopoeias. The new issue from Dublin was written in English instead of in Latin as hitherto, while the troy grain and the avoirdupois ounce and pound were introduced for the first time. In 1851, there was a final issue of the *London Pharmacopoeia*; and after that, the three books were gradually incorporated into the *British Pharmacopoeia* which was published in 1864, and has been re-edited at intervals ever since.

The most drastic of all revisions was that of 1932 when under the Chairmanship of Dr. A. P. Beddard, the expert committee transferred 350 preparations to the Codex, while on the other hand, many new infusions and other preparations were added. In some cases biological standards of assay for several drugs and their preparations have been also included. Certain standard preparations are now kept in the National Institute for Medical Research in Hampstead, and the quality of a drug is determined by comparison with these. This standard holds good throughout the British Empire. The question of substitutes is also dealt with. For example it is laid down that in places within the Empire where olive oil cannot be obtained these two substitutes may be used for it; the 'Katchung oil' of India from the seeds of *Arachis hypogaea*, and the oil from the seeds of *Sesamum indicum*, much employed in the East Indies.

It is possible that in the future, pharmacy will become to a great extent internationalized. For some time, things have been moving in that direction, and as long ago as in 1900 a congress was initiated by the French and was held at Paris to discuss the unification of pharmacopoeial formulae for drugs. The result was the formation of a Federation of International Pharmacy, and meetings of this body have been held annually ever since. One day there may be an International Pharmacopoeia, for it is realized as a defect in the present system that the various tinctures and extracts do not mean the same thing in the practice of the different countries. Dr. Rosenthaler gives as an instance of this variation the following preparations of aconite: 'root in U.S.A., Japan and Russia; leaf in Denmark; fresh juice inspissated from the leaf in Greece, and alcoholic extract of root in Italy and Spain'.

Every country naturally has its own Pharmacopoeia, but that of the French is the most widely used, as it is official in Turkey. Also, it includes 250 preparations, and is about double the size of any other. In England the remedies of Homoeopathy are mainly those of the Pharmacopoeia though they are given in different dosages and with a different principle. Those of the herbalists are always of vegetable origin; many of them are official, but many more include the native simples taken from the native Flora. Several herbalists' firms culti-vate the plants of wild as well as foreign species, for the demand for them in popular medicine is considerable and could not be met by collection alone. Thus, Messrs. Potter and Clarke have one of the largest drug plant farms in the country, and Messrs. Heath and Heather of St. Albans who began their work after the war have a large and increasing trade in herbal remedies. The story of herb cultivation in England and Europe will be told in Chapter ix.

FURTHER ORGANIZATION

The Pharmaceutical Society of Great Britain owed its inception to the initiative of a little group of men who met at the house of Mr. Joseph Bell in Oxford Street on March 20th, 1841. Their first committee was formed in the following April. The object of the Founders was to form a national institution for the advancement of pharmacy as distinct from the practice of medicine. It was realized that pharmacy embraced so many sciences and had become so much more complicated that in the public interest it demanded the ex-clusive attention of its members. One of the ablest and most energetic of the Founders was Daniel Bell Hanbury to whom, with Mr. Joseph Bell, the success of the undertaking was largely due. Another notable early member was Jonathan Pariera. The Society obtained its charter from Queen Victoria on Feb. 18th, 1843; and eleven years later, an Act of Parliament admitted all fully qualified chemists into the membership of the society subject to the findings of an examining board.

Nine years before the Charter was obtained by the pharmacists, the medical profession instituted a new body of control in the British Medical Association. This was brought into existence under the leadership of Sir Charles Hastings in the Infirmary at Worcester in 1832, since which date orthodoxy of a distinctly die-hard type has regulated their counsels. The only thing that has not been regulated and which goes its way unrestrained is the sensation press which panders in so many directions to the lower elements in the community. Occasionally a 'headline' has resulted in a chemists' boom, as for instance in the cholera outbreak in England in the early nineteenth century. A paragraph appeared in the daily press to the effect that the disease could be kept at bay by a poultice of mustard and linseed on the feet, camphorated spirit rubbed on the stomach, and thirty drops of either oil of cajeput, peppermint or cloves taken internally. The public liked the sound of the cajeput, and there was such a run upon it that the price rose to 20/- an ounce. The chemists could scarcely be blamed for profiting by the occasion and advertising in their windows 'Complete set of all the articles required for cholera'. *Verb. Sap.* The story is a typical example of how a 'stunt' can be organized in the spirit of the land of push and go-getting.

As a matter of fact, quackery is indigenous in any society where trade is carried on among people at different educational levels. In spite of a tightening control, it continued to flourish openly all through the seventeenth century when the trade in 'secret' remedies called patent by those who had exclusive rights in them was at its height. These quack formulas appeared at a time when the price of drugs was extremely high, and some of them 'caught on' by the mere expedient of a popular price. But others were issued with a more ambitious aim, and there are remarkable stories of the impositions practised upon wealthy people. All through the sixteenth and seventeenth centuries it was fashionable to dabble in panaceas just as monarchs of the older days had dabbled in theriacs. One celebrated remedy was known as the Duke of Portland's powder because he was 'cured of gout' in Switzerland by its means. The powder was a blend of gentian root, leaf of germander, birthwort and centaury. Another powder which has had a long and established reputation was called Dover's powder after the Bristol doctor of Charles II's time who invented it. This, which is a blend of 'composition powder' with ipecacuanha, potassium sulphate, etc., is still prescribed in catarrh.

The French kings were especially generous in their remuneration for a remedy, and Madame Nouffer sold a 'patent' medicine to Louis XIII for a considerable sum. The prescription contained a well-known vermifuge (oil of male fern), and this had to be followed by a queer compound of resin, calomel and scammony. Louis XIV not only bought Tabor's secret remedy for fever but also another specific which was found to contain antimony; after which the latter drug became a fashionable medicine. These remedies were at least more honest than the Goddard's drops sold to Charles II, for they turned out to be merely a concoction of human bones.

Although no legislation has ever succeeded in putting down quackery, the sale of poisons gradually came to be restricted, though it was not before 1851 that the so-called Arsenic Act was passed into law. In 1908 there was a creation of licences for the sale of certain poisonous substances by pharmacists; and in 1932 a new Dangerous Drugs Act was passed in accordance with the Geneva Convention to tighten up the existing law. The output of cocaine and diamorphine is now strictly regulated, and the latest records show that between 1926 and 1931 the output of morphine has fallen by one half. This is one of the matters that has been most successfully dealt with through International co-operation through the League of Nations.

It was in the seventeenth century that the relations between the apothecaries and the physicians seem to have been at their very worst. It was probably inevitable, as the apothecaries — who had grown into a very powerful body — had become more educated; and from being merely compounders of medicines they had encroached upon the physicians' preserves in extending their practice to medicine, surgery and midwifery. It was also complained — and not without reason that they charged scandalous fees. One typical instance is quoted where a charge of thirty shillings was made for twenty-five pills. With the amenities common to the age, the physicians and apothecaries assailed each other in scurrilous pamphlets while the public cheered and took sides. One of the Apothecaries' champions entered the argumentative lists with the assertion that during the Fire of London their society had at least remained at its post, while the physicians, to a man, had run away. It will be realized that in view of this long continued quarrelling and quackery, the dual organizations of 1832 and 1841 marked a considerable advance towards a higher tradition of civil responsibility.

CHAPTER VI

THE ENGLISH HERBALS

MEDICINE IN THE SIXTEENTH AND
SEVENTEENTH CENTURIES

CIMICIFUGA RACEMOSA
from *Medicinal Plants*, Bentley & Trimen

By courtesy of Messrs. Churchill

IN every European country from the fourteenth century onwards, the fathers of botany were contributing in some degree towards the classification of the vegetable kingdom. When this description of the plants and their affinities was linked to their therapeutic uses, a herbal came into being. The writers of these herbals were mainly concerned with the medicinal 'virtues' of plants; but it was in this way and through their efforts that botany became a science.

In 1516 Conrad Gesner, the physicist and naturalist after whom the N.O. *Gesneraceae* was named, was born in Switzerland. Some details of his practice have come down to us, particularly his use of *Nux-vomica* which was known to the Arabians but after their time seemed to have dropped out. The catalogue of plants which he published in 1542 was not a herbal in the strict use of the word, for he cared more for garden varieties and species than for medicinal plants; but as a naturalist he rendered good services to science, and would have done more had he not unfortunately fallen a victim to the plague in 1565.

His friend and contemporary, William Turner, the Dean of Wells, was one of our earliest herbal writers. He had learnt some medicine at Bologna, and was an enthusiastic botanist. His English herbal gave the names of herbs 'in Greek, Latin, Dutche, Englishe and Frenche wyth the common names that herbaries and apothecaries use'. The book was dedicated to Queen Elizabeth in 1551, and his descriptions were so faithful and scientific that he was called the Father of English botany. He had great faith in the 'virtues' of his native flora; 'herbes soveraigne and strange' he called them, though one may suspect that his own predilections sometimes ran away with him, as for instance we find him bracketing coriander seed with the more powerful hemp for the soporific property of 'taking men's wittes from them'. But the herbal — of which there are several editions — is a most interesting production with its quaint language and charming woodcuts. Many of the prescriptions aimed at the dispersal of 'devils and despair', the good old betony being, as usual, highly esteemed.

His contemporary, Rambert Dodoens was born at Malines in 1518, and has been already mentioned as Professor at Leyden. His book on the history of plants was translated into English by Henry Lyte, an Oxford enthusiast who founded one of the earliest botanic gardens in England. The translation called the Pemptades was dedicated to Queen Elizabeth, and had a preface by William Clowes, her physician, who aptly recalled 'the many great men, like Mithridates, who had considered writing about heroes a fit occupation for gentlemen and wights of worthy fame'.

This was the century when specimens of new plants brought from abroad were exciting great interest in England and elsewhere, and this constant importation no doubt contributed to the foundation of many botanic gardens and the increase of herbal literature. Between 1533 and 1598 the Botanic Gardens of Padua, Florence, Bologna, Paris and Montpellier were planted, that of Padua being stocked with many Egyptian plants collected by Prospero Alpino. From 1628 to 1678 the Gardens of Jena, Oxford, Upsala, Leyden, Chelsea and Edinburgh came into being, and were followed by those of Amsterdam and Utrecht.

One of the first herbals to incorporate many newly imported species was that of Nicholas Monardes, a Seville physician of the sixteenth century. In her *Old English Herbals*, Miss E. Sinclair Rohde gives some beautiful reproductions from this work which was widely translated and gave a unique account of many of the drug plants of Spanish America. 'Joyful news,' said the author, 'out of the newe found world wherein is declared the rare and singular virtues of diverse and sundrie herbes.' He, it appeared, had been in correspondence with 'a gentleman of the Peru' from whom he had learnt much about the native materia medica. The most interesting thing in the book is an account of the use of 'hearbe tobaco' by the Indians who called it 'picielt', and accompanied its use by religious ceremonies. His comment shows a shrewd insight into the occult beliefs that underlaid such ceremonies. The natives, he suggests, were self-deceived as to the effect of the herb upon their senses. 'Instead of receiving wise counsel in their trances and exaltations,' he writes, 'it may have been the devill that prompted them.' And later he adds that 'they may have made themselves drunk because they liked it'.

He says also that the Indians taught the Spaniards to use tobacco as a wound herb; and that although it was introduced into Spain 'to adornate gardens with the fairnesse thereof', yet it was more used 'for its meruelous medicinable vertues than for its fairnesse'.

Monardes' *Herbal* was the first that dealt with the American flora; but early in the seventeenth century, an American, 'John Josselyn, Gentleman', of Boston, prepared a book in which he described many of the native remedies. He tells us how they brewed their beer and flavoured it with liquorice (like our stout) as well as with sassafras and fennel. Wounds were treated with 'wild cats' grease' and then with powdered root of the white hellebore. The Boston gentleman was doing in his garden exactly what our English herbalists had tried to do in the Old World a century earlier, after America had been discovered by mistake, and the geographical expansion had led to the importation of novelties. He was making a herb bed with our culinary herbs, mint, thyme, etc., and for some unknown reason he could not get thyme to grow.[1] His garden very properly ranked among 'New England rarities', but later on, some of the *Mayflower* settlers became good physicians, and in their own words 'began to rescue pharmacy from the Indians, old women and clergymen'. In 1646 a store of pharmacy was set up in Boston.

IMPORTED DRUG PLANTS

It was not only from the States that new plants were brought to England and to Europe in the sixteenth and later centuries. From South America came the most important of all the new discoveries, quinine; and about the same time guiacum, sassafras and ipecacuanha were imported.

Guiacum proved a reliable remedy in gout, rheumatism and

[1] See John Josselyn's *Two Voyages to New England*.

various cutaneous diseases. The resin comes from the wood of *Guaiacum officinale*, Linn. (*Zygophyllaceae*, the Bean Caper Order). Sassafras was brought over by the Spaniards to Seville, and was so much believed in that it became the custom to carry a bit in the pocket as a disinfectant. From the root a volatile oil, rich in safrole, is distilled, and used as an alterative and rubefacient. The plant, *Sassafras variefolium*, Klotz., belongs like the Camphor tree and cinnamon to the Laurel Order. Balsum of Tolu, a resin obtained from the stem of *Myroxylon Toluifera*, H.B. & K., was another of the medical plants which came from the coast of Central America. It has long been used in chronic bronchial affections. The Balsam of Peru which has similar properties but is more commonly used in the perfumery trade, comes from another tree of the same Order, *Myroxylon Pereirae*, Klotzsch., *Leguminoseae*. This grows in San Salvador and from thence was shipped to Peru by the Spaniards; hence its name. Ipecacuanha was imported with a reputation for the cure of dysentery and was at first a 'secret' remedy. Afterwards it was sold as so many formulas were, to the King of France. It is one of the drugs whose reputation has been enhanced under modern tests, for in 1912 Rogers confirmed its curative value in amoeboid dysentery, while it is also commonly used as a diaphoretic and expectorant. The medical property is in the alkaloid, emetine, and the drug comes from the root of *Psychotria Ipecacuanha*, Stokes, a native of Brazil belonging to the N.O. *Rubiaceae*, and to the group lately separated by botanists into a separate Order, *Cinchonaceae* which includes the tree whose bark yields quinine. The *Cinchona* tree was not discovered by Europeans until 1639, and was therefore not known to Monardes, but its discovery was the most epoch making event in the medicine of that age. The *Cinchona* trees grow on the heights of the Andes, and the properties of the bark had probably been known for centuries to the natives. The genus was named after the Countess Cinchon, wife of the Viceroy of Peru, who, while living in that country, had contracted a fever and had been cured by the use of the bark. She returned to Spain in 1640, bringing the bark with her, and this was the first occasion of its importation into Europe.

Ten years later the Jesuits popularized the remedy in Spain, and it became known as 'Jesuit's bark'. In 1682 Louis XIV bought a reputed 'secret remedy' from Sir Robert Tabor who had acquired a great reputation for the cure of intermittent fevers. The king then made it public; and the ingredient, which was Peruvian bark, was called the 'English remedy'. It was not until 1742 that Linnaeus in his *Genera Plantarum* named the species Cinchona. The barks vary, and are classified in materia medica. The grey or 'silver' bark gets its colour from the lichen growing upon it. This grey bark was first known in Spain. In common with many other medicinal plants, the *Cinchona* trees differ according to their place of cultivation, and the Bolivian trees give a more valuable yield than those from New Granada. It was estimated that in the years between 1849 and 1851 three million pounds of bark were exported from Bolivia. This was the *Calisaya* bark from *Cinchona Calisaya*, Wedd: The red bark — the *Cinchonae rubrae cortex* of the British Pharmacopoeia — comes from *C. succirubra*, but the B.P. recognizes the bark of the following as official under the title 'Cinchona'; cultivated trees of *Cinchona Calisaya*, Weddell; *C. Ledgeriana*, Moens; *C. officinalis*, Linn.; *C. succirubra*, Pavon; and hybrids of the last two species with either of the first two.

The alkaloids are obtained from the bark, by first treating it with lime, to release the free alkaloid from the salt in which form it is present, and then extracting with alcohol or petroleum ether. Of the alkaloids which are extremely complex, quinine is the most important. Others are quinidine, cinchonine and cinchonidine, and the B.P. directs that a bark should contain not less than six per cent of these alkaloids, one half of which must consist of quinine and cinchonidine. Quinine is a highly valuable disinfectant and germicide in intermittent fevers and malaria. As an anti-pyretic, it is valuable in typhus and pneumonia, while quinidine is now used in auricular fibrillation of the heart.

The drug appeared in England at an opportune moment, for ague, as Defoe tells us, was the scourge of the land, and the apothecary who cured Charles II of it made his fortune. As the importation increased, it was realized that the supply was endangered by the ruthless stripping of the trees in South America, and La Condamine suggested its transplantation into other countries. This was begun and carried on until, by the year 1860, *Cinchona* was established in India, and twenty-five years later, Ceylon became the source of the world's supply. Then the Dutch set to work, and made their great plantations in Java from whence 90 per cent of the world's supply is now obtained while Amsterdam has replaced London as the centre of the market. The work of collecting the bark and transplanting the trees proved a most strenuous undertaking, many men engaged in it becoming crippled, and other losing their lives. The man who worked the hardest gained no recognition in his own day, but his name, Charles Ledger, is perpetuated in the valued species *C. Ledgeriana*.

Despite the amount of work done in the swamps and malarial zones in the British tropical possessions, it seems that we still want 800,000 ounces of the drug yearly (representing roughly $8\frac{1}{3}$ million pounds of bark). In Burma, Madras and Bengal, production has lately been increased, but in the war, the Dutch put all their supplies at the allies' disposal. The fact that this indispensable drug was swept off the market at that time, and in view of the virtual monopoly held by the Dutch, it has been thought that other countries should try to put *Cinchona* under cultivation. The French and Italians are working at this experiment with several hybrid species.

Quinine, together with the suppression of the mosquito has, of course, by checking the scourge of malaria, led to the advance of white civilization in many tropical areas of the world.

The importation of drug plants which began in Queen Elizabeth's time and continued for the next two hundred years brought us, among several ephemeral remedies, others which were lasting. After quinine perhaps the most important was *Podophyllum Peltatum*, Linn. Although it did not become official till 1820 it is now included in probably every pharmacopoeia in the world. This species came from North America, but the other medicinal plant, *P. Emodi*, Wall., is indigenous to Northern India. Both varieties are official. *Podophyllum resin*, B.P., is obtained as a precipitate when an alcoholic extract of the rhizome is poured into acidified water. The drug — which is however a variable one — is still the subject of present day research, but is of proved value, and forms an ingredient of many 'liver' pills. In herbalism it is called mandrake root.

Cimicifuga racemosa (Nutt), N.O. *Ranunculaceae,* the Black Cohosh or Snakeroot, came from North America and has been retained as a useful remedy in rheumatism.

Hamamelis Virginiana, Linn., of the *Hamamelidaceae* was named by the settlers in Virginia and was called 'Witch-hazel' in about 1700. The twigs were used in the eighteenth century for discovering precious metals just as those of the Hornbeam and other trees are used for water divining in England. The Natural Order is strongly astringent, the trees containing catechin or tannin in the bark.

Grindelia squarrosa (Pursk.), Duval, and *G. Camporum,* Greene, were imported in 1811 from North America and were used in bronchial asthma.

The Beth root, *Trillium pendulum,* Willd., N.O. *Liliaceae,* long used by the Indians, was adopted by the settlers in North America. It is an interesting and beautiful plant, the rhizome containing a very complex system of glucosides, tannin and resin. It is still used in herbal medicines as an astringent.

Logwood and quassia were imported from Central America. In seventeenth century medical books, *Picraena excelsa,* the source of quassia wood, is extolled as a tonic, febrifuge and anthelmintic. The chips are still employed in herbal pharmacy.

The fruits of *Phycolacca decandra, Phytolaccaceae,* called Poke berries, were brought from America where they had long been in use as purgatives. Herbalists recommend them in rheumatism.

Two other American plants were for a time used medicinally. One was the resinous shrub, *Drimys Winteri,* named after Captain Winter who sailed in Drake's ship. This had long been in use among the Indians as an anti-scorbutic and stimulant. It was used here as a substitute for cinnamon bark, but is now disregarded. The other was *Vitis quinquefolia,* Planch., once called *Ampelopsis,* the 'Virginian Creeper' which was brought here in 1629 and has become such a popular vine for clothing bare walls. A balsamic resin with a bitter principle in the stem and fruit gave it medicinal value as a cathartic, and it found a place in the Edinburgh Pharmacopoeia till it was superseded.

In Queen Elizabeth's reign we hear for the first time of the cultivation of liquorice in England. The plant had been known to Theophrastus who said that it grew near Lake Maeotis and was used by the Scythians for asthma and coughs. Turner mentions it in his herbal. Liquorice is the dried rhizome from several species of *Glycorrhiza*, *G. glabra*, *G. glandulifera*, and *G. echinata*. N.O. *Liliaceae*. The first is official in England, but the two latter species in the U.S.A. The plant has always succeeded well in England. Gerard and Culpeper both speak of the 'good profit made' from the crop; and some is still grown in Yorkshire.

Among our native and naturalized plants which were in great vogue among the herbal writers and which have more or less remained in use, were the Lily of the Valley, *Convallaria magalis*, Linn., *Liliaceae*, and the balm, *Melissa officinalis*, Linn., *Labiatae* (not to be confused with 'Balm of Gilead').

In the collection of prescriptions called the London Dispensary of 1696 it was said that 'an essence of Balm given in Canary wine every morning will renew youth, strengthen the brain, relieve languishing nature and prevent baldness'.

Equally remarkable eulogies were conferred upon this sweet and homely herb in European practice, for many claimed that its use tended to longevity, and the 'Carmelite water', made of balm flavoured with nutmeg, lemon, and angelica root was habitually drunk by distinguished and — apparently — long-lived people.

Balm is frequently drunk as a 'tea' at the present day, and is used by herbalists in feverish colds.

The lily of the valley is still used on the Continent in cardiac debility. It has two water soluble glucosides, convallamarin and convallarin, with slightly purgative and diuretic properties. Gerard and his successors followed Dodoens in recommending it for 'renovating a weak memory' and for 'comforting the heart and vital spirits'. How longingly and hopefully they flew to their herbal remedies in that age! 'Afflicted in mind, body and estate', yet they saw themselves surrounded by a fruitful and variegated vegetation from which 'comfort' could be drawn. The good old word is so significant and homely. It hints that, not infrequently the root of the trouble was traceable to the tormented mind.

Another liliaceous plant — a native of the Mediterranean countries — which has sustained its reputation both here and abroad is the Squill, *Urginea Scilla*, Steinheil. It produces abundant mucilage, and contains oxalate of calcium together with a bitter principle. Squill is in constant use as an expectorant and energetic diuretic in dropsy resulting from cardiac disease. It resembles digitalin in its action.

ENGLISH GARDENERS AND HERBALISTS

The most renowned authors of our herbal literature in the sixteenth and seventeenth centuries formed an interesting little group who were closely associated with the gardeners of that period such as Franqueville, Tradescant, Lobel, Goodyer and Coys in whose famous garden in the parish of North Okington in Essex the Yucca first flowered in this country. Other members of this friendly coterie were Thomas Penny, a London physician, Richard Garth, Thomas Johnson and Sir John Salusbury of Llewern. Penny, who imported several plants into England and was called a second Dioscorides for his botanical knowledge, was a friend of the foreign botanists, Clusius, Cameranius and Gesner. Garth received from Clusius the Solomon's Seal which he 'very lovingly imparted' to Gerard; and Thomas Johnson, an excellent herbalist, whose *Inter Plantarum in Agrum Cantianum* is in Magdalen College Library, Oxford, was an apothecary of Snow Hill. Sir John Salusbury and his son Sir William Salusbury of Llewern in Denbighshire, were gentlemen of very ancient lineage and stormy reputation, but the former did a notable work in compiling from the works of Fuchs, Turner and Dodoens, a herbal which gave the names of the plants in Welsh.

John Goodyer seems to have assisted all these other members of his circle out of his unbounded energy and enthusiasm. Elias Ashmole, the antiquary, has left it on record that 'having entered upon the study of plants he went a simpling on June 6th, 1648, to see Mr. Goodyer, the great botanist at Petersfield'. The house now bears a tablet inscribed

John Goodyer, Botanist and Royalist
1592 — 1664, lived here.

He was a copious translator, and rendered into English the commentaries of Matthiolus, the materia medica of Dioscorides, and the works of Theophrastus. The last specimen of his handwriting, Professor Gunther tells us, referred to a resin ointment similar to that recently included in the B.P. In 1664 he bequeathed his Botanical Library to Magdalen College, Oxford. He it was who first wrote an account of that 'wonderfull increasinge vegetable', the Jerusalem artichoke.

Matthias Lobel — or properly de l'Obel, — superintended the Botanic Garden of Lord Zouch at Hackney, and later became gardener to James I. A man of some learning, he had studied with Rondelet of Montpellier and with a great patron of botanists, Christof Plantin of Antwerp. He was one of the first to see that the foundation of a natural system of classification must be natural affinity, and he influenced the work of the French botanist Kaspar Bauhin, whose *Phytopinax* appeared in 1623. Dr. Church claims that this work prompted Sherard's subsequent studies, and therefore led to the Sherardian Professorship of Botany in Oxford.

William Coys, the 'excellent herbalist of happy memorie', also left some literary notes upon materia medica, though he was more renowned for his garden and for his generosity in giving rare plants to his friends, especially to John Goodyer. A most interesting recipe for beer is preserved by Lobel who got it from Coys. 'The most agreeable and wholesome of all German and English cerevisia or beer,' said the latter, and forthwith proceeded to explain from his first-hand investigations the action of yeast in producing alcohol from malt. Lobel published Coys' notes upon this subject in 1605. The other necessary ingredient, the hop, was already there, having been introduced, as someone oddly observed, 'with peacocks and heretics' between 1520 and 1524.

ENGLISH HERBALS

THE HERBAL LITERATURE

Although Goodyer and his contemporaries, both Flemish and English, greatly influenced the study of botanical classification which was founded upon the medicinal properties of plants, it was left for Gerard and Parkinson to produce herbals that were literature. Although the famous work of John Gerard actually appeared at the end of the sixteenth century, its fame spread over the seventeenth, and has lasted to our own day. Gerard was a young man at the time that London was humming with exotic stories of foreign travel, and he was no less thrilled than Monardes had been by the introduction of the various plants. He too listened to the tales of the tobacco, *Nicotiana Tabacum*, Linn., which was said to have obtained its name from the Mexican word *tabacum* for the pipes in which the dried leaf was smoked. These pipes and others like them can be seen in the Wellcome Museum of Medicine, and it seemed that the word *tubbag* was applied to any herbal compound that was used in smoking. Tobacco came to be regarded by the Spaniards as a sort of cure-all. It was tried for syphilis and for many other diseases. The pure alkaloid, nicotine, is even in minute doses one of the strongest and most rapid poisons in the world.

Ginger also, which had been hitherto only known in its dried state, was now brought over in the fresh root of *Zingiber officinale*, Rosc. Gerard's interest in all these things was unending. He began to receive from many countries roots and seeds which he tried to grow in his garden in Holborn. The ginger failed, which vexed him, for he viewed his treasures with the professional eye, and had recommended ginger in particular for 'the loosening of the belly'. He also tried to grow dates, as many have done since and with the same result, that they germinated and sprang up to about two feet until the frost touched them. In the same optimistic spirit he 'expected the success' with the rare white thyme. He tried to inspire the Barber Surgeons' Company with his own enthusiasm, but failed to induce them to start a garden for medicinal plants. So for a time he contented himself with his own garden, of whose plants he issued a catalogue in 1596.

His idea, however, was destined to bear fruit, later on, on the foundation of the Apothecaries' Garden, or 'Physick Garden' of Chelsea. The picturesque history of this old foundation is given in Mr. F. D. Drewitt's *Romance of the Apothecaries' Garden at Chelsea*, and in Mr. Henry Field's *Memoirs* of the same subject. Sir Hans Sloane, who had been cured of tuberculosis, devoted his means to the service of medicine. He was a broad-minded man, a friend of Sydenham, and he helped to popularize the use of quinine. He was also closely associated with the Society of Apothecaries. After the Great Fire which destroyed both the Apothecaries' Hall in Blackfriars and that of the College of Physicians, the Apothecaries became financially embarrassed. They sold their plate, and rebuilt their Hall at considerable expense. They also desired to keep up appearances consonant with their position, and they maintained a four-oared barge, gaily decorated with banners. By 1713 however, they found themselves without funds, while the barge required mending. They therefore taxed their members. It was at this critical time that Sir Hans Sloane made his gift to the Society of the Physick Garden: the date was 1722.

Chelsea Manor, thus acquired by Hans Sloane, was a country site with three rivers and cornfields. The trickling ghost of the Westbourne is to-day imprisoned in the iron tube over Sloane Square Station. The dedication of the garden was, in Sloane's words, 'to the manifestation of the power, wisdom and glory of God in the works of creation, and to encourage the study of botany among medical practitioners'. Already there was one other garden which had been started by Tradescant at South Lambeth, but there the interest was mainly horticultural and nearer to the older type of Botanic Garden, such as those of Padua and of Florence made in the sixteenth century. The Apothecaries' Garden was devoted solely to the medical plants of every country, and many rare and interesting things were received there. One packet sent by the Curator in 1732 deserves to be remembered: it was a little packet of cotton seed, and it was the progenitor of the cotton plantations of Georgia. In the same year a botanical event happened in the Physick garden: one of the four Cedars of Lebanon which De Jussieu had brought from

Syria planted in a spare hat and watered with his shaving water during the voyage — this little cedar of hope and enthusiasm produced a cone! For some years indeed the gallant trees did all that was required of them, but they have gradually weakened under the influence of the climate and the London smoke.

Soon after the foundation of the new Physick garden, the Apothecaries' Society instituted a botanical fellowship which became very popular under its resonant title of *Socii iterantes*. Its members met for excursions all round the country with the object of 'simpling'. The society was, in fact, the precursor of our Field Clubs and Natural History societies. The records suggest that the meetings were on more spacious and convivial lines than at the present day; there is a Dickensian touch about some of them; and evidently the members got some fun as well as botany out of the excursions. They seem also to have inspired the great Swedish botanist, Linnaeus, with a similar taste, for he too instituted a 'herborizing' society at Upsala where the members were summoned by trumpet and drum.

To return to old Gerard, who was as good a field botanist as he was a gardener. His own herborizings took him far round the country that encircled the city of London; and he gathered his mallow and penny-royal in the fields that are now Gray's Inn.

In 1597 he brought out his herbal. In 1583 a certain Dr. Priest, of the College of Physicians, had been commissioned by John Norton, the Queen's printer, to translate Dodoen's *Pemptades* from the Latin into English; but before completing the work, Priest died. This was the book which came into Gerard's hands and was the foundation of his herbal. He altered the general arrangement from that of Dodoens to that of Lobel, and added a commentary of his own, together with a delightful dedication to William Cecil, Lord Burleigh.

'What greater delight,' he asks, 'is there than to behold the earth apparelled with plants as with a robe of embroidered worke set with Orient pearls and garnished with great diversitie of rare and costly jewels?' He adds, however, that 'though the delight is great, the use is greater and joined to necessitie'. At the end he reverts to his own garden with loving pride. 'To the large and singular furniture of this noble island,' he says, 'I have added from forreine parts all the varieties of herbes and floures that I might obtain . . . I have laboured with the soil to make it fit for plants, and with the plantes that they might delight in the soil. What my successe hath been and what my furniture is I leave to the report of them that have seen your Lordship's gardens and the little plot of myne owne.'

The 'credit' he assumed would have been greater had he not issued what was practically the herbal of Dodoens without due acknowledgment. However, it must be remembered that all the men of his day systematically borrowed from ancient sources, and he quotes as freely from Dioscorides as any faithful Latin herbalist of early centuries. Nor was the herbal his only work, for he also issued a *'Catalogus arborum, fruticum et plantarum'*, which was a comprehensive piece of work even in his day.

Although the materia medica of the herbal was largely traditional, there was much freshness in its presentation. He described his simples in a charming, original manner, and told his public how to use them and what to expect from the use. As a rule, he made use of the fresh herb; the juice or extract, after being 'stamped' out of it, was mixed with ale, or sometimes converted into an electuary with honey. A dried herb was 'brayed to a powder'. Thus the flowering twigs of the broom were brayed on the strength of a recommendation from Sir Thomas Fitzherbert who had cured his jaundice by this means. The broom had been used from antiquity, though its chief use — as a diuretic — was probably not clearly realized, and its chief alkaloid, sparteine, was not known. Henry VIII is reported to have taken it 'against a surfeit', or perhaps as we might say, for slimming. The properties of salicin were evidently still unknown, for Gerard only used the willow as Dioscorides had done 'for cornes and other risings in the feet'. Digitalin was not in use, and the foxglove was therefore dismissed with the remark that 'it had no place among medicine according to the Ancients'.

Gerard had no truck with charms and 'such foolish toyes'. On the one occasion when he had a 'grievous ague, and was persuaded by 'fantasticke people' to hang one round his neck, he protested roundly that he recovered by the grace of God and not by any such treatments.

In one place he warns his readers against the 'quackery of unlearned physicians, overbold apothecaries, and foolish women'. A misogynist touch seems to be latent in the herbal. For instance, in quoting a North country saying about the valerian that

> They that will have their heal
> Must put Valerian in their keale

he suggests, perhaps slyly, that 'some woman poet or other' may have been responsible for the tradition.

There are many pleasant touches throughout the herbal concerning the wildings and their seasonal background. The Cuckowflower, he says, 'comes in April and May when the Cuckow begins to speak her pleasant notes without stammering'.

And of Traveller's Joy — later named by Linnaeus *Clematis vitalba*, he writes, 'The floures thereof come forth in July: the beauty thereof appears in November and December. This plant is commonly called *Viorna quasi vias ornans*, of decking and adorning waies and hedges where people travel, and thereupon I have named it the Traveller's Joy'.

All such comments reflect an ardent, poetic, if sometimes self-regarding personality. The herbal retains its freshness for the chief reason that it is literature. Our splendid language which owes its richness to its varied sources, and its flexibility to its freedom from gender and case, was never finer than in this country when English prose was being formed. There had been little attempt at prose literature before this time, and the translation of the Bible in 1611 had an all-important effect upon its development. Yet among many other contributory causes we must include such works as the *Religio Medici* of the 'beloved physician', Sir Thomas Browne (1605 — 82), and the earlier writers of the herbal literature, Parkinson and Gerard. For its sustained fertility of expression, its quaint humour, and its occasional periods of delicate beauty, the prose of Sir Thomas Browne which has been justly called fugal from its consummate handling of a theme has been appreciated by scholars of every succeeding age. Sir Thomas brought to his work a questing mind as well as his religious instinct: in *The Garden of Cyrus* he shows himself occupied with problems of growth and form which are still unravelled: he was in many respects the disciple of Bacon and had the analytical mind of his Master. Our own century has lately honoured his memory by a reprint of his works in an edition de luxe.

John Parkinson brought out his *Paradisus terrestris* in the same year that Thomas Browne took his degree at Oxford; the year 1629. He was thirty when Gerard's herbal was published, and like his contemporaries he too was keenly interested in the new importations, and his delight was in making them grow. He had a medical training, and achieved distinction in that he became physician to King James I. His first book, the *Paradisus*, he dedicated to the queen. In his herbal which did not appear till eleven years later, he followed all the old traditional lines as Gerard had done, though without any obvious borrowing from foreign sources; and from certain expressions we gather some points of difference between the two men. In his earlier work he wrote of plants without any reference to their 'virtues', and they constituted for him an 'earthly paradise'. It would not have occurred to him to use Gerard's phrase about 'their uses being greater and joined to necessity'. He always strikes one as being in the first instance a gardener. His books have for the modern reader a sunset touch of happiness combined with a delightful style. His own garden in Long Acre, was, he tells us, 'well stocked with rarities'; and in the *Hortus Kewensis* of 1810, we read that he introduced seven new species, and was first to mention the arrival of thirty three more.

All through the Elizabethan time interest in gardening had been growing, both here in England, where private gardens like Sir Thomas More's became famous, and in France where Catherine de Medici had set the fashion in an artificial and flamboyant style. It was also the period when the great battle was beginning to be waged between the Formalists and Romantics which was to last two hundred years. In his garden of pleasure Parkinson took the greatest interest in what he called 'the outlandish plants' that could be 'noursed in oure Englishe Ayre'. Among them was the double daffodil from Spain, one of the many narcissi which were imported in this century from Southern Europe and from Turkey. Gerard had already popularized our native *Narcissus Pseudo-Narcissus*, Linn., which he had found growing 'in a poore woman's garden' and which proved a very easy bulb to propagate. Its medicinal use by the Arabians has been mentioned, but the English herbalists did not apparently value it for its virtue. Both Parkinson and Gerard were on terms of intimacy with the best gardeners of the day. Gerard speaks of the white bryony root being given to him by Mr. William Godorous the queen's chief gardener, 'that very curious and learned gentleman', Parkinson's great friend was John Tradescant, senior, gardener to Charles I, who brought him 'many dainty plants from beyond the seas'.

Parkinson's herbal, the *Theatrum Botanicum*, though it never attained the popularity of Gerard's, was, as in fact he himself claimed, 'more ample and exact than any before'. Its style is more austere and less joyous than the *Paradisus*, but it was much more comprehensive, for no less than 3,000 plants were included in its descriptions. This was the most complete classification in any English herbal until that of the botanist Ray appeared in 1686. Many of the prescriptions were those in ordinary use, and included the native simples which have ever since been used in herbal practice, but among them also were certain of the newer remedies imported at that time from the West Indies and America. *Nux-vomica* was among them, though Parkinson seems to have prized it only as an insecticide. Sarsaparilla was in use, and remained in use as a blood-purifier for some centuries. It appeared in the B.P. in 1885, but afterwards ceased to be official and is now used mainly by herbalists. This climbing *Smilax ornata*, N.O. *Smilaceae*, is an interesting plant of the South American swamp flora. It was found so difficult to collect that it was soon put under cultivation, and supplies now come chiefly from Jamaica.

Many of Parkinson's patients seem to have been afflicted with incipient baldness. His contemporary herbalists had counselled them to rub their heads with onion and then stand in the sun, but he recommended southernwood (the common *Artemesia* of our gardens) mixed with salad oil. The root of the Madonna lily, *Lilium candidum*, Linn. was another hair tonic in repute. Bulbs were used fresh and dried.

Perhaps the thing that strikes the modern reader most in all these seventeenth-century herbals is the preoccupation with what was called 'melancholy'. Sir William Osler once called our attention to the large literature which dealt with this subject and to Burton's *Anatomy of Melancholy* in particular. Sir William defined the state as one 'in which man was so out of gear with his environment that life had lost its sweetness'. Now it is surely significant that Burton began to live his silent sedentary life at Christ Church, Oxford, in the year 1599, and was therefore writing about mental affliction in the same period when the herbal writers were trying to find simples to meet the case. It was also characteristic of an age seething with political unrest that Burton began his book with a lengthy treatise on the causes of melancholy, medically observed, and ended it with a curious flight into a realm of ideal harmony in the chapters on love and religion. 'The most elaborate treatise on love ever written,' said Sir William. This extraordinary book which has been reprinted many times down to our own century, was no doubt largely a personal and 'human' document; but taken in conjunction with the innumerable prescriptions in the herbals, it suggests that the changing structure of society was being reflected in a widespread depression. The herbalists therefore set great store by those simples which they deemed applicable for the relief of 'mind, body and estate'. They prescribed what we should call tonics or even stimulants of a vegetable origin, but they did so in such delectable language that hope must have been given with the bottle. The borage was one of the plants most relied upon 'to comfort the heart'. 'It is a herb,' said Gerard, 'of force and virtue to drive away sorrow.' And John Evelyn who was as much interested in simples as in 'sallets' recommended sprigs of borage in like manner 'to revive the hypochondriac'. Flowers of the Salad Burnet were given by Gerard 'to make the heart merry and glad'; and as for saffron, every medical writer extolled its powers. 'The virtue thereof,' said Christopher Catton, 'pierceth to the heart, provoking laughter and merriment.' And Lord Bacon added, 'It maketh the English sprightly'. The botanist Ray echoed the herbalists, saying that 'it had long enjoyed the reputation of comforting the heart and raising the spirits, going far towards the relief of those who are melancholy'. Similar virtues were ascribed to rosemary and balm. 'Balm,' said John Evelyn, 'powerfully chases away melancholy,' while Parkinson recommended strawberries to comfort the fainting spirits, and all agreed that flowers of rosemary in a cordial increased the powers of the mind. Many such phrases ringing with confidence, and often embedded in memorable prose, grace the herbals of the seventeenth century.

Though none that appeared after the *Theatrum Botanicum* were of equal rank, it is interesting to note the large output of herbal literature which continued all through the seventeenth and eighteenth centuries. In 1673 John Archer wrote his Compendious herbal. In 1694 John Pechey's *Compleat Herbal* was issued. In 1702 Dr. Mead published his *Account of Poisons*, and these were followed at intervals by the herbals of Miller, Patrick Blair, Elizabeth Blackwell, Short's *Medicina Britannica*, and the herbal of Dr. John Hill.

Culpeper's *Herbal* also belongs to the seventeenth century, and reflected more than any other the 'popular' side of medicine. He himself was not without credentials, for he had been at Cambridge, and was later apprenticed to an apothecary. Also he seems to have has a lovable streak in that he ministered to the poor in his own fashion and was well spoken of. But his simples were mixed up with astrology of the degenerate kind, and the trail of the charlatan is manifest in his work. He had some highly individual preferences: for one thing he could not bear orchids; he said that Nature had played the fool with them. He had a sharp tongue, and in his denunciations of the *London Pharmacopoeia* he was as fearless as Paracelsus had been in his day. Yet, he retained the old belief in the Doctrine of Signatures which taught that plants revealed their virtues by some outward mark, sometimes connected with a star or planet. Thus *Euphrasia officinalis*, the Eyebright was used (and is still) for the eyes because of the dark pupil-like spot on its corolla. Lungwort (*Pulmonaria officinalis*) has spotted leaves which seemed to suggest a lung, and it was therefore used in chest troubles. The *Scrophulariaceae* as a family were given in scrofula because of the gland-like tubers attached to their roots; and the spotted medick (*Medicago maculata*, syn. *M. arabica*) was used for heart disease because its leaflets, according to an old herbalist 'bear the icon of a heart in its proper colour'. As a matter of fact, many of the lesser herbals were coloured by superstition. *The Art of Simpling*, for instance, written by William Coles in the seventeenth century, included some quaint observations laid down in all good faith concerning the lower animals. A donkey which had unfortunately caught the prevailing melancholy from its masters was said to have cured itself by eating Asplenium fern. Yet even this herbal which was no more than a treatise upon various herb plants had something of the literary charm of its period. 'Very wonderful effects,' said the preface, 'might be wrought by the virtues which were enveloped within the green mantles wherewith the plants were adorned.' The book dealt with the more easily obtained species which could be distilled at home, for the vogue of the 'still room' so characteristic of the eighteenth century was in sight, and aromatic herbs were in great request, not only for 'pomades divines' but for various hygienic uses.

All this time English and European travellers were constantly enlarging our knowledge of foreign species. The elder Tradescant was the first to publish an account of the Russian flora after a voyage to Archangel. Up to 1665, medical organization had been backward in Russia, but in that year, a Physick Garden was planted in Moscow, and the Russian Government sought the assistance of physicians from abroad. After 1700, when Peter the Great was transforming the Byzantine-Tartar state into a European Empire, many apothecaries were invited from Switzerland and other countries. All over Europe, during the seventeenth and eighteenth centuries, a considerable literature dealing with medicinal plants came into being, and writers began to make lists of the drug plants native in their own land or even in special districts.

The first local English flora to chronicle the plants of a particular district was written by Thomas Johnson, who in 1629 and 1632 published descriptions of his two botanical expeditions to Kent, and of his excursions to Hampstead. Later, he published lists of all the plants found in both places (A recent work on Thomas Johnson was published in 1933 by H. W. Kew and H. E. Powell).

At the end of the seventeenth century a local flora was brought out by James Petiver, enumerating the plants which he and his friends had noticed on one of their herborizings round London. The description of the adventure shared on one occasion by Petiver and his friend John Sherard, would make an interesting item for the Selborne Society. It took place in 1704. The two *socii iterantes* started in a post chaise with two horses, accompanied by a servant with another spare horse. They appear to have dismounted occasionally to herborize, and when they arrived at their destination, which was the house of an hospitable friend near Sevenoaks, they were so well entertained with 'venison pasty and the strongest drink in the county' that they went no further that day. On the day following, they made a public exhibition of their finds, and started again only to get entangled in the roads which were probably only cart-tracks, near Wadhurst. This experience seemed to discourage them, for after a further convivial entertainment, they made haste home regretting that they 'had no more opportunities for simpling by the way'. They did, however, finish their 'voyage' with a pleasant tour round Kent.

In 1775 Dr. Withering published his memorandum upon the foxglove which had been hitherto little employed; and this was followed by works on medical botany by Dr. Woodville, Jonathan Stokes, Thomas Cox and Dr. Stephenson. Of these the most important and finely illustrated was that of William Woodville. It was mentioned in a rather flamboyant eulogy of the Edinburgh Dispensary written by Dr. John Thornton of Guys in 1810. 'The university of Edinburgh,' he wrote, 'has, like the city of Thebes during the life of Epaminondas, emerged from obscurity to a splendour unparalleled in literary history.' He went on to cite the public work of such men as Munro, Rutherford, Cullen, Black and Duncan; especially of the latter who had issued 'a useful and perfect Pharmacopoeia'. The only herbal which he treated with respect was that of 'the able and ingenious Woodville'. All the rest, whether written by herbalists or doctors he held in contempt, saying that they were a disgrace to medicine and dangerous to the community; that their figures were inadequate and their descriptions 'so gross and vulgar that false properties were bestowed upon common and trivial plants'. Woodville, he affirmed, had cleared away some of the rubbish from this Augean stable, but much more remained to be done.

From all this we perceive that the decline of the herbal witnessed in the early nineteenth century was the result of the large output of inferior work which began in the seventeenth, and led to a strange and unhappy reaction against medical botany as a branch of knowledge. By 1830 the reaction came to be recognized in the medical schools where the properties of plants were often frankly disregarded. In his *Alphabet of Medical Botany* issued in 1834, Dr. James Rennie of King's College, London, stated that medical botany had become 'a word of reproach entailing sarcasm and contempt as if a knowledge of the means whereby diseases could be cured might enfeeble the mind'. He added that in his own experience, a doctor whom he described as 'a most successful practitioner and an ornament to the profession' was scoffed at in a London hospital for 'knowing a nettle under a hedge'. He also states that some attempts had been made to establish a botanical class in the London medical schools, but it was given up as no one was willing to attend it. And Woodville himself writes in the same sense saying that 'only a few practitioners have a distinct knowledge of the different species'.

The herbalists therefore had obviously fallen upon evil days, in respect both to instruction and literature; but were things any better in the orthodox professions of medicine and pharmacy? Let anyone read some of the accounts of the medical practice, more especially of the seventeenth century, and judge for themselves. Still, every age has its Seer and Forerunner, and the seventeenth century produced the man who came to be known as 'the English Hippocrates', Thomas Sydenham.

SYDENHAM AND HIS ENVIRONMENT

This illustrious physician who prepared the way for a profound modification in practical work was born in 1624, and trained at Montpellier. By his accurate observation of nature and his insistence upon the *vis medicatrix naturae*, he did more than any man of his age to free science from mediævalism. Many of his sayings are commonly recorded, such as 'at the bedside alone you can learn disease'. Of gout, which he studied closely, he said, 'the radical cure is yet a secret, nor do I know when or by whom it will be discovered'. There is a curious passage upon melancholy. 'The strength and steadiness of the mind during its union with the body chiefly depends on the firmness of the spirits which are subservient thereto and border upon immaterial or spiritual beings.'

Four years after his death — he died in 1689 — his treatise on the cure of disease was published, followed by an epitome of his works. As he is nearer to our own time than the latest of the herbal writers, a few of his prescriptions have their interest for us. Here is one for a throat gargle.

Elm bark, six drachms. Liquorice root, ½ oz. 20 stoned raisins. Red roses, two pugils. To these after being boiled in a pint of water, add two ounces of simple oxymel and of honey of roses 'to make a gargarism'.

The purgatives he used were tamarinds, senna, rhubarb, and syrup of roses. He rarely prescribed jalap or scammony. He it was who first popularized quinine (Peruvian bark) in about 1676, though it had been previously used by Brady and Prujean. 'Of all simples' he said, 'Peruvian bark is best; for a few grains morning and evening strengthen and enliven the blood.'

In an interesting passage, he discusses the subject of the simple and its blending. 'A skilful mixture of some kinds answers the end of digesting the humours better than any single simple . . . for every ingredient contributes something towards curing the disease . . . I give preference to electuaries made after the manner of Venice treacle because the fermentation of the simples together improves their virtue . . . But I freely leave the choice of such ingredients and the form in which they are to be given to the judicious physician.'

Gout seems to have baffled him more than anything, and he has left what seems to have been a highly experimental list of the plants he tried. They include angelica root, sweet flag, wormwood, horehound, germander, ground pine, feverfew, St. John's wort, tansy, chamomile, caraway, juniper berries, saffron, and several of the 'sweet herbs'.

He adds a note on their preparation. They were to be 'gathered when in utmost perfection, and dried in paper bags' before powdering. Some of his sick room comments such as 'A patient dies from over-officiousness' display a naive common sense. And again, 'I thought I acted the part of a good physician and an honest man when I did nothing for six or eight days together in scarlet fevers'.

There were occasionally, no doubt, some natural nurses in his day, born for their job, but their share in a patient's recovery is not mentioned.

Sydenham was one of the first to recognize the importance of the germ theory which had been faintly foreshadowed by Girolamo Fracastoro of Verona (born in 1483), who believed that infections were caused by minute bodies having the power of multiplication; just as Lucretius in 60 B.C. had guessed at 'some flying seeds that caused disease and death'. The first experimenter who actually isolated a germ was Leeuwenhöek in 1675; but after both he and Sydenham had passed away, the matter dropped out of science until it was revived through bacteriology two hundred years later.

In his clinical work Sydenham introduced some new and afterwards permanent preparations. One was the 'black draught', a compound infusion of senna; and the other was a laudanum pill made from opium and saffron extracted with canary wine. His memory is the more to be respected when we consider the contemporary records of his age with regard to practice which was disfigured by incredible superstitions, and such nostrums as fox's lungs, powdered gem stones, worms and ants. There is no more amazing scene in history, if it be true, that than related of Charles the Second's deathbed, when fourteen doctors were said to have stood and wrangled round the monarch's bed before they first bled and then administered an emetic to the dying man. John Freind (1675 — 1728) who wrote a history of medicine, may have had scenes like this in mind when he wrote that 'contemporary doctors were mountebanks whose impudence was equal to their guilt in tormenting people in their last hours!'

In the materia medica many herbs came under a ban as being

connected with evil influences, a belief which has persisted in several occult schools at the present day; while on the other hand, some were still hung up to scare away the witches, for the belief in witchcraft was never productive of more hideous consequences than in the seventeenth century. Morbid ideas also centred round a dead body, and ointments were made from the moss that had attached itself to a dead man's skull. For toothache, a tooth was taken from a rotting corpse on the gallows and inserted into the patient's gum. More horrible still was the practice of stabbing a cat to death and giving the blood to a child in convulsions. No wonder that Dr. John Brown in the *Horae subsecivae* wrote of 'the mass of errors and prejudices among which Sydenham was placed when the practical part of his art was overrun with vile and silly nostrums'. In fact, it is evident that all this time in spite of the advances in chemistry wrought by Boerhäave and Boyle, pharmacy only slipped downhill, while medicine, still dominated except for Sydenham's influence by the dead hand of mediævalism, and retarded like all progress, by the incessant wars, could not make much headway. In many respects the seventeenth century was a heroic epoch: it set on foot great social enterprises; it brought differentiation into scientific study, and some important discoveries were made. Yet its pharmacy is an offence to our self esteem, for it portrays us after twelve centuries on much the same level as the Saxons.

Another and more lamentable aspect of this and the succeeding centuries was the growing hostility between religion and science. It had its roots in an unhappy past. The unspeakable wars of religion (1618 — 1648) used barbarous methods of persecution by which the Churches were disgraced. Christianity itself was obscured by the passionate adherence to archaic elements in its presentation, and science was treated as an enemy. Thus there grew up the hostility which destroyed what should have been an equal speed of progress. From the conflict, science emerged the stronger, and it has ever since pursued its work, often disinterested, generally beneficent and civilizing, until the tragic impasse of the present day, when its discoveries are for the first time being exploited, less for racial progress than for racial suicide.

The helplessness of every nation in the face of ruinous epidemics had been one of the tragedies of the Middle Ages. It is brought home to us with special emphasis in the case of the bubonic plague. Professor Oman has pointed out that the epidemic of 1348 which was brought from the East by a Genoese ship and spread all over Europe deflected history by wiping out in Greenland the only people who had any knowledge of North America. It also had another far-reaching effect for England as it caused the conversion of much of the arable land into pasture. From the sixth to the eighteenth century this scourge had been endemic in Europe with occasional fierce outbreaks, and all that could be done was to light fires as Hippocrates had done, and burn aromatic herbs in fumigation. 'Appalled and doubtful,' as Lucretius had said, 'mused the healing art.'

All through the ages these stark and calamitous outbreaks had been accepted as part of the natural — or divine — order, with a resignation which alone seemed relevant to an occasion which no one understood. But the terrible thing was that this attitude persisted long into the seventeenth century, especially in Scotland which was described by Buckle as 'living at that time in a total night'. It is worth reading the extraordinary description in his *History of Civilization* of the diseases of that period, and of men's attitude to them. 'The smallpox,' he writes, 'being one of the most fatal as well as one of the most loathsome of all diseases was especially sent from God', and on that account, the remedy of inoculation was scouted as a profane attempt to frustrate His intentions. (As late as 1850 the use of chloroform in childbirth was resisted in England upon similar grounds.) 'Other disorders all owed their origin to the anger of the Almighty . . . He was always punishing . . . Every fresh war was the result of his special interference: it was not caused by the meddling folly or insensate ambition of statesmen, but it was 'the immediate work of the Deity.' Not only the humanity but the native common sense of these naturally intelligent people who were afterwards to set an example in education that put others to shame, was at that time overlaid by the fear and gloom which darkened their religion.

They were still marooned in it when the cholera epidemics began.

The world-wide attack that started in India in 1817 came here by way of Russia, and spread to Europe and America causing a death roll of approximately a million. In 1853 there was another outbreak which spread rapidly in the slum areas of Scotland where filth and penury abounded. This was the occasion of the famous correspondence between the Scottish clergy and Lord Palmerston, the former asking that a day of fasting should be observed to stop the visitation. Palmerston's reply diplomatically suggested that measures should be taken to free the poorer districts from those sources of contagion which infallibly breed pestilence.

Meanwhile in London, corpses were being removed in carts as in the old days of the Black Death, and it was at last discovered that the 'Broad Street pump' had been contaminated by a cesspool.

Thirty years later, the cholera *spirillum* was isolated by Koch, and in 1874 a Japanese discoverer isolated the *Bacillus pestis* which lives in the stomach of the flea whose host is the black rat. Incidentally it must be remembered that the introduction of the brown rat into England and the consequent disappearance of the black species was a factor in the conquest of the plague.

The attitude of the Scots, like that of the Church which remained the controlling factor in European history for so many centuries, was part of the tragic misunderstanding by which the gulf between science and religion was widened. The *rapprochement* which is increasing on both sides at the present day is indicative of a change partly resulting from the growth of problems new to the world. They are forcing men to seek fellowship under stress of a common failure, and to look, as Plato said, 'to the universal polity whose troubled image we behold in the polity which we know'.

We generally restrict the word creative to the supreme products of the artistic imagination, but no less creative is the one hundred per cent enthusiasm that has led men to the peaks both of religion and science. It remains to create a Kingdom of right relationships in which both shall at last be brought through an extended vision into harmony with the other forces of human life.

CHAPTER VII

MEDICINAL PLANTS
OF THE
BRITISH FLORA

CHAPTER VII

WE have seen that the science of botany arose with the herbals, but many centuries passed before a rational basis was found for classification. Observers from Aristotle to Linnaeus had concentrated upon some structural plan which they defined as underlying the myrian species. It was like the quest of philosophy for the One in the Many and the Many in the One. The first system of botanical classification had been constructed by Andrea Caesalpinus (1519-1603) in his treatise on plants. Through the eighteenth and nineteenth centuries, the labours of many botanists were pooled. After Mohl, de Jussieu, Ray, de Candolle, Pereira, Bentley and Lindley, the so-called Natural System was evolved extending the previous work of Linnaeus; and after the appearance of Dr. Lindley's *Flora Medica* in 1838, the therapeutic side began to take its proper place in scientific literature.

Meanwhile, though the present Natural System which is obviously based in most instances upon well marked and permanent characteristics may not prove to be the last word in classification, yet it must always be the foundation of all future work in systematic botany.

To the Natural Orders then we shall adhere in this chapter upon the native flora which will perhaps be found a suitable pendant to the story of the English herbals. Among the many excellent works which are written upon English botany are the following: Sowerby's *English Botany;* John's *Flowers of the Field;* Babington's *Manual of British Botany;* and Bentham and Hooker's *Handbook of the British Flora.* Many of the plants enumerated in this short survey will justly be considered as weeds; for the most insignificant, like the Groundsel and the Shepherd's Purse have the true weed's proclivity for a dust heap as if it were the optimum of a plant's desire. Others like the Good King Henry seem to follow man's footsteps, beating a track from wood or common to his flower bed wherever he may build. Yet all these weeds were at some time or other esteemed as 'worts' by our ancestors, nor are they all superseded at the present day. Many hundredweights of them are still marketed by the herbalists who go so far as to claim that the use of a mineral remedy is 'contrary to Nature', a belief which can however scarcely be substantiated in the face of recent discoveries which shew that many metallic elements such as silver, tin, magnesium and copper exist in small amounts in the body where they may play an important part.

But apart from extravagant claims, there is no doubt whatever that the plant remains as it has always been of the highest value in alleviating the ills of mankind, and further, that the folk-lore concerning its use has often anticipated science. From the botanist's point of view, it surely adds to the pleasure of his 'herborizing' when he is conversant with this long remembered and venerated lore.

NATURAL ORDER, RANUNCULACEAE

The Celandine, *Ranunculus Ficaria*, Linn., is a firstling of spring; a pretty little plant with nine pointed petals which display their brilliant gold for about seven hours a day in sunshine. It has not been observed to set seed, but propagates freely by bulbils in the leaf axils. The tuberous roots are the base of many ointments, and the plant has been called Pilewort from the appearance of its tuberous roots.

The two Hellebores, *H. viridis* and *H. foetidus* belong to this order but are seldom used to-day.

The word 'Hellebore' is a word of confusion, as it has been and still is applied, not merely to a number of different species of the same genus, but to plants belonging to two entirely different and unrelated genera. The Hellebore of the ancients was possibly *H. lleborus orientalis*, Lam., but the plant which came to be used most for magical and medicinal purposes was the Black Hellebore, or Christmas Rose, *H. niger*, Linn., frequently grown as a garden plant in this country. The part used medicinally consists of the rhizome and roots, but it is little employed to-day except in homoeopathy, as it is a very dangerous drug. It owes its poisonous properties to certain glycosides which it contains. Green Hellebore, or Bear's Foot, *H. viridis*, Linn., and Stinking Hellebore or Setterwort, *H. foetidus*, Linn., are native; at least, of the first, var. *occidentalis* (Reut.) is a native plant. They are both very poisonous.

White Hellebore, *Veratrum album*, Linn., has also been known and used medicinally, and for poisoning, from early times. This is a member of the N.O. *Liliaceae*; and owes its poisonous properties to its alkaloidal content. The American Green Hellebore, *Veratrum viride*, Ait., is a related plant with similar alkaloids. (The veratrine of pharmacy given to reduce high blood pressures, comes from the seeds of *Schoenocaulon officinalis* whose product is known as *cevadilla*.)

There was an interesting article by Mr. Redgrove on Hellebores in *Folklore and Fact* in the *Gardeners' Chronicle* for Jan. 9th, 1932.

BERBERIDACEAE

The pretty shrub, *Berberis vulgaris*, Linn., is not found every day in woods and copses, but when it is found, it is unmistakable from our familiarity with the many hybrids of our gardens.

It is the only British species. The bark has been mentioned as identical with the Indian rusot. The inner layers of the stem bark are of a beautiful yellow colour: they yield the alkaloid berberine, and are used, chiefly in herbal medicine, for jaundice and indigestion.

PAPAVERACEAE

The Opium poppy, *Papaver somniferum*, Linn., may occasionally be found in waste places and cornfields as a naturalized plant.

The Greater Celandine, *Chelidonium majus*, Linn., is used by herbalists as an alterative, diuretic, and purgative. They also recommend the fresh juice to destroy corns and warts.

FUMARIACEAE

Fumaria officinalis, the Fumitory, is still in use. It was formerly boiled in milk 'for blotches, weals and pushes', besides being esteemed for 'melancholy'.

CRUCIFERAE

The large wholesome family of the cresses is marked by antiscorbutic and pungent properties. Lately, the fact that their mustard oils protect a plant from mould has been made the basis of a very interesting experiment by Professor Virtamen of Finland who is applying this to agriculture in the storage of acid silage. Except for the Mustards themselves, few Crucifers are now employed in pharmacy, but many of the old worts will be found in the Order. *Capsella Bursa-pastoris*, Moen., Shepherd's Purse, is still used by herbalists in kidney complaints and dropsy. It has often been confused with Penny Cress, *Thlaspi arvense*, Linn. Both plants are widely distributed and were known to the Greeks. Penny Cress was included in the ancient Mithridate and was called Mithridate Mustard: it is not nearly such a common weed in England as the *Capsella* from which it may be distinguished mainly by the rounder wings of its seed cases.

Several of the *Lepidums* or Pepper-worts are found in our flora. The following were medicinal: *Cochlearia officinalis*, Linn., the Scurvy Grass; *Subularia aquatica*, Linn., the (rare) Awlwort; *Senebria Coronopus*, Poiret, the Wart Cress; and *Erophila verna*, Meyer, the tiny Whitlow-grass. Gerard's account of this insignificant wilding is an example of his close and loving observation. He noted 'the verie little white flowers, the small, flat pouches which being ripe, fall away, leaving the middle part standing a long time after, which is like white satin'. Erophila's ancient name was Nail Wort; it is one of the flowers that rely almost exclusively on self-fertilization.

Cardamine pratensis, Linn., the Cuckoo flower, was named from *cardia*, the heart, and *damao*, to strengthen. *Sisymbrium Allaria*, Scop., is misleadingly called Hedge Mustard, but is better known as Hedge Garlic, for its big crinkled leaves have a strong garlic smell. Turner, in his herbal, said that in England and Germany it was used for saucers, and he praises it as an aid to digestion.[1]

Brassica nigra, Koch., is the Black Mustard, and is an uncommon plant occurring sparingly by willow-bordered streams. It grows in most latitudes and has been known and prized by the earliest races. The seed pods are said to contain about 1000 seeds from which the volatile oil is distilled.

Another wort that has lost a once brilliant reputation is the rather uncommon *Sisymbrium Sophia*, a native of the real Hedge Mustard, *S. officinale*, Scop. A dusty looking weed of waste places, it was nevertheless so highly valued that it was once picturesquely called 'the wisdom of surgeons', from its supposed healing powers. The rise and fall of reputations in the herb community is probably more evident within our own flora than anywhere else.

Cochlearia officinalis, the Scurvy Grass, is the subject of a tale told by Lind in his treatise on scurvy. A sailor, it was said, being rendered helpless by the disease was sent on shore to die. Seeing this plant growing near him, he managed to bite off a portion of it and found himself benefited. In the end he recovered. The plant may be recognized on the coast by its fleshy, kidney-shaped leaves and loose branching heads of white flowers. It is not considered indigenous.

The Sea Kale, *Crambe maritima*, Linn., and the Sea Cabbage, *Brassica oleracea*, Linn., both occur on the cliffs by the sea in some parts of Britain. The latter is one of the few plants whose name, from *bresig*, a cabbage, is of Celtic origin, and both plants were doubtless included in the early British dietary. In the modern world, the Crucifer that is perhaps most prized outside of the cultivated vegetables, is the watercress, *Nasturtium officinale*, R. Br., the only one of its genus that has white blossoms. It was known to the Greeks; and modern science has justified its reputation. It has an essential oil, with traces of iodine and salts of potash. 'The mess of water-

---

[1] H. S. Redgrove has recently called attention to its utility as a salad. See *Gard. Chron.* May 13th, 1933.

cress' as Herrick called it, is one of the most valuable ingredients in our salads.

VIOLACEAE

The little pansy, *Viola tricolor*, Linn., which flowers by the corn-fields, was called by the monks *Herba Trinitatis*, and is still used as a cordial. The leaves of the sweet violet, *Viola oderata*, Linn., have been esteemed from ancient times; herbalists credit them with valuable antiseptic properties and allege that they are capable of allaying pain, in — and even arresting the growth of — cancer.

TAMARICACEAE

Towards midsummer the Tamarisk throws up its sprays of pink blossoms in various places in the south-west, but it is not a native. The plant (*Tamarix gallica*, Linn.,) is said to have been introduced here from the Mediterranean by good Archbishop Grindal in 1590. Writing of it in 1596, Richard Hakluyt says: 'many people received good health from this species.' In Denmark it was made a substitute for hops.

CAROPHYLLACEAE

The Pink Order is not a very important one in medicine. *Saponaria officinalis*, Linn., the Soap-wort, is used in herbalism as an alternative to sarsaparilla. The Pearl Wort, *Sagina spetala*, Ard., has dropped out in practice, as also have the Sandworts; but the Stitchworts, or at least the smaller Stitchwort, *Stellaria media*, Vill., one of the commonest of wayside weeds, is sometimes used as a demulcent. Its common name is Chickweed which is confusing since the Cerastiums are known as Mouse-Ear Chickweeds. It is an instance of the frequent overlapping and iteration in popular botany. *Veronica officinalis* of dry pastures, is still used in herbal practice for catarrh, and was formerly a 'tea plant' used both here and on the continent where it was called 'Thé de l'Europe'.

LINACEAE

Linum usitatissimum, Linn., the Flax of commerce, is not a native plant, and the only member of the family formerly used in English medicine is the tiny Mountain or Purging Flax, *Linum catharticum*, Linn. One wonders how enough of it could have been gathered for its medicinal property. The generic name comes from the Celtic word *lin*, a thread.

MALVACEAE

The plants of the genus *Gossypium* are the most important in this Order by reason of the cotton producing species, but the roots of Mallows are mucilaginous and have long been used for their emollient properties. *Althaea officinalis*, Linn., is the marsh mallow: the name comes from the Greek *althomai*, to heal. The plant is widely cultivated on the Continent for a sweetmeat and for medicine. The roots which grow fleshy like parsnips under cultivation, are eaten in Palestine, recalling the passage in the Book of Job, 'flung into the wilderness and cutting up mallows for support'. The fruits of the common mallow, *Malva sylvestris*, Linn., are the 'cheeses' of the country children.

HYPERICACEAE

The plants of this Order are generally aromatic and resinous, and although none of the species has been called '*officinalis*', the common St. John's wort, *Hypericum perforatum*, Linn., has long been used as a pulmonary. The beautiful little *H. pulchrum*, Linn., of dry pastures is probably the species called 'Baldur's blood' from its crimson tinted buds. The name preserves the association of the pre-Christian festival of the summer solstice when bonfires were lighted about the 24th of June and the plant hung up to ward off evil spirits. When the Feast of St. John the Baptist took the place of the pagan rite, the St. John's wort was still burnt in the bonfires of midsummer. Gerard in speaking of its 'oyle as a pretious remedy for deep wounds made with a venomed weapon' adds a sinister comment that 'in time of wars no gentlewoman should be without St. John's wort'. The handsome species, the Tutsan, *H. Androsaemum*, was also called '*toute-saine*' from its medicinal properties.

RHAMNACEAE

To this Order the Buckthorn, *Rhamnus catharticus*, Linn., belongs. The berries were formerly much used, but the remedy has been superseded.

LEGUMINOSAE

The Pea and Bean Order is a large and highly beneficent group. The yellow Broom, *Cytisus Scoparius*, Linn., has long been used in medicine, and 'broom tops' are still used in pharmacy as a diuretic, though no longer official in the B.P. Sparteine sulphate is a useful derivative, used in blood pressure. The diuretic properties of the plant are due, not to this alkaloid but to a neutral substance they contain known as 'scoparin'. Gerard used the flower buds in a 'sallet'. The bulk of medicinal plants belonging to the *Leguminosae*, like cassia, acacia, liquorice, etc., come from abroad.

ROSACEAE

Many astringent plants used in herbalism belong to the Rose Order. One is Meadow Sweet, *Spiraea Ulmaria*, Linn., one of the

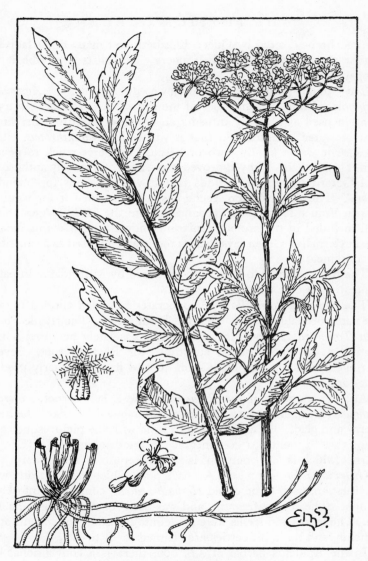

VALERIANA OFFICINALIS

scented herbs desired by Queen Elizabeth and many other ladies in Tudor times for strewing their floors. Herbalists prescribe it for dropsy.

The tough-stemmed, yellow-flowered Agrimony, *Agrimonia Eupatoria*, Linn., is a member of the same N.O. In the country it is often used as a tea by infusing an ounce of the dried herb in a pint of water. Gerard said that it was called *philanthropus*, either because it was a kindly herb or because its burrs stuck to people as if it loved them. Pliny approved it as a herb of 'princely authoritie'; and Gerard quoting him, adds that it was excellent for 'naughty livers'. The Anglo-Saxon leechdoms recommended it for wounds, and in France it has been recognized from the Middle Ages and is still included in the aromatic mixture known as *Eau d'arquébusade*, used externally. Green says that its root was even used as a substitute for quinine.

The herb was said to have been first used by Mithridatus Eupator: hence the specific name.

The use of a *Potentilla* by Hippocrates has been alluded to, and the name probably derives from the Latin *potens*. The fragile *Potentilla Tormentilla*, Nest., the Tormentil, has lately acquired a new dignity as an experimental substitute for Rhatany root. Several astringent remedies are made from it, and it was formerly used in fever and cholera.

Another member of the *Rosaceae* is the Salad Burnet, *Poterium Sanguisorba*, Linn., which Gerard recommended 'to make the heart merry and glad'. He also put it into wine with the picturesque comment that 'it yielded a certain grace in the drinking'. The Greater Burnet which is less common, is still in repute as a vulnerary.

Geum urbanum, Linn., the Avens, a plant which varies greatly with its situation, used to be called *Herba benedicta*, contracted into Herb Bennet. The root is fragrant, and was used for flavouring wine and ale. The leaves and stems were made into infusions for consumptive patients, and tonic properties are claimed for it to-day.

In the Apuleius herbal of A.D. 600, there is a conventional but unmistakable drawing of the Blackberry, *Rubus fruticosus*, Linn., whose leaves have been used in medicine for centuries. Bramble fruit was in fact, included in early editions of the *London Pharma-copoeia.* Gerard gave both leaf and fruit as an astringent. The wild raspberry, *Rubus Idæus*, Linn. (the specific name from Mount Ida where it grew) was utilized by the Greeks medicinally. So were the roots and leaves of the Strawberry which are astringent, and used to be given in dysentery.

Another valuable genus of the great Rose Order includes *Pyrus Aria*, Ehrh., the Whitebeam; *Pyrus aucuparia*, Ehrh, the Mountain Ash; and *Pyrus communis*, Linn., the Wild Pear occasionally found in woods. The latter was known to Pliny who said that of the many varieties not one was digestible! Mountain Ash berries used to make a drink which John Evelyn called 'incomparable'; they were recommended for scurvy.

Of *Pyrus Malus*, Linn., the Wild Apple, Pliny enumerated about 22 varieties. Cider is mentioned in Anglo-Saxon MSS. and it is thought that the tree was brought here during the Roman occupation. 'It is virtuous in medecyn,' said the old herbalists, and its value is abundantly recognized in the modern dietary.

The hips of the Dog Rose were once employed as an astringent, and the haws of *Crataegus Oxyacantha*, Linn., the Hawthorn, prescribed by Dioscorides, were long retained in the B.P. and are still used in France for kidney disease, and by English herbalists as a cardiac tonic.

The two *Alchemillas*, *A. vulgaris*, Linn., Lady's mantle, and *A. arvensis*, Scop., Parsley Piert, are both highly esteemed in herbal pharmacy. They are astringent and diuretic.

The former was named by Tragus, the German botanist, and mentioned in his *Hist. Plant.* in 1532. The latter was once called Parsley Piercestone from its influence on gravel or stone in the bladder, and the name was corrupted into Parsley Piert.

CUCURBITACEAE

The White Bryony, *Bryonia dioica*, Jacq., belongs to the Cucumber Order. Its scarlet berries which, with the strikingly decorative tendrils, persist long into the Autumn, are emetic and unwholesome, though the young shoots have been eaten as a vegetable. The French name for the plant '*nâvet du diable*' suggests however that the results have been unexpected.

White Bryony root is much used in herbalism for bronchial affections, but the Homœopath uses the European species, *B. alba*, Linn., for rheumatism. Gerard said that 'stamped with wine' *B. dioica* should be used for boils. The White Bryony has been confusingly called the false Mandrake. In Henry VIII's time the root was cut into a semblance of the human shape, fitted with eyes, and sold as an amulet. The popular superstition credited it with magic power and high prices were paid for it. Green in his *Universal Herbal* of 1832, says that a mould was fitted over the growing root of a young Bryony and left all the summer, after which it would be found that the rapidly growing root had acquired a roughly human shape, and it was then 'shown for mandrakes to the common people'. The root when fresh, is succulent and fleshy with an unpleasant smell and acrid taste. The cells contain a bitter principle with phosphate of lime and other constituents.

UMBELLIFERAE

A species of this wide and varied Order commonly found in the woods is the Sanicle, *Sanicula europoea*, Linn., called by Culpeper 'a present help to man and beast', and retained by herbalists for blood impurities. Four very poisonous plants of the Order which occur wild in Britain should be known to botanists, for many mistakes have been made in identification. The most familiar is the Hemlock known by its graceful leaves and smooth spotted stem. Hemlock seed — the fruit of the plant — was official in the B.P. before 1908, and the tincture was retained in the *Ext. Conii Liquidum* of the Codex. Its use was as an anti-spasmodic, but the tincture was said to vary in strength, for the plant is one whose properties vary considerably with position and soil. A useful test for hemlock fruit is *liq. potassae* which causes it to give out a foetid odour. The alkaloid, *conine*, is one of the strongest vegetable poisons. *Cicuta virosa*, Linn., is the Cowbane or Water Hemlock, an extremely poisonous plant which is fortunately rare. A very common relative is Hemlock Water Drop-wort, *Oenanthe crocata*, Linn., a stout plant with tuberous roots which have been taken for parsnips. *Aethusa Cynapium*, Linn., the Fool's Parsley, is the fourth poisonous Umbellifer, but it is a slender little weed not likely to be taken for any other.

Coriandrum sativum, Linn., used by Hippocrates, is not a native. It is thought to have been brought here by the Romans, and was once largely cultivated in Essex on the good, heavy soil so congenial to many crops. Coriander is much used in pharmacy preparations of senna and rhubarb; it is also sold to the makers of curries, mixed spices, and liqueurs.

Foeniculum vulgare, Mill., Fennel, has long been used for the oil from its seeds. The fruits from cultivated plants of this species are official in the B.P.

The lusty growth of *Angelica sylvestris*, Linn., is familiar by the water sides. Its furrowed stem is tinged with purple, and the white umbels have a pinkish tint. It is often taken to be the Angelica of the confectioner as well as of the pharmacist, but the plant which gave its heavenly name to the species is the foreign *Archangelica officinalis*, Hoffm. Opinions differ about the medicinal properties of this long revered species. The story of Warburg's tincture in Wootton's *Chronicles of Pharmacy* adduces evidence to show that quinine was more potent in malaria when mixed with the essential oil of Angelica. Kirschbaum, a German chemist, has moreover experimented with the oil, and suggests that its musky smell may be due to the presence of 'the lactone of 15 oxy-pentadecylic acid'; a suggestion which, though it leaves the ordinary reader cold, appears to be linked with other technical discoveries indicating that the plant may contain something more potent than the ancients guessed or the moderns knew. The oil is a highly aromatic stimulant, and is used in the manufacture of liqueurs and in fine perfumery. Probably its whole story remains to be told.

Carum Carvi, Linn., the Caraway of commerce, may occasionally be found wild, but only as an escape from former cultivation. Nor are any of the species which yield gum-resins British plants. The common parsley, *Carum Petroselinum*, B. and H., is sometimes met with on waste ground, but is not a native. *Crithmum maritimum*, Linn., is the Samphire of our cliffs. Many will remember Shakespeare's allusion in King Lear to the 'dreadful trade' of the Samphire gatherer who hung half way down the cliff on the coast at Dover. A terrible accident befel the last of the gatherers, since when the trade in Samphire has passed away. The plant used to be in great request, and was either boiled or pickled, or eaten raw in salads.

Equally pungent is the Scottish Lovage, *Ligustrum scoticum*, Linn., which grows in the north. It is used by herbalists as a carminative.

RUBIACEAE

This Order includes some plants of great service to man as food, dyes and medicines. Among the latter are quinine, coffee and Ipecacuanha, all of which are plants of hot latitudes. There is no group whose genera differ more widely in their characteristics. In Britain they are only represented by small, herbaceous things such as Madder, Bedstraw and Woodruff which have no special properties for the pharmacist; but the cleavers mentioned among the plants of Dioscorides, is still employed in herbalism.

VALERIANACEAE

Valeriana officinalis, Linn., the Valerian, is a native of dry places in the woodland and is considered by some botanists identical with *V. sambucifolia*, Mik., which is commonly found by brooks and in ditches. The red-flowered spur valerian, *Centranthus ruber*, D.C., which grows so abundantly on walls, dry railway banks, etc., is not used medicinally.

Formerly, when we depended on our own supplies, Valerian was cultivated in Derbyshire, and several hybrids are still grown in our drug farms as well as on the Continent.

Valerian has been in use from pre-Christian times, and retains its place in every pharmacopoeia for its action in nervous complaints. Dr. Manson, writing in the *British Medical Journal* in 1928, said that 'it was perhaps the earliest method of treating the neuroses'. He considered it was worthy of further research into its properties and action upon the nervous system, for the extract alleviated mental misery without any deleterious habit-forming propensities.

In 1929, Dr. James Grier read an interesting paper before the Pharmaceutical Society, dealing with the history and value of the plant. Valerian and the volatile oil of Asafoetida, he said, had long been used in the treatment of hysteria and the nervous troubles of women. Recently the drug had been used for shell-shock in men (with the effect in 1918 of trebling the price of the drug) and also for the simple, nervous restlessness of children. Formerly and in recent times it had been held that the action of valerian and asafoetida were purely psychological, associated with the repulsive colour and taste, and with the preconceived ideas held in mediæval times as to their actions. Nervous diseases being due to evil spirits, the logical thing was to cast them out by spells, charms, fumigations, and the taking of repulsive drugs; nor were these methods by any means ineffective. The Valerian-asafoetida combination may have had a remedial effect on both mind and body, for psycho-therapeutists are aware that both must be considered and treated as a whole. The volatile oil of Asafoetida contains sulphur compounds. Valerian oil contains, among other constituents, esters of valeric, butyric and other acids, including bornyl esters. It also contains camphene, terpineol, etc.

Dipsaceae. The Devil's bit, Scabious, *Scabiosa Succisa*, Linn., is indelibly connected with native folk-lore. Its little round heads are locally called 'blue buttons and bonnets', but the older name referred to the curious 'premorse' or bitten off root which in pharmacy was esteemed for all kinds of ailments. Parkinson's comment is amusing: 'Fabulous antiquity (the monks and friars being, as I suppose, the first inventors of the fable) said that the Devill envying the good that this herbe might do to mankind, bit away part of the roote, and thereof came its name.'

COMPOSITAE

This Natural Order is one of the largest in the vegetable kingdom. In about 1840 M. Lasègue observed that its members constituted one tenth of the plants then known, and Lindley estimated their number as 9,000 species. Many more have been found since his day. Structurally, the Composite is considered the crown of the vegetable kingdom, as it has attained its maximum degree of specialization in its rayed and tubular florets, exquisitely wrought into a conspicuous head. Medicinally, the Order is a variable one, but a bitter principle, serviceable as a tonic, pervades the greater number of species, many of which also possess a volatile oil. *Anthemis, Arnica,* and *Artemesia* were all known to the ancients: some valuable roots like the Jerusalem artichoke (*Helianthus*) and some equally useful leafy vegetables like the lettuce, belong to this family.

Several of the 'weeds' of the *Compositae* are in use in herbal medicine.

Achillea Millefolium, Linn., is the Yarrow which in the days of tournaments was called Knighten milfoil and soldier's woundwort, and was kept ready for use in the monasteries. As a vulnerary and styptic its credit has diminished, but it is still much used here and in the U.S.A. as a tonic and diaphoretic. Linnaeus extolled it for rheumatism. The *Senecios* as a species are suspect, as many are very poisonous. The leaves of the Groundsel, *Senecio vulgaris,* Linn., are acrid, but the leafy stem formerly made the base of emollient poultices. The manner of using the herb varied curiously in different ages. Some old writers deemed it unfit for internal use, while in Culpeper's practice it was used as a vermifuge. Others reckoned it anti-scorbutic. Most herbalists however warned people against over-doses.

The showy yellow Ragwort, *Senecio Jacoboea,* Linn., is no longer a wort of any consequence, but its near relative, the Marsh Ragwort,

S. aquaticus, Hill., may occasionally be used. It used to be called St. James' Wort as it flowered about July 25th, St. James's Day. It was held in repute for 'healing greene woundes'. Other curious names for it were Stammer wort and Stagger wort. All the *Senecios* were also regarded as 'Flea worts', but other genera of the *Compositae* were better known as Flea-banes. The *Erigerons* for instance possessed this title. There are only two native in the British flora; but *Erigeron canadensis*, Linn., a naturalized North American species, is retained by the herbalist for kidney troubles.

The *Pulicarias* are likewise Flea-banes. The name comes from the Latin *pulex*, a flea. These plants are no longer put to any special uses either as worts or insecticides, but the uncommon *Pulicaria dysenterica*, Bernh., was evidently a wort in the bad old days of prevailing ague. It is a plant of moist places with bright yellow daisy flowers and downy leaves.

Our native *Artemesias* have an interesting history. *Artemesia vulgaris*, Linn., the Mugwort, is common on waste land; much commoner than the Wormwood, *Artemesia absinthium*, Linn. It was once a substitute for hops, and was also made into a tea in the west of England when Indian tea cost seven shillings a pound. Dr. Fernie states that Wormwood was first prepared as a drink by a French physician named *Ordinaire* at the close of the eighteenth century. His *tisane* was devoid of alcohol, but the absinthe which is the modern liqueur is made from *A. absinthium* and other flavouring ingredients in an alcoholic infusion. It is a powerful stimulant. Infusions of Wormwood were strangely declared by Dioscorides to be a remedy against intoxication. Gerard used it as a vermifuge. It has been suggested that the dangerous properties of absinthe come not so much from *Artemesia absinthium* as from the mixture wrought into the infusion.

Tanacetum vulgare, Linn., the Tansy, makes a brave show in the English landscape where it recalls the flaming masses that are so common on the banks of the Rhine. It is more largely used in German than in English medicine as a blood purifier and anodyne in gout. Its essential oil possesses poisonous properties. Among other Composites, *Lapsana communis*, Linn., the Nipple-wort, and *Ser-*

ratula tinctoria, Linn., the Saw-wort, have evidently disappeared from popular pharmacy. The Burdock, however, remains in favour. The root of this hefty plant, *Arctium Lappa*, Linn., is dug up every autumn, and in powdered form is used in skin troubles as well as inwardly. The Dandelion, *Taraxacum officinale*, Weber, was until quite lately, included in the B.P. for use in atonic dyspepsia, the fresh root being used as a 'bitter'. The smaller roots are employed to make dandelion coffee. Leaf as well as root contains the bitter substance taraxacin with insulin; the leaves are often palatable in salads and should not be bleached. The plant was cultivated in Germany before the war, and the imported root was often the size of a parsnip. The Coltsfoot, *Tussilago Farfara*, Linn. (generic name from *tussis*, a cough), used as an inhalation by Dioscorides, has been called 'Nature's best herb for the lungs'. Cough mixtures are often made from it, and a simple infusion makes 'Coltsfoot tea'. The powdered leaf is still employed in the old Roman way for smoking. To the N.O. *Campanulaceae* belong the two native *Lobelias*, one of which, the beautiful *L. urens*, Linn., hitherto only known in Devon and Cornwall, is said to be on the increase, for it has lately been recorded for Dorset, Sussex and Hants. The other native Lobelia is *L. Dortmanna*, Linn., which frequents the northern lakes. Both species contain the same narcotic and poisonous substances as the medicinal *Lobelia inflata*, Linn., of America, used in whooping cough and asthma.

APOCYNACEAE

The only native representative of the genus *Vinca* are the periwinkles, *V. major*, Linn., and *V. minor*, Linn. They possess a strong astringent property and are still used in popular medicine. Herbalists are claiming many cures in diabetes by treatment with the extracts.

GENTIANACEAE

One of the loveliest of English flowers, the Bog-bean, *Menyanthes trifoliata*, Linn., belongs to this Order and was for many years official in pharmacy. The tonic properties extracted from its sturdy root stock are common to all the genera in this family. In Sweden and Germany the plant was once used as a substitute for hops, and medically as a substitute for quinine in ague. In England it was the practice to cut up the roots and bottle them in sherry until required.

Another Gentian is the Centaury (named after the old Centaur) *Erythraea Centaurium*, Pers., It is fairly common on hill sides or in woods where it branches out into shrubby plants with bright pink blooms fading to white. The finest clumps I ever saw were in a woodland clearing near Bolney in Sussex. It is employed by herbalists in dyspepsia.

The Gentian of the B.P. is *Gentiana lutea*, Linn., from the Alps and the Jura, but the two native species, *G. Amarella*, Linn., and *G. campestris*, Linn., used to be constantly used, and are mentioned by both Culpeper and Gerard. The roots and stems are still prepared by herbalists as a bitter. Culpeper proclaimed the 'vertues' of these two native plants to be 'not a whit inferior to that which cometh across the sea'. Nevertheless, the latter has entirely superseded all other species in official medicine. The rhizome and roots are collected in autumn and carefully dried. It affords a very useful tonic, a simple bitter which has no action beyond that which belongs to the bitter quality related to its sugar compounds. In the *Gardeners' Chronicle* of Sept. 5, 1931, Mr. H. S. Redgrove writes, 'In the past the plant has been credited with many marvellous medicinal virtues. It was an ingredient in the once celebrated antidote supposed to have been invented in the sixth or fifth century B.C. by the philosopher Pythagoras, and was included in the formula for three of the four amazing concoctions which, on account of their supposed importance, were once termed the 'Four Officinal Capitals'.

It is also employed in the French *apéritif* called 'Suze'.

Our native Marsh Gentian seems to be almost extinct; and Linton in his Flora of Derbyshire links it with the Turk's Cap Lily and the Cyclamen as disappearing plants. Professor Salisbury in his book on our 'Waning Flora' suggests that the beauty of some of these species has been their undoing, and that additional by-laws should be framed to deal with unscrupulous tourists. It is a matter in which the support of public opinion is manifestly needed.

BORAGINACEAE

Several plants of this Order were in constant use in the Middle Ages. *Symphytum officinale*, Linn., the Comfrey, had a long tradition in medicine, for the Greeks gave it its name from *sympho*, to unite, from its healing properties. It has a mucilaginous juice, and is still much used in chest troubles.

Pulmonaria officinalis, Linn., the Gromwell, recalls the Doctrine of Signatures, for its spotted leaves were supposed to resemble the lungs. Hence its use in consumption.

The hairy old Borage, *Borago officinalis*, Linn., is the herb in which Gerard trusted for the relief of melancholy, and which Pliny had christened '*euphrosyne*' for the same reason. 'I, Borage bring alwaies courage,' is the loose translation of a Latin tag. The herb was reputed a blood purifier: 'it engendereth good blood' said Gerard. A generation ago, the young leaves were put into salads, and the herb — which has a scent rather like cucumber — was used in cooling drinks. A sprig is frequently used in the modern claret cup.

SOLANACEAE

All the members of the Potato Order possess pungent, bitter or narcotic properties, and are frequently poisonous if improperly used. Herbalists use the leaves of *Solanum Dulcamara*, Linn., the Bittersweet or Woody Nightshade, as a diuretic, and the twigs were formerly official and used as an alterative. The closely allied but smaller species,

the Black Nightshade, *Solanum nigrum*, has similar poisonous properties in its berry. Both plants are dangerous to children whom the
berries may attract, but it should always be remembered that they
are *Solanums*, and do not belong to the same genus as the real 'Deadly
Nightshade', *Atropa Belladonna*, Linn., which used to be more
common in limestone districts than it is now; for much of it was
harvested for atropine during the war. Still, it propagates itself by
underground suckers and is not easily destroyed. It is often found
in the neighbourhood of the ancient abbeys where it was once cultivated, such as Furness where the neighbouring valley, Bekansgill,
was called the valley of the Nightshade. This plant together with
perhaps its relative, the Henbane, is thought to be commemorated
in the seals affixed to the title-deeds of Furness Abbey. The specific
name originated in Italy where women used the drug to dilate the
pupils of the eyes. The large shrubby plant with purplish bell
flowers followed by luscious looking black berries is not likely to be
mistaken for any other. All parts of the plant contain the alkaloid
hyosyamine which is easily converted into atropine, and both leaf
and root are official in the B.P. and probably in every other country.
Atropine sulphate and atropine salicylate are two forms in which the
drug is administered. Atropine stimulates the central nervous
system, and checks profuse sweating in intestinal colic. Hypodermic
injections are given in spasmodic asthma and whooping-cough.
The medicines made from Belladonna leaf and root also relieve inflammation and congestion and are given in the collapse of pneumonia and typhoid.

The henbane, *Hyoscyamus niger*, Linn., is less common in England.
The plant is unmistakable and rather unattractive from its small
and its sticky leaves. The B.P. recognizes only the leaf of this one
species, though the continental supplies were often mixed with others.
The Green Extract is prepared from the young leaves gathered in
June, and the drug is now standardized by assay to contain 0.05 per
cent of the alkaloids of hyoscyamus. Hyoscine is a more powerful
hypnotic than atropine in cases of cerebral excitement. It is a spinal
sedative and relieves pain in cystitis. It is probably one of the oldest
narcotics in the world. In modern surgical practice it is given by

injection for anaesthesia, and in combination with morphine it is given to induce 'twilight sleep'.

The Thorn Apple, *Datura Stramonium*, Linn., which is used in asthma, is only occasionally found in waste places in Britain but when found its white drooping bells will make it easily recognizable. Its alkaloids are inconstant, but they are mainly hyoscine and atropine. The drug is used in paralysis agitans and in asthma. All extracts used in modern pharmacy derived from the above plants are classed together as cerebral excitants. They act upon the nerve endings and the involuntary muscle. Pilocarpine, caffeine and theobromine belong to the same group with lobeline, nicotine, conine and gelsemine.

Mandragora officinalis, the Mandrake, is not a British plant, but it should be mentioned in this group to which it belongs. It has the same narcotic poison as the others, and was formerly used as an anaesthetic. It is constantly confused with the herbalists' Mandrake root which is *Podophyllum*, and with the White Bryony root mentioned in an earlier chapter.

About this true Mandrake many of the fables of antiquity circulated. For instance, it was supposed to utter a dreadful shriek when pulled from the ground. Whoever heard the shriek died. Hence to collect it, a dog was tied to the plant and tempted with some meat. The dog pulled up the plant and died, while the collector remained at a safe distance. The dog is of course, represented in the picture of Dioscorides and the nymph.

It was also held that there were two different forms of the Mandrake, male and female.

LABIATAE

This beautiful family at once suggests the kitchen garden with its fragrant and aromatic culinary herbs. Sage, Winter Savory, Tarragon, Rosemary, and Marjoram are all plants of the Mediterranean regions. The medicinal Thyme is *Thymus vulgaris*, Linn., our little garden favourite, but the native British species is

ATROPA BELLADONNA
Deadly Nightshade

T. Serpyllum, Linn. The foreign plant has been cultivated in England ever since the sixteenth century and perhaps earlier, but the Greeks knew it, and there are several references to it in Roman literature. According to Pliny it was generally used in fumigation. Old English writers said that 'it yielded most and best honie'.

The crystalline phenol called thymol is obtainable from *Thymus vulgaris,* but the chief sources of natural thymol are the Ajowan seeds of *Carum Copticum.* In modern pharmacy the bulk of the thymol used is synthetic. It is a powerful antiseptic and valuable in medicine. Our own native Thyme possesses the same properties but in an inferior degree.

The Marjoram, *Origanum vulgare,* Linn., is common all over England, and its delightful crimson flower heads appear towards the end of the summer. 'Swete margerome' was beloved of the old herbalists, and was used for strewing the rooms and for fumigation as well as for a 'tea'. It is still in use in herbal medicine. The essential oil of Marjoram is distilled on the Continent from *O. Majorana,* Linn., a native of North Africa. This species is said to be the one known to the early Aryans, and sacred to Vishnu.

The Sage has been in repute for many centuries as a throat gargle. In their *Traité de Botanique,* le Maout and Descaine say of it, 'Le Sauge réunit tous les autres principes medicamenteux que possèdent séparement les autres Labiées: des proprietés stimulantes, toniques, et astringentes qui lui ont valu son nom de *Salvia officinalis.*' Linn. At the same time, oil of Sage, unlike oil of Rosemary, contains a poisonous property. The dried herb is used as a gargle for relaxed throats, and *S. Sclarea,* Linn., the Clary Sage, a European plant, is also cultivated, but mainly for perfume. Sage is put into tooth powders, and its volatile oil is an ingredient in embrocations for rheumatism.

The Rosemary, so beloved all through the ages, was acclimatized here before the Conquest. Sir Thomas More grew it in his famous garden at Chelsea, and it was always regarded as a symbol of love and fidelity. The oil distilled in France is an ingredient in Eau de Cologne, and is employed by herbalists for headaches and as a nerve tonic.[1] Its use for the hair is well known, and there are few better hair stimulants than a simple infusion made at home. Together with Rue, it was put into those pathetic bunches which were carried into the assize court to guard the judge from the pestilential infection brought by the wretched prisoner from his cell. The botanical name of the Rosemary is *Rosmarinus officinalis*, Linn. The sweet, honey-scented Balm, *Melissa officinalis*, Linn., is sometimes found in southern England, but is considered as an escape from former cultivation as it is really a European plant.

The little Self-heal, *Prunella vulgaris*, Linn., is esteemed by herbalists for relaxed throats. Another plant in great repute in popular medicine is the Skull Cap, *Scutellaria laterifolia*, Linn., but this is a European relative of our common Labiate, *S. galericulata*, Linn., the graceful little herb of the riversides. Among the Mints, the herbalist's Pennyroyal, *Mentha Pulegium*, Linn., is not so common as in Gerard's day when he found it 'about the holes and ponds of the place near London called Mile's End'. It is easily recognized as it is the smallest of the family and has the strongest smell. It was called Pudding grass and hysteric grass, and was considered a very strengthening and wholesome herb. It is still cultivated in cottage gardens and used as a 'Tea' herb. The Mint of the kitchen garden is the Spearmint, *M. Spicata*, Linn., but though Gerard spoke of finding it by the river side where it 'rejoyced by its odour the heart of man', it is not reckoned a true native, but is thought to have been brought here from the south of Europe by the Romans. There were several references to its culinary use in classical literature. Hippocrates, Pliny and Ovid all mention it, the second in a very odd connection recommending it as 'being proper for students to wear on their heads in a crown to exhilarate their mental faculties!' The Hebrews must have esteemed it equally as it was part of the tithe of mint, anise and cumin made by the Pharisees.

There is a variety of the Spearmint distinguished as *crispa* which is cultivated in Roumania and in other countries with *M. Pulegium* and the Peppermint, *M. piperita*, Linn. The distilled oils of several

[1] The solid volatile oil (or stearoptene) of Rosemary has been lately found to be practically identical with that of camphor.

of the Mints have been used in medicine for ages as the whole family possesses some stimulating and carminative properties. The oil of Spearmint is a frequent ingredient in tooth pastes.

The Germanders are represented in England by the interesting Wood Sage, *Teucrium Scorodonia*, Linn., of the *Labiatae*, Linn., and three rare other species. *T. chamaedrys* is a naturalized plant, and *T. Botrys*, Linn., is probably only naturalized also.

The Wood Sage has long held an honoured place in the country materia medica. In the west of England it is made into an infusion which may well be a good and wholesome drink when the bitter taste is softened. In Jersey it used to be called ambrosia, for it was used there — and indeed in England also — instead of hops. Its wrinkled leaves when freshly gathered smell just like hops, but when stale they emit a curious memory of garlic. The plant was once called garlic sage.

Teucrium Scordium, Linn., the Water Germander which is smaller with purple flowers, is only found — and then very rarely — in wet places, but was once commonly used as a tonic. This of course suggests that its disappearance was connected with its use in pharmacy. The question of a possibly over-worked simple becoming extinct is a difficult one, for there is another side to the inquiry prosecuted by Professor Salisbury and other botanists in that some of the rarer forms are on the increase. *Teucrium botrys*, the cut-leaved Germander, for instance, hitherto only known in Kent, Surrey and Gloucestershire had lately appeared in Hampshire where it is doing well.

VERBENACEAE

With the Verbain, *Verbena officinalis*, Linn., we recapture a host of memories which come flying across the world with a flavour of ancient magic. The plant was sacred in Persia, in Rome, and among the Druids. It is the only British species of the *Verbenaceae*, and its straggly, wiry branches with their small lilac flowers are not likely to be mistaken for any other plant. Even in 1568 Turner spoke of it with reverence as the 'holy herb' or *Hierobotane* that was used 'agaynst inchantementes'. The old fears and personifications of evil clung about it for many centuries, for the Welsh in the Middle Ages called it Devil's bane, and after cutting it in the dark, brought it into the churches to use as a sprinkler of holy water. It is still utilized in herbalism.

SCROPHULARIACEAE

To this Order belongs the Fig-wort, *Scrophularia nodosa*, Linn. It is a strange looking plant and one of the very few in England fertilized by wasps. Herbalists use it as a diuretic.

The medicinal Speedwell, *Veronica officinalis*, Linn., of dry pastures is gathered for catarrh and for a tea.

The Eyebright, *Euphrasia officinalis*, Linn., has for many centuries been esteemed for outward application to the eyes when there is an inflamed condition, but apparently it was once used internally as well, for Dr. Bayley who held the Physick Chair in Oxford in 1561 mentioned a drink made of Eyebright in meade or beer. Herbalists still recommend it in lotions. The Mullein, *Verbascum thapsus*, Linn. also remains in herbal use for its emollient properties.

The only plant of the Order in official medicine, and a very important item in every Pharmacopoeia, is the Foxglove, *Digitalis purpurea*, Linn. For a long time its active principle remained unknown, but in about the middle of the nineteenth century, a whole series of glucosides were extracted, digitoxin, giloxin, digoxin and gitalin. The extract of the plant itself continues also in use. It has now been found that the yield from *Digitalis lanata*, Ehrh., an Eastern European species, is more powerful than the standard leaf hitherto in use. The plant is cultivated in England and on the Continent, the cultivated kinds having proved to be as potent as the wild. The tincture is employed as a diuretic in cardiac and mitral disease. It is a strong protoplasmic poison, and paralyses the sensory nerves, but it stimulates the nutrition of the heart, and is an invaluable remedy in failing circulation.

THE PHYSICK GARDEN

POLYGONACEAE

Rumex acetosa, Linn., the common sorrel, is anti-scorbutic, and its leaves have been used in salads. *Polygonum aviculare*, Linn., the Knotweed, is a herbal astringent medicine, and *Polygonum bistorta*, Linn., (said by Turner to be the *Herba Britannica* of the Romans) is employed in a similar way. The root contains tannic acid, and with that of *Fagopyrum sagillatum*, Gilis., the Buckwheat, it has been used for food more especially by the peasants in Eastern Europe.

CHENOPODIACEAE

This is an important Order, for it gives us some of our most important vegetables and some excellent foods. For centuries *Chenopodium ambrosioides*, Linn., ver. *anthelminticum*, Gray, has been used in America as a valuable vermifuge, and its essential oil, Chenopodium oil (B.P.) has come into prominence as a remedy against the Hookworm disease of the intestinal canal. Its active constituent is ascaridole. The oil was in fact one of the substitutes used in the war when thymol was not obtainable, and it was probably used by the old herbalists as its former name was *Herba Sanctae Mariae*. Since 1917, its use in medicine has become established in Ceylon and other hot countries where the Hookworm disease is prevalent, and it is also used in veterinary practice. Several species of *Chenopodium* are now cultivated in Holland and in the Dutch dependencies. In Roumania, *Chenopodium ambrosoides* has hitherto been collected, as the wild plant has sufficed, but it grows in greater quantities in the United States, and is known as the American Wormseed. In England twelve species of *Chenopodium* occur, either wild or naturalized, the strongest as to its properties being the 'Stinking Goose-foot', *Ch. Vulvaria*, Linn., which also grows mainly by the sea, and whose odour is said to be fishy, which means that the fish is no longer young. This species has been used in nervous troubles.

The two commonest of the family will be found inland, or indeed anywhere, from the garden to the manure heap. They are the Good King Henry, *Chenopodium Bonus-Henricus*, Linn., and the White Goosefoot, *C. album*, Linn. The leaves of the former were used for poultices. It was called 'All-Good', and 'Smear-wort'. Gerard speaks of its power to 'scour and mundify' the chronic sores which appear to have been so unpleasantly frequent in those days before Lister was born. The White Goose-foot was called 'Midden Myles' and 'Dirty Dick' because of its partiality for manure heaps in the farmyard: many such names testify to the close observation and rustic humour of the English peasant. But this plant and the Good King Henry were really more valued as vegetables both here and in New Mexico where they grow freely and are boiled with other foods. The young leaves of the Goose-foot are quite palatable, and probably very wholesome. Those of the Good King are often eaten in the country as a substitute for the Spinach which is another member of this generous family, indigenous in the Levant, and introduced here in the Middle Ages. But the most valuable as a food stuff is the *Chenopodium quinoa*, Willd., called by the natives in the Andes Quinoa. They use the mealy seeds in large quantities.

In some places on the coast we may find the Sea Beet, *Beta maritima*, Linn., of the same Order, but the only British species. The flavour of Spinach is really present in its great glossy leaves which are often made use of as a vegetable in France. It has given rise through cultivation to the varieties of *Beta vulgaris*, Linn. (the Mangel Wurzel) which yield the commercial sugar. The cultivated 'Beet root' has been known from the time of the Greeks when it was given as an offering to Apollo: the root is rich in glucose, and since its cultivation for sugar which began in Essex in 1910, large quantities of refined sugar have been produced by the factories of the Eastern counties and Nottinghamshire. Culpeper used it for the hair, and — as usual — for 'weals and pushes' in the skin.

Lastly there are the Saltworts and Glassworts of the allied species, *Salsola and Salicornia*.

The Prickly Saltwort, *Salsola Kali*, Linn., is a creeping succulent with jointed stems, and the Glasswort, *Salicornia Europea*, Linn., has the same fleshy joints which fit into each other in such a remarkable way. Both species abound in soda, and it was from allied plants of the *Chenopodiaceae* that the 'soda cakes' of the Middle Ages were obtained, being imported into Europe for glass manufacture from the East. Dr. Campbell Thompson tells us that the Assyrians who were experts in glass and pottery also got their soda from *Chenopodium* ash. In England cattle are sometimes turned out to graze upon these saltings.

URTICACEAE

All along the paths and hedgerows, the common Stinging Nettle, *Urtica dioica*, Linn., thrusts its feet into stony soil where nothing else would flourish. The name comes from *uro*, I burn, with obvious allusion to the acrid property contained in the leaf hairs. The young shoots are wholesome and have been much used in France, both in hard times when food was scarce and in the ordinary menu. The French chef, M. Soyer, used to recommend them as a vegetable, though one may guess that with his Gallic genius he probably 'wangled' his dish to make it palatable, for though we are told that nettle tops are a substitute for spinach nothing could be more unlike that delicious vegetable than the nettle boiled in the common way. Still, if one gives up extravagant claims, there is a good deal of evidence in the country as to the blood purifying properties of the herb. Strong infusions of the leaf are used for burns and for nettle rash.

Dried nettles have been sold in herbal practice for centuries. Dr. Fernie says that in the year A.D. 1400 there was an entry made in the Churchwardens' account of St. Michael's at Bath for nettles that had been sold to a certain Laurence.

There is another Stinging Nettle in our flora which is apt to be mistaken for the common one. This is *Urtica urens*, Linn., often found on waste places: it is very similar to *Urtica dioica* but it grows scarcely a foot high and is not so hairy. The two species have both been used in medicine and for urtication. A third species which, though not native, is to be sedulously avoided in the few places where it still springs up on neglected ground, is one of the venomous plants of the nettle Order and has a bad sting. Its name is *Urtica pilulifera*, Linn. In appearance it is a coarser looking plant with larger teeth at the leaf margin, and its flower clusters bear rounded fruits. It is thought to have been brought here by the Romans. As a whole, the plants of the genus *Urticaceae* in England contain innocent species such as the two indigenous nettles and the *Paritaria*, Pellitory of the Wall; but in hot countries, the Nettle group, especially in the East Indies, is in the highest degree inimical to the animal world. A sting often causes death. The acrid juice in our own common nettles is, of course, harmless, and is destroyed in boiling. What the Romans did with their importation we can only conjecture from a remarkable passage in Parkinson which is worth quoting at length.

'The nettle, (*U. pilulifera*) hath been found,' he says, 'naturally growing time out of mind both by the town of Lidde by Romney, and in the streetes of the towne of Romney in Kent where it is recorded Julius Caesar landed with his soldiers and there abode for a certain time . . . It is recorded that the soldiers brought some of the seede with them and sowed it there for their use, to rub and chafe their limbs when through extreme cold they should be stiffe and benummed; being told before they came from home that the climate of Britain was so extreme cold that it was not to be endured without some friction or rubbing to warme their bloode and to stirre up natural heat.'

One wonders whether these forebodings were realized and if the nettles came into use.

CANNABINACEAE[1]

Humulus Lupulus, Linn., the Hop, is said to have been introduced here in 1524; and soon afterwards an amusing petition was sent to Parliament denouncing the use of this 'wicked weed which will spoil the taste of our drink and endanger the people'. It seems that alarming stories had got abroad of harvesters who had inconveniently

[1] This Order is by some botanists combined with *Urticaceae*.

fallen asleep while in contact with the plant, and no doubt this would be looked upon as a danger from more than one point of view. John Evelyn, writing a century later, makes the odd comment that 'the changing of our wholesome ale into beer had doubtless altered our constitutions'.

However, the Hop remained. It might have been said of its twining stems as it has been said of the spider, that 'she taketh hold with her hands, and is in Kings' palaces'. From August onwards, these wiry stems which travel clockwise, making one revolution in two hours, thirty one minutes, may be seen in the hedgerow while the cultivated hops are being stripped into their bins. There, they occasionally testify to their relationship with the resinous Indian Hemp and its allies, for on some of the pickers they produce an irritation of the skin. The 'hop' is an aggregate of leafy bracts surrounding the flower seeds: each bract has at its base a yellowish, aromatic gland containing a volatile oil and a bitter product called lupuline. The first historic instance of a hop pillow being used is that of King George III who obtained relief from it in insomnia. Simples are often made from the flower heads in infusion.

The sub-order, *Salicineae* among the catkin bearing trees includes *Salix* the Willow, *Populus*, the Poplar, and *Betula*, the Birch. The products of many of the Willows have been used for generations in pharmacy, and various species yield the crystalline glucoside, salicin. The product of *Betula lenta* and its close resemblance to the salicylate obtained from *Gaultheria* will be mentioned again in Chapters viii and x. This product, methyl salicylate, being quickly absorbed by the skin, is largely used in ointments blended with lanolin for rheumatism. An injection is also used for varicose veins.

In modern pharmacy sodium salicylate ($NaC_7H_5O_3$) is obtained by acting on sodium carbonate with salicylic acid.

Aspirin, whose formula is $C_9H_8O_4$, is obtained by the action of acetic anhydride or acetyl chloride on salicylic acid. It was brought into use in 1899.

These valuable drugs are antiseptic, and will check an attack of rheumatism in its various forms. They are also used in migraine though in this they are generally less efficacious than phenacetin.

LORANTHACEAE

Viscum album, the Mistletoe, is one of the strangest plants in our Flora. Its French name is *Gui des Druides*, recalling the Celtic derivation from the word *guid*, a sacred shrub.

Mistletoe is unique as a stem parasite which remains green and is therefore in active vegetation all the year round. Still, as it does extract such nourishment as it requires from its host, it must be regarded as to some extent injurious. It has great powers of assimilation: some specimens have yielded twice as much potash and five times as much phosphoric acid as the wood of the host.

Medicinally it has been used for many centuries. Our Saxon forefathers seem to have regarded it only through a vague symbolism as being good for 'the falling sickness' (epilepsy), because it grew 'upside down'; but Le Maout tells us that the Brazilians used their native species more intelligently, and found the leaves anti-syphilitic and remedial in oedematous swellings.

Physicians in Dr. Rudolf Steiner's clinic are claiming good results with it in cancer.

The Scandinavian legend of the death of Baldur, the Sun God, smitten with a mistletoe dart, seems to be unconnected with the Druidic veneration. It may be — as Pliny hinted — that the sacredness of the oak was extended to anything that grew upon the tree.

DIOSCOREACEAE

This Order includes the black bryony, *Tamus communis*, Linn., as well as the yams whose large tubers are made into food in hot countries. The word 'bryony' in Greek signifies a rapidly growing plant. The black roots were used for a cathartic in old days, and the homoeopath retains the plant as a diuretic. Externally, the root is often applied for bruises, and was formerly called Black Eye root.

THE PHYSICK GARDEN

IRIDACEAE

Crocus sativus, Linn., is the Saffron Crocus mentioned in Hebrew medicine. It was said to be naturalized at Saffron Walden in Essex where it was cultivated, but it is no longer found there, and cannot be considered a British plant.

LILIACEAE

Convallaria magalis, Linn., the lily of the valley, has probably disappeared from many places simply through the destruction of the woodland for building. The root is still sparingly used in England and extensively in France for a heart tonic. The genus *Scilla* is represented here by three of the Squills, but the medicinal Squill is a European species.

Several species of garlic are described in the English flora, but the medicinal garlic is *Allium sativum*, Linn., which is not native. To the same order belongs the beautiful meadow saffron, *Colchicum autumnale*, Linn., said to have been used in medicine by the Egyptians. It was once common in Herefordshire, but its poisonous nature made it obnoxious to farmers, and it has been gradually destroyed. Its name is misleading; first, because it is not a Crocus, and secondly, because the name Saffron refers to the commercial product of the true Crocus, *C. sativus*.

Colchicum corm and seeds are official in the British Pharmacopoeia. The bulk of the supplies come from Southern Europe, several tons being imported every year.

The alkaloid, colchinine, is a slow poison whose action is not thought to be entirely understood, but its value as a medicine has been attested for centuries. It acts upon the white corpuscles of the blood increasing their activity, and is given in gouty affections to-day just as Alexander of Tralles gave it in the sixth century. The seeds are especially potent and are required by the B.P. to yield 0.3 per cent of the alkaloid instead of the proportion of 0.25 per cent required

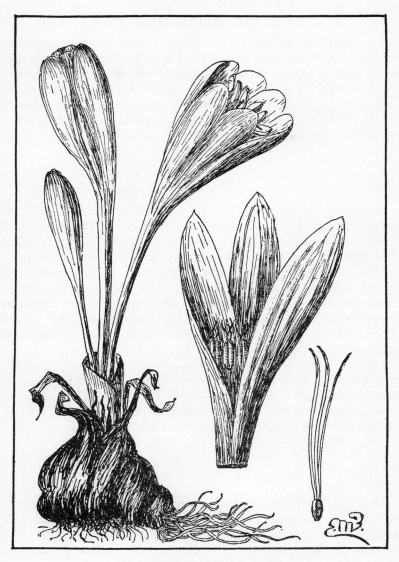

COLCHICUM AUTUMNALE

Meadow Saffron

to be yielded by the corm. The medicine was known to the older herbalists who however often rejected it as 'corrupt and venomous', while Gerard warned patients against its poisonous properties as in improper doses it might be harmful. It was said to have been popularized in England by Baron Stork in 1763, and in the reign of Louis XV it was included in a famous quack remedy called Eau médicinale d'Husson.

CONIFERAE

An interesting account of the Juniper will be found in Mr. Redgrove's *Spices and Condiments.* Juniper berries, the product of *Juniperus communis*, Linn., are always in demand. Herbalists utilize them as a stimulant and diuretic, and they are also useful in veterinary practice and in the manufacture of gin. The foreign juniper, *J. sabina*, called savin, was much cultivated in English gardens in the sixteenth century. *Oleum sabinae*, distilled from the shoots, is sometimes used in skin diseases. The fruits of the yew, *Taxus baccata*, Linn., have sedative and anti-spasmodic qualities, and have been used in epilepsy.

The concrete oleo-resin called Terebinth extensively used in pastilles, etc., is obtained from *Pinus palustris* and other species. Creosote is a product of the distillation of Wood Tar. The exudations from *Cedrus libani*, the Cedar of Lebanon, and *C. Deodara*, are still made use of for external applications in Indian pharmacy.

PTERIDOPTERA

Dryopteris Filix-mas, Linn., Schott., is the male fern common in England, but rarely harvested because it abounds in masses in Transylvania, and is moreover cultivated elsewhere. The extract from its root stock is the oil of male fern, or distol, long valued as a vermifuge and anthelmintic.

MEDICINAL PLANTS OF THE BRITISH FLORA

LYCOPODIACEAE

The Club moss, *Lycopodium clavatum*, Linn., is used for the dusting powder obtained from its spores. This is applied to excoriated surfaces, and used for coating pills.

THE ALGAE

The marine Alga, *Gelidium Amansii*, Kutz., is the East Indian seaweed called Agar-agar whose constituent carbohydrate, glose, has a powerful gelatinizing action, and is frequently blended with *Cascara Sagrada*. Several of the genus *Ulva*, called 'Laver', are used in the coastal regions of Britain and other countries as food.

Chondrus Crispus, known as Irish or carrageen moss, is still used in herbal medicine for chronic catarrh, and yields a thick and possibly nutritious substance when boiled. The Irish say that its constant use confers longevity. Its relative, *Gracillaria lichenoides* is used in India as a substitute.

In Scotland and Ireland the Dulse, *Rhodomeria palmata*, has been used for centuries as a vegetable with blood purifying properties, and several species of *Fucus* were formerly employed in scrofulous diseases.

Litmus, much used as a chemical test in pharmacy, comes from *Rocella tinctoria*, D.C., a marine Alga of warm latitudes.

LICHENS

Cetraria islandica is the still popular Iceland moss used by herbalists in catarrh, as a mild mucilaginous tonic.

FUNGI

These lowly members of the vegetable kingdom are in England largely overlooked for any utilitarian purpose and although several mushrooms are edible, the common *Agaricus canpestris* is the only one used to any extent as food. It is a pity that we have no institution comparable with the French system which provides a free inspection of all the Fungi brought from the country into the 'Halles' where experts examine and pass them on. As it is, the great proportion of our 5000 species many of which are wholesome are perforce wasted. The Hebrews, Greeks and Romans made use of a good many species for food as we know from Celsus and Pliny. Medicinally, three kinds chiefly have been used: *Polyporus officinalis*, the White Agaric; *Lycoperdon gigantea*, the puff-ball; and *Claviceps purpurea*, the ergot, parasitic on the rye.

The powdered drug made from the *Polyporus* is rich in phosphorus, and yields what is called agaric acid, formerly used to check profuse sweating. The puff-ball has a reputation for arresting haemorrhage, and a tincture of 25 per cent has been given as a nerve sedative. *Fungus Sambuci*, parasitic on the elder, was made into a lotion for conjunctivitis, but none of these remedies are much thought of at the present day.

With ergot the case is different, for it is official in most of the Pharmacopoeias in the world. The fungus is known as the enemy of wheat or rye. The spores remain on the ground in the winter, and then they are blown about in the spring they attach themselves to the young shoots of the growing crop. There they quickly penetrate the tissue and absorb the nutriment. A spike thus affected looks black and shining, the grain being transformed into a hard, purplish mass. When the crop is grown for medicine the ergot is collected directly the rye is mature after which it is very carefully dried at a moderate temperature and kept in a closed vessel. The drug yields two complex alkaloids, ergotoxine and ergotamine besides glucosides and a fatty oil. It has a stimulating effect upon the muscles of the body, and is often used in parturition. Its use is one of the most remarkable examples of the reverse side of the medal in which a naturally destructive organism becomes an agent of service to man.

THE TRADE IN MEDICINAL HERBS
EUROPEAN CULTIVATION, AND NEW ENTERPRISES

KING ARCESILAS OF CYRENE SUPERVISING THE WEIGHING AND DESPATCHING OF A LOAD OF SILPHION

The picture is on the inside of a Laconian cup, probably made by Cyrenaic potters in the middle of the sixth century B.C. when beautiful work was done in the Spartan tradition in a black figured technique upon a fine white surface

The illustration is from Furtwangler-Reichold's book, *Griechische Vasenmalerei*, and reproduced by courtesy of Messrs. Brückmann of Munich

Photo by Miss L. M. Bonar of the Edwards Library, University College

CHAPTER VIII

THE picture reproduced by courtesy of Messrs. Brückmann, is an early and interesting portrayal of a medicinal plant in commerce. The species thus represented on a Laconian cup was also struck upon the coinage of Cyrene in the same century. It is thought to be the *Thapsia Silphion* which was said to be exported from Cyrene to Greece in large quantities. It belonged to the *Umbelliferae*, and its gum resin may have been similar in effect to that of the Persian *Galbanum* used in Asia Minor in nervous disorders.

The following extract is taken from *The Treasury of Botany*: 'The plants belonging to this genus (*Thapsia*) of the *Umbelliferae* were in very ancient times celebrated for their medicinal properties, the Cyrenean *Silphium* or *Laser Cyreniacum* being generally supposed to have been the produce of one of them. . . . *Thapsia Silphion* often regarded as a variety of *T. garganica*, is found on the mountains in the neighbourhood of the site of the ancient Cyrene, and is supposed to have formerly produced the gum-resin known to the ancients as *Laser Cyreniacum*, sometimes called *Laser-dulcis* to distinguish it from *Asafoetida*, both of these plants being included by the Greeks under the name of *Silphion* as were other *Umbelliferae*. Representations of it occur on the coins of Cyrene.'

Dr. Pereira in his materia medica gives a further account of the *Thapsia* taken from Roman sources. Pliny said that in his day the *Laserpitium* as it was then called, had not been found in Cyrene for many years because 'the publicans who rent the pastures dug it up for food for cattle'.

Only one 'stalk' was collected and sent to Nero. He also states that another *Laserpitium* was brought from Persia as a substitute. On his showing therefore, the original plant became extinct. By tradition it was said to be 'worth its weight in gold', and was regarded as a cure-all.

THE PHYSICK GARDEN

The exportation of a valuable drug plant had no doubt become an important matter between the older civilizations, for we know that marketing of drugs and spices was carried on by the caravans that went to and fro across the Libyan desert or the Mesopotamian plains. Drugs and spices were also marketed or bartered by the 'merry Grecian coasters', or 'the shy traffickers, the dark Iberians' along the Mediterranean shores. In all this ancient commerce the 'drug' and the 'spice' came under the same heading.

Were these products harvested and exported from the countries where they grew, or were they cultivated? Probably a country that had the monopoly of an important plant started its cultivation, though nowhere do we hear of any cultivated medicinal crops, other than those mentioned in the second chapter as under the care of the Hindu physicians who grew them round their dwellings.

Yet, as civilization increased, the growing communities would naturally realize the advantage of being self-supporting with regard to various crops of economic value, and centres of the drug plant industry might be expected to arise where easy export and a fertile soil made such centres profitable. In many cases where a plant was indigenous and easily grown as well, a population might quickly produce more than they needed to consume. The fertile sunny lands with varied soils and climate — like Roumania at the present day — possessed a clear advantage as producers; and thus from early times, this natural fertility has been the determining factor in the world traffic that has grown up round the plants of pharmacy. To a great extent it is so still, though, since the war, the advance in synthetics, and more systematic collection instead of cultivation, have altered the conditions more especially in the European area.

THE LONDON DRUG MARKET

A visit to the showrooms at the London Docks would reveal the international character of the trade, in a scene, which, if it has lost the picturesqueness of King Cyrene's days, nevertheless still retains its individuality. Before the war, London was the international clearing house for crude drugs, and most of the foreign drafts for overseas exports passed through the city. To-day the bulk of the foreign shipments go direct to the Continental ports; and partly owing to trade depression and partly to the high dock charges in London, there are fewer consignments of drugs than there used to be. Nevertheless the scene in the warehouses to which the whole-sale buyers flock to inspect the bales is a characteristic one.

It was after one such visit to the Cutler Street Warehouses that the Poet Laureate was moved to inscribe the following verse upon a fly-leaf: —

> You showed me nutmegs and nutmeg husks,
> Ostrich feathers and elephant tusks,
> Hundreds of tons of costly tea
> Packed in wood by the Cingalee
> And a myriad drugs which disagree.
> Cinnamon, myrrh, and mace you showed,
> Golden paradise birds that glowed,
> More cigars than a man can count
> And a billion cloves in an odorous mount.

The term 'drug' embraces all the bottles of essential oils, the dried flowers or seeds in tins, and the crude drugs, barks or resins which have not undergone any refining process since they were collected and dried in their own country. In the sorting rooms we see the cases of rhubarb root that was dug up in China in September and dried in the sun, or the bales from Java containing two different grades of quinine, large sections of trunk and root, and smaller chips called quills.

Other large cases contain sarsaparilla root from Jamaica, and the dried leaflets and seed pods of Senna from India and the Sudan. From India too come the square blocks of opium wrapped on oiled paper, and the best quality myrrh sent from Bombay.

Multitudes of tins and bottles contain volatile oils. Most of these are colourless, but the oil of chamomile is a beautiful blue colour, while those of juniper, cumin, and nutmeg have a golden tint. The cinnamon oil from Ceylon retains the warm aromatic taste of the parent bark, while the oil of Wintergreen from North America has the characteristic odour of methyl salicylate.

Drug Sales are an old institution. They began in 1704 as quarterly auctions for East Indian produce, and in those palmy days profits as high as 95 per cent were realized by the dealers. Then came the Dutch competition which forced prices down. Finally, fortnightly sales were instituted, first in East India House and in Garraway's Coffee House in Change Alley, and then in the Sales Rooms in Mincing Lane where they are still held.

The next stage, when the 'crude' drug passes into the factory of the manufacturing chemist deserves notice owing to the high specialization of the modern power-driven grinding machines which are at work throughout the year. Equally efficient are the modern stills used for essential oils. In many cases, crude oils are re-distilled with steam, but some, like oil of Limes, are obtained by expression, and there is an ingenious apparatus called the *écuelle*, in which the fruits are rotated in a copper pan. Refinements of technique are also applied to the analysis of the oils by means of such instruments as the polarimeter and refractometer.

In the latest Pharmacopoeia, stringent tests for purity and for determination of the constituents, i.e. for assay, are laid down, and modern chemical analysts are doing all in their power to check the adulteration which, especially in the case of expensive volatile oils, was formerly too prevalent.

THE TRADE AFTER THE WAR

During the war of 1914-18, although we still received bales from the Far East and India, the large consignments from Central Europe were entirely stopped, so that, as a result, prices soared to famine height. The unprecedented dislocation that ensued in the trade together with the fact that for 40 years Germany had had the monopoly of the synthetic drug industry which she had built into a large organization, led to a national movement in several countries for increased home production. Nor was the movement influenced entirely by the shortage alone. In England, at any rate, conscientious pharmacists had for some years been expressing dissatisfaction with certain features of the drug trade. In 1867 one particular complaint was urged by Mr. Daniel Hanbury who pointed out how ruthless grubbing up of native supplies affected the market by making a drug scarce and expensive. In other cases a monopoly in the hands of a few operated with a similar restricting effect, while complaints were made from time to time about the inferiority of the imported produce. Mr. Hanbury pointed out that many consignments came over in ill condition, and badly packed; that plants were sometimes picked at the wrong season; and that some, like chiretta, hemedesemus and jalap were frequently unsound or uncertain in quality. A few years later, in 1873, he called attention to the vexed question of the drug called *Pareira Brava*. This name, properly *Parreira brava*, meaning wild vine, had been given by the Portuguese to the plant *Chondrodendron Tomentosum*, Ruiz and Pavon, *Menispermaceae*, used as a tonic and diuretic in inflammation of the bladder. In commerce however, its place had been taken by the spurious roots and stems of *Cissampelos Pareira* and other plants from Jamaica.

It was increasingly felt that the drug plant trade needed renovation, especially in regard to those exotic species which could only be cultivated in warm latitudes. Mr. Hanbury and others also expressed the opinion that it had been a mistake for English growers to abandon the cultivation of so many easily grown medicinal species.

In England, therefore, a movement to supply the existing demand for medicinal plants was initiated in 1916, but as the organizations were run by private enterprise at a time when people were fully occupied in other ways, and as government support was not forthcoming, the effects were only temporary.

Abroad, on the other hand, in countries which had hitherto relied mainly on imports but which were also very suitable for medicinal herb cultivation, it became realized that increased cultivation might pay. Some countries in Central Europe fell back upon organized collection, as in many districts some of the more important plants like henbane and belladonna grow wild in masses.

In France swift and energetic action was taken under an Interministerial committee, and an appeal made to the Government and to the goodwill of the nation. The response was immediate, but the work necessarily slow. There were the usual delays in the administrative services, and the usual lethargic comments from people who thought it easier to buy what others produced than to have all the trouble of growing it. The shortage, they pointed out, would be only temporary, and then the foreign markets would be re-opened.

But largely thanks to the work of M. Perrot, Professor of Materia Medica in the University of Paris, an industry was worked up; and in 1928, the results of the increased cultivation in France and her colonies was published, together with an account of similar enterprises in other countries. The pamphlets published by the 'Office National des Matières Premières végétables pour la Droguerie, la Distillerie, la Pharmacie et la Perfumerie' are exceedingly interesting. Some deal with the results of the ten years' work in France, and others with the similar efforts elsewhere. From the moment of its inception in April, 1918, the French committee went ahead by virtue of its clear-sighted and vigorous organization. The leaders saw that close co-operation between science, commerce and industry was necessary for success. They set themselves to study the needs of the markets and the fluctuations in price; they organized the collection of indigenous plants, and began to experiment with exotic species to ascertain whether they might be successfully grown in France or Northern Africa. Above all, they understood propaganda. Each year M. Perrot — who meanwhile had been appointed Director of the National Committee — went lecturing up and down the country to arouse interest in the work and to give technical instruction in its details. Doctors, students, pharmacists, small growers, were all brought into the movement, which had as its central aim the freeing of the country from the necessity of foreign imports. The intelligence, skill and imagination with which the adventure was carried out reminds one of the similar enterprise of the Danes in working up their agriculture in the nineteenth century. Finally, the committee organized a film which was lent by the Ministry of Agriculture to the various centres of collection or cultivation.

TRADE IN MEDICINAL HERBS

THE DISTILLATION OF VOLATILE OILS

In this film — which, by the way, was a financial success — pictures were shown representing all the activities of the industry, the distillation of orange flowers, rose and jasmine at Grasse; the peppermint and hyssop fields of Brittany; the picking of lime flowers by the aid of a novel and ingenious ladder; the extraction of iodine from seaweeds in Brittany; and the culture of pyrethrum[1] in Provence, showing the action of the insecticide in agriculture.

For the first few years the Committee turned their unremitting efforts towards the increase of home cultivation, selling the produce at a price low enough to compete with foreign imports. Journeys were taken in order to study the culture of foreign plants and their properties, such as the production of gum arabic in the Sudan, of the stimulant 'Kat' from *Catha edulis*, Forsk. (N.O. *Celastraceae*), in Abyssinia, or the sandalwood trees of Mysore from which the fragrant oil is distilled. At home, a Congress of Lavender was held at Grasse with the object of working up the French lavender industry. Grasse has for many years been the centre of the distilling industry for the winning of essential oils used in commerce. All through the year this work is carried on, first with violets and narcissi, then with roses and orange flowers, and later with lavender, geranium, tuberose, etc. In the winter the staff are again occupied with cinnamon and clove. It is estimated that about twelve billion pounds of flowers are gathered each year.

The methods of winning the essential oils vary. Rose, lavender, orange flowers, rosemary, and various aromatic roots, barks, and seeds are distilled with steam, and as the essential oils form a layer distinct from the water, they can be separated in the receiver.

In some cases the water which distils over along with the oil is itself very fragrant, as certain constituents of the oil are water-soluble. This is notably the case with roses and orange-blossoms; and in this

---

[1] This insecticide is *Chrysanthemum Cinerarioefolium*, D.C. as distinct from the other Composite, *Anacylus Pyrethrum*, D.C. till lately official as an analgesic.

way genuine rose-water and orange-flower-water are obtained. Other so-called waters of an aromatic character are quite different in their mode of production, and are weak alcoholic solutions of essential oils and other aromatic materials. Lavender water provides an instance of the latter kind.

A process called *enfleurage* is used for the most delicate blossoms, especially for jasmine and tuberose which gradually evolve the perfume emitted through the decomposition of their glucosides as they lie upon layers of lard. When at length the lard is saturated with the essence, this is extracted with alcohol.

There are four general methods in use for winning essential oils, namely (*a*) distillation with water or steam, (*b*) expression as applicable to essential oils contained in rinds of *Citrus* fruits only, (*c*) *enfleurage*, and (*d*) extraction with volatile solvents. The products of the last two methods are employed only in perfumery and not in medicine. The latest development is fractional distillation, whereby the essential oils are separated from certain constituents, terpenes and sesquiterpenes, and are thereby rendered more easily soluble in weak spirit. The essential oils are far from simple in composition; on the contrary, they are extremely complex, and are made up of many constituents. In modern industry they have been separated into groups, many possessing useful antiseptic powers and some valued as carminatives. Other useful substances can be isolated from them in a more or less pure state, as for example, carvone from caraway oil, anethole from star-anise oil, eugenol from clove oil and cinnamon leaf oil; safrole from sassafras oil, menthol from crude Japanese peppermint oil, cineole from eucalyptus oil, etc.

In several cases an essential oil has been built up synthetically, although in no case as far as we know at present has the identical fragrance of the original leaf or flower been recaptured. What the Arabians would have called the elusive spirit or 'quintessence' of the plant's being is hardly to be caught even when the molecules of the synthetic product are identical.

Lavender grows in the South of France, and the species yielding oil of the best quality is *Lavendula vera*, DC., N.O. *Labiatae*. Inferior oils are got from *L. spica*, Cav., and from several hybrids.

The largest plantations of lavender are in the Drome, the Hautes Alpes and the Basses Alpes.

After the war, the gathering of wild plants was hampered by the exodus of the population from many districts, and it was decided to increase the cultivation of the best oil-producing varieties. The industry, especially round Marseilles, has now been enlarged with a corresponding increase in the output of the oil.

Oil of lavender has carminative properties, and until 1914 was official, but it is not much used to-day except for making lavender water and for perfuming soap and other toilet requisites. The earliest reference to *L. vera* appears to be that of the Abbess Hildegarde of the twelfth century, but Dioscorides referred to the species *L. stoechas*. This very interesting and pretty plant still flourishes at Hyères whose islands were named the Stoechades. Gerard and Parkinson extolled the compound tincture, which was used externally as a rubefacient for stiff limbs and sprains. The French consider it stimulant and tonic, and it was proved antiseptic in the war. Mrs. Grieve in her interesting pamphlet upon the uses of lavender tells us that lavender oil was much used in the hospitals for swabbing wounds.

In the manufacture of otto of rose, France has now to a large extent attained the high place formerly held by the Bulgarian product, though there is still a good demand for the Bulgarian otto. A variety of *Rosa centifolia*, Linn., is being widely cultivated for the purpose. The rose-water obtained in distillation has been, as we know, used for many centuries as an ingredient in cold cream and other toilet preparations.

Oil of rosemary from the familiar and delicious plant *Rosemarinus officinalis*, Linn., is produced in large quantities in the South of France and is a frequent ingredient in eau-de-Cologne and other perfumes. Another — indeed one of the most important essences used in eau-de-Cologne is the oil of Neroli from the bitter orange flowers distilled at Grasse. The young shoots and leaves of the Bitter orange tree, *Citrus Aurantium*, Linn., var. *Bigaradia*, HK., yield a less delicate oil called *'petit grain'*, also in great demand commercially.

Bergamot oil is obtained by expression from the peel of the fruits of *Citrus Aurantiacum*, var. *Bergamia*, Riss. The oil owes its properties to its linalyl acetate, the acetic ester of linalol. It is a very expensive product, and is an ingredient in the de luxe varieties of eau-de-Cologne, the ever popular scent which was said to have been invented before the eighteenth century by Jean Marie Farina, a trader in Cologne. But Mr. Redgrove tells us in *Scent and All About It*, that there were various stories about its origin, and law suits over the trade mark just as there were various formulae for its composition. The following is one of the more expensive recipes.

Rectified spirit from wine	1,000 parts
Bergamot oil	3°.5
Lemon oil	5°.0
Neroli oil	4°.75
Rosemary oil	2°.5

with lavender oil and orange-flower-water.

The most important products isolated from essential oils and used in perfumery are linalol, nerol and geraniol. The chemical formula for all these closely related oils is $C_{10}H_{17}OH$: and so accurately is their composition known that many are now made synthetically. The history of one particular synthetic called ionone is interesting, for it was accidentally discovered. For many years the scent of the violet has been wooed in the laboratory at Grasse and elsewhere; but as the yield from the natural flowers is so small, two chemists, Tiemann and Kruger, experimented to try and get a synthetic violet scent from orris root. They isolated a substance called ivone which had a definitely violet-like fragrance. Then they tried to produce this synthetically by combining citral with acetone. The result was a new and unexpected substance, nearer in its fragrance to violet than ivone had been. This they named *ionone*, and it is now the base of all the violet scents on the market.

Geraniol is obtained from the fragrant pelargonium leaf or scented geranium. The plant is cultivated round Grasse, and its essential oil won by distillation. The French oil is the finest on the market, and the industry in all these products is a very important one.

Several varieties of *Citrus medica*, Linn., the Citron, are used in

LAVENDULA STOECHAS

medicine: the rind and juice, like those of the lemon (*C. Limonum*, Osbech,), are anti-scorbutic. The essential oils of the lemon and the lime are also fragrant and used commercially.

FRENCH PHARMACISTS AT WORK

M. Perrot's committee followed the example of Germany in instituting post-war centres of research in pharmacology. One interesting case is afforded by the familiar monkshood, *Aconitum Napellus*, Linn., whose extracts (from the root) have long been recognized as unstable while several of the allied species are therapeutically inert. The official monkshood grows wild in large quantities in Central Europe whence we import it into this country; but despite the variability of the species and its hybrids, it is safe to consider the familiar plant of our gardens as unalterably poisonous. During the war, many of its native places in Europe were destroyed, the plant being ruthlessly grubbed up for the market's demands. Hence, cultivation became more essential than before, and it is now being carried on in England, in the Pyrenees, and elsewhere. Even so, and although the propagation is done by the root stock, the medical instability in the content has not been overcome, and it is obvious that from the point of view of drug-plant farming, this uncertainty in the yield is a disadvantage. In the French laboratories therefore, research is being directed to this problem.

The reference to the widespread destruction of a wilding for its marketable value reminds us of another case in which there has been a greater wholesale destruction.

Adonis vernalis, The Pheasant's Eye, N.O. *Ranunculaceae*, has long been valued on the Continent as a heart tonic, and is still in good repute in the French materia medica. In England, our herbalists use it as a cardiac tonic. It is a pretty red-flowered plant, very much like our own single representative of the species, *A. Autumnalis*, Linn.

The genus was known to Pliny who took it from Hippocrates, for an allied species, *A. aestivalis*, Linn., was mentioned in some early Greek herbals. Before the war, *Adonis vernalis* was imported from Central Europe into France where it had been tried as a substitute for *Digitalis*. In 1921 M. Perrot made inquiries in the Cervennes, and found that in every district where the little plant had flourished, it had been pulled up by the peasants who were naturally anxious for gain and had discovered that the *Adonis* was marketable. The Comité Interministérial des plantes medicinales in France therefore took instant measures to prevent further devastation, and have begun a tentative cultivation of the *Adonis* at St. Nizier and elsewhere.

This possible destruction of a wild crop is a subject intimately bound up with the whole question of the plant and its gathering, especially in the smaller countries like France and England. It shows us the necessity for cultivation where some of the wildings are concerned.

There is also another rather unsuspected side to the question. Some plants when they are taken out of their native state, prove intractable in the oddest way. For instance, there is the *Arnica montana*, Linn., known to both Greek and Roman, and employed in pharmacy, old and new. This Composite is called 'Panacea' on the Continent, from its power of absorbing the effects of swellings and bruises. In the Alps and Auvergnes, it grows wild, covering large tracts of country, but since the war, the difficulty has arisen that the native population has dwindled and gatherers are scarce. The French are now trying to put it under cultivation, but at present it has not done very well.

In 1928 M. Perrot dealt with the results of his ten years work in a pamphlet published by the Office Nationale. In it he showed that, on the whole, the results had been encouraging despite the fact that the slender subsidies given by the Government had dwindled every year. In the summary of the whole situation, he once again stressed what he had said at the outset, that the real need of the industry was an International Bureau to control the produce and the sale of drugs. On the other hand, it was realized that in the present tormented state of the world, such an idea must remain visionary, while the difficulties of the medicinal plant industry were for several reasons beset with difficulties peculiar to this branch of agriculture. For one thing, the fluctuations in prices depend in their turn upon seasonal conditions which are reflected in the market. A scarcity one year with a corresponding rise in prices may be followed by an excess the following year which will make marketing uncertain. The greatest detriment of all is the lack of co-operation between the various branches of the trade whose interests are not identical. A further difficulty arises from the fact that the drug houses refuse to take any but large consignments, a practice which is also detrimental to pharmacy, as mixtures and adulterations are liable to be overlooked. In fact, from many causes, the industry is a peculiarly difficult one, and this report of the French committee showed clearly that it will never be satisfactorily worked until there is more efficient co-operation, both between the several marketing groups and between the producing countries. For even when each country produces perhaps two-thirds of its necessary crops, there will always remain certain things which cannot be produced owing to differences of climate and latitude. Nevertheless, the French enterprise in this direction has been of extraordinary interest: among the exotic species which they have tried to grow and are growing are the following: *Camphor, China Rhubarb, Liquorice, Podophyllum, Hydrastis, Cimicifuga, Grindelia,* and *Hamamelis.* Nor was it merely a question of importing the plants and of preparing the plantations; in every case the horticulturist and the chemist worked together, the former testing the effect of various soils and artificial stimulants upon the crop, the latter testing the results in the laboratory. The French pioneers in this endeavour are entitled to claim precedence in forming an alliance between industry, commerce, science and production. 'The goal which we have in view,' said M. Perrot in his Report of 1929, 'which is the production in our own country of the maximum of necessary drug plants, can only be reached gradually and after long and delicate study. A crisis had been brought about by new methods which have transformed pharmacy; . . . the individualism which obtained in former times, has passed away.' He then went on to give a short outline of the results obtained in the other European countries. The sketch was graphic, and even a few of its details suffice to show how

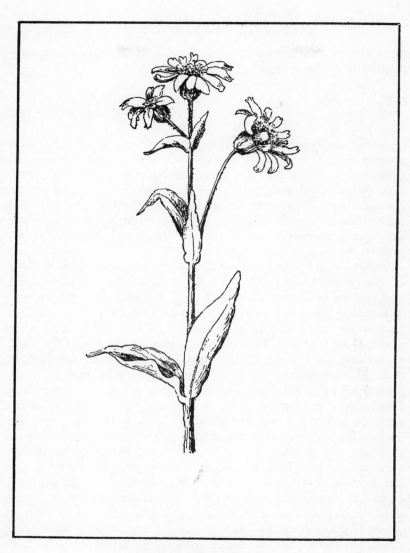

ARNICA MONTANA

many factors are involved in this taming of the wild plant to the necessities of civilized man.

THE REVIVAL IN CENTRAL EUROPE

Among the European states Roumania has long been known as the country of the volatile oils and the bee plants. She has a varied climate and a fertile soil. On the commercial side she is well placed with geographical propinquity to the other European countries, and facilities for transport are given by the Danube waterway and the railroads. In spite of the increasing interest in the oil industry she remains essentially agricultural, and the record for her medicinal plant crops is uniformly a high one.

Before the war, the Roumanians did a large export trade in many of the essential oils used in perfumery which are obtained from such plants as *Salvia Sclarea*, Linn., *Hyssopus officinalis*, Linn., *Coriandrum sativum*, Linn., and *Carum Carvi*, Linn., the source of the caraway oil which is used in liqueurs and which now comes chiefly from Holland. They also cultivated the lovely scented roses, *Rosa damascaena*, Mill., and *R. rugosa*, Thumb., which are used for making rose-water and in *confiture de roses*. *Chrysanthemum cinarariae-folium*, Vis., and allied species which are grown for the insecticide, formed another of their crops, and years ago they used to supply America with the flower and stalk of *Cnicus benedictus*, Linn., the Blessed Thistle, for making beer (as a substitute for hops).

At the end of the war, the country found herself as usual with the clock put back for some years, with her export trade ruined, and her land gone out of cultivation. She had therefore to fall back upon her own native resources for the medicinal plants that grew wild. It was like poor Poe flinging himself upon the earth after an attack of insanity, and in some measure all the countries were doing the same. Here again, Roumania had a natural advantage. Her flora in its richness follows the curves of her varied climate, and some of the most needed herbs grow in immense quantities. For the moment, therefore, she applied herself to the collection of the wildings which is not such an easy matter as it sounds. Gathering cannot be done haphazard by people who lack knowledge, and those who have it often in times of poverty will prove unwilling to undertake rather arduous work for little pay. Still, it filled in the gap before cultivation could be begun again, for as we have said, the Roumanian produce was in many instances richer in medicinal properties than any other, and a reputation for good stuff soon gets established in the drug market. When the industry was again set in movement, greater attention was paid to special crops like peppermint which will grow where cereals will not flourish. Coriander, caraway, rue, and *Verbascum phlomoides*, Linn., — (a mullein whose flowers are used alternatively with those of the English mullein, *V. Thapsus*, Linn., for their demulcent properties), were all planted in greater quantities. The castor-oil plant was also tried in big plantations in Bessarabia, and proved easy to grow and — an equally strong point — to collect, for the peasants can be entrusted with the gathering, and the market is now enlarged owing to the use of the oil in machinery. Altogether, one may expect Roumania to be one of the foremost countries in drug plant cultivation, not only because of its natural advantages, but also because, as early as 1904, an experimental station, the first of its kind, with a bio-chemical laboratory, was established in the country. Good work was done and is still being done there. The esperiments showed among other things that atropine could be obtained from the hyoscyamine present in *Datura Tatula*, Linn., a plant of the *Solanaceae* as well as from belladonna itself. This *Datura* grows in abundance on the hillsides. Another drug plant which is found in masses is the male fern; *Dryopteris felix-mas*, Schott, whose roots yield the vermifuge long used in pharmacy.

Roumania is also scoring in respect of the homely but indispensable peppermint, *Mentha piperita*, Linn. The mints were, as we have said, known to the Chaldeans as 'kindly healing herbs', and they belong to one of the most distinct and valuable groups in the vegetable kingdom. Their flowers conform to a type, the corolla with two segments, the upper ones forming an arched protection for the stamens, and the lower ones forming a *labium* or lip from which the group receives its name, *Labiatae*. Their leaves are studded with glands containing a volatile oil which is almost always aromatic and wholesome. Our thoughts rest upon the *Labiatae* whenever we think of our herb gardens, for they have given us our sage, mint, and lavender, our hyssop, marjoram, and thyme. They are among the ancient remedies whose use has been ever more justified by research, and peppermint oil is one of the most familiar.

The true peppermint is known as the Mitcham plant; it is *M. piperita*, Linn., a species native to Britain and believed to be a hybrid between *M. spicata*, Huds., and *M. aquatica*, Linn.

There is little or no peppermint grown in Mitcham to-day, but some is grown in the vicinity; and the term 'Mitcham peppermint' is applied to any peppermint grown in the E. or SE. of England from the Mitcham strain of plants. There are two forms distinguished as 'red' and 'white'; but the latter appears to have gone out of cultivation. English distilled oil from Mitcham peppermint is unique in flavour. It is expensive, and hence much subject to adulteration with inferior oils. Its chief constituents are menthol and menthone, but many other substances exist in the cellular tissue, including acetic acid and terpenes of antiseptic value.

The oil is official in the B.P., in the United States, and many other Pharmacopoeias.

Japanese peppermint is wrongly named. It is distilled from a variety of *M. arvensis*, var. *piperascens*, Linn. It is rich in menthol; but this is mainly removed by freezing and marketed separately. The oil is otherwise very poor in flavour, leaving an after-taste of fish; nevertheless large quantities are sold for flavouring. The Franco-Mitcham and Italo-Mitcham oils are distilled from plants raised from the Mitcham strain grown in France and Italy. The oils are generally considered inferior in flavour to the English oils, but propagating centres for the 'Mentha-Mitcham' have now been established in France and Italy. The oil from Roumanian plants on the other hand is now said to be equal to the English standard and to be fetching an equal price.

The story of Roumania — whether of her food crops or medicinal crops — is a very interesting one; and it may be added that it is the only country where the slaughter of wild birds is entirely forbidden.

TRADE IN MEDICINAL HERBS

In Italy after the war, lavender plantations were started in association with local distilleries which were worked in the same neighbourhood and at a profit by the peasantry. From this initial effort co-operative societies came into being; and in 1922, the Italians increased their drug plant cultivation much as the French had done. Indeed, they had better support from their government, and they are now engaged in several cultural experiments, the most interesting of which is the castor-oil plant.

The fact that *Ricinus communis*, Linn., belongs to the Spurge Order, the *Euphorbiaceae*, suggests its poisonous properties, and one whole seed would be a fatal dose. The Hindus and the Egyptians (who cultivated it and used it externally, as well as for a laxative) crushed the seed in water and made poultices for headache. For internal use the seed was mixed with 'beer'. Blended with some kind of fat it was warranted to make the hair grow luxuriantly. The plant, which grows tall in tropical countries, is very handsome with its large leaves and flower spikes which produce a violently explosive capsule.

An amusing story was told by Mrs. Lee, in her book, *Trees, Plants and Flowers*.

She was sitting at a table in Egypt when two flowering spikes of the *Ricinus* were brought in for her to see. She laid them down, one on each side of the table, and went on writing until a stinging blow on the face, followed by another and a third, made her think that someone was shooting at her from the window. She bolted through the door only to discover that it was the castor-oil plant fulfilling its destiny by expelling its seeds all over the heated room. The albumen and embryo of the seeds contain the oil, which is – rather unusually for a fixed oil – soluble in alcohol.

The ancient physicians could not have foreseen that their plant would one day acquire a new value through its use in aviation, but this has happened in recent years. In 1928 the Italians decided to put about 4000 acres of the allied species *R. sanguineus* and *R. Gibsoni* under cultivation, as the Air Ministry, wishing to reduce the importation of mineral oils, had hit upon the castor-oil as a promising substitute. The results from the Verona fields are very satisfactory, showing a high yield of the oil. Before the war, Russia grew the plant in large quantities in the Caucasus, and many acres are grown in Hindustan.

Further experiments in Italy are being carried on with some of the North American drug plants. With *Rhamnus Purshiana*, D.C. (*Cascara Sagrada*), which seems to be very adaptable in many climates, they are doing very well. A more ambitious attempt is being made to acclimatize the camphor tree.

EXPERIMENTS IN RUSSIA

From the point of view of natural advantages in respect to certain crops, Russia holds a high place. There, both land and labour have always been cheap, while in the case of at least two important plants, liquorice and *Artemesia Cina*, Berg., the source of santonin, the medicinal yield has proved higher from the wild plants than from the cultivated crops elsewhere. Santonin is widely used as an anthelmintic against the round worm, *Ascaris lumbricoices*. Before the war the exportation of liquorice (from *Glycyrrhiza glandulifera*, W. & K.) was enormous, quantities being taken by China, America, and Germany. The Russian fennel, also, like the Roumanian, yields four to five per cent of volatile oil as against one per cent from the Indian produce. Russian Coriander is also richer in oil than the English or Continental varieties, and is exported in great quantities.

The medicinal flora is large and widely distributed. Valerian is common on the Steppes; *Rhus Cotinus*, Linn., the sumac, abounds in the Crimea; *Matricaria Chamomilla*, Linn., in the Ukraine; and the ergot of rye (*Claviceps purpurea*) occurs on cereals in great quantities in the north and north-west provinces. The opium poppy is now being largely cultivated, with an average yield of from nine to fourteen per cent of morphine. In the Karlov district and elsewhere, the culture of mustard is being undertaken on a grand scale, and the saffron crocus is being grown for the market in Daghestan. The castor-oil plant is another successful crop.

TRADE IN MEDICINAL HERBS

It seems likely that Russia may take a very important place among drug-producing countries, for since 1920 she has attacked the problems of the industry with great vigour, and was the first country to insist upon a meticulous standard of excellence for her exports. Her lead in this direction has had important effects upon the trade and has led to better standardization. Her home organization was also excellently carried out, by the formation of small co-operative societies for growing and collecting.

AUSTRIA

The country in which the most desolating changes have taken place, in regard to this particular industry, is Austria. Before the war, she exported millions of tons of dried herbs, and England, France and the United States were among her constant customers. Now the trade is almost unimportant, as some of the most fertile portions of the old Empire have been separated, and are beginning to organize a trade of their own. In 1920, attempts were made to recapture some of the former trade and to organize renewed efforts, but it was uphill work. Three herbalist firms, however, founded a society, and put about ninety acres under cultivation, with peppermint, marsh-mallow, and thorn apple. Some of the farmers and smallholders also began to grow certain crops. In Haute Austria there is a varied and suitable flora, and there, urged by poverty, the peasants undertook herb gathering for a livelihood. The Austrian government, co-operating with the pioneers of the herb growing and collecting movement, gave help in the propaganda, and pamphlets were widely distributed giving instruction as to picking and drying. One pamphlet called 'The Ten Commandments' dealt with plants that might be collected every month in the year, but the money paid was so small that it could not command a steady stream of pickers. Gradually, the Austrians set themselves to cultivate once more, and one of the first crops chosen was the marsh-mallow, so familiar in that delightful French mixture of mucilage, gum arabic, sugar and white of egg known as *pâté de Guimauve*.

The source of this mucilage is *Althoea cannabina*, Linn., known as *Guimauve à feuilles de Chanvre* (or *Guimauve Faux-Chanvre*). The Chanvre is the hemp, and the name is based upon the shape of the leaf in this species. Its medicinal property, the mucilage in its roots and seeds, is used on the Continent in diseases of the mucous membrane, and the plant is always in demand, so that its cultivation is profitable. The garden hollyhock is another plant of the Mallow Order (*Malvaceae*), and it also possesses some extremly tough fibres in its bark.

RESULTS IN GERMANY

Germany, better able than her unfortunate ally to pick up the broken threads of her industries, began in 1917 to encourage both picking and cultivation. A horticultural society was formed with a periodical bulletin, and the co-operation of scientists, gardeners and druggists was invited. A big training college at Münich was the first of several well-organized societies under the auspices of the Imperial Bureau of Health. Rural institutes made small experimental gardens, and the Germans, who before 1914 had been foremost in drug plant cultivation, now set themselves to re-establish the trade and to find out in the first place how to turn their indigenous flora to the best account. At the same time, it is noteworthy that they took steps to protect the wild plants from too drastic collection. The flora of the Hartz mountains is rich in medicinal species, and large collections could be made of foxglove (for digitalin), of deadly nightshade, male fern, thorn apple and henbane. Meanwhile, many acres were once again put under cultivation, the peasants often sharing a plot and being responsible for the harvesting. Thus in 1925 a large acreage was devoted to peppermint, and men, women and children could be seen weeding the trenches in the intervals of the cutting which takes place twice a year. The crop was then dried slowly in the shade before being sent to the menthol distillery.

Valerian is another crop worked by the peasants on co-operative lines. The wild plant is brought from its native ditches and set in the cultivated land. It has been found that the plant does better if it is transplanted a second time, and good dressings of super-phosphate of lime or sulphate of ammonia are given during growth. The root, when dug up, is dried in the sun. German horticulture is not an easy matter, for the climate is not always favourable, many of the crops being liable to injury by frost. It is said that the only herb crop that can be grown without difficulty and in the poorest soil is coriander, but there is little demand as the market is overstocked with the Russian product.

Probably the most valuable work done by Germany since the War has been in the Commission of vegetable chemistry which is at work upon the distribution of the native plants and the possible substitu-tion of one for another in times of scarcity. The French are also at work upon this subject which is full of interest scientifically. As a general rule it is commonly held that the peculiar properties of a genus exist throughout its various species and not to any great extent elsewhere. To this rule, however, there are numerous exceptions, one of the most remarkable being afforded by oil of wintergreen. This had long been known as the product of *Betula lenta*, Linn., the sweet birch of the United States, belonging to the Natural Order *Betulaceae*, an Order of trees and shrubs having marked character-istics of their own. Afterwards it was found that the North American shrub *Gaultheria procumbens*, Linn., N.O. *Ericaceae*, yielded an oil with a large proportion of methyl salicylate closely resembling that of the sweet birch. Another striking instance of totally unrelated plants yielding very similar essential oils is afforded by the anise and star-anise mentioned in Chapter II.

When, after the war, the importation of European plants was still for a time disorganized, the question of substitutes came to the front with new significance. New experiments were tried, and some of the results were as startling as in the case of the identical oil from the wintergreen and sweet birch. The French pharmacists claim that the humble weed *Potentilla Tormentilla*, Neck., has properties similar to those of the South American Rhatany root, a plant of an unrelated Order. In like manner, the properties of the Senega snake-root (*Polygala Senega*, Linn.), are now said to exist in the remote *Saponaria officinalis*, Linn. Perhaps there are more duplicates of this nature than have been suspected. M. Perrot in speaking of these discoveries pointed out the many unexpected results that have followed the development of pharmacology, with a side issue upon the economics of the case. Though certain foreign species, he said, could not and perhaps never would be replaced, it was proving possible to find substitutes for others hitherto considered as unique. To the botanist this inquiry is 'intriguing'.

FRENCH CULTIVATION OF EXOTICS

Some foreign species are being put under cultivation by the French in their African colonies, such as camphor in Algiers, and 'Buchu', the best known South African drug plant, *Barosma betulina*, Bart. and Wendl. This shrub, which is extensively used as a diuretic, is one of the *Rutaceae*. It is now being grown in Morocco.

Experiments are also being made with some North American plants. One of these, *Hydrastis canadensis*, Linn., is the source of the hydrastis root so largely used in America as a bitter, having a supposed beneficial action on the mucous membrane. (It is now rejected from the B.P.) The plant — called the Golden Seal — is not at all easy to grow out of its native habitat, as a few growers in England have found to their sorrow, but the French cultivators are still undaunted, and the final issue of the experiment is not yet known.

The American *Podophyllum peltatum*, Linn., has on the other hand proved accommodating. So has *Cimicifuga racemosa* which was first brought to Europe in 1860, and is still doing excellently in its new conditions. It is a beautiful plant, and with its hybrids, is often seen in English gardens.

The two species of lobelia, *L. inflata*, Linn., and *L. syphilitica*, Linn., are also giving interesting results. They belong to the N. O. *Campanulaceae*, and grow in North America. The former is called Indian Tobacco or Poke-Weed. It is official in England, and is one of the most potent drugs known, the narcotic juice being strongly poisonous. It is also used as a sedative and expectorant in

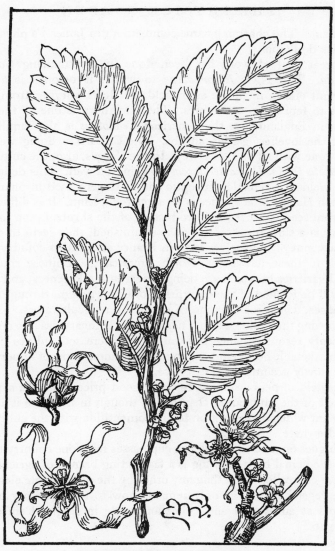

HAMAMELIS VIRGINIANA
Witch Hazel

herbalism. The charming name commemorates James I's physician, Mathias de l'Obel.

A great deal of work has been done in acclimatizing *Cascara Sagrada*. The N.O. *Rhamnaceae* to which it belongs is a very important one in medicine as it yields products varying from purgatives to febrifuges and tonics. The buckthorn is one of the best known in England, but the American *Ceanothus* is also familiar as one of the loveliest garden shrubs. The *Cascara* is doing well (as it has done with us in Yorkshire). In the Vosges, also, the culture of *Hamamelis* (N.O. *Hamamelidaceae*) is going on well. This delightful shrub yields the reliable antiseptic and astringent used in pharmacy as Witch Hazel. The species is *H. virginiana*, Linn. It is difficult to rear from seed, so that the introduction of the shrubs into a foreign country is a slow process, but once established, they seem to give a good account of themselves both in France and in this country.

Add to these natives of North America the Chinese rhubarb, several varieties of which are being grown in the Pyrenees, and some idea will be formed of the enterprise, often carried on through great difficulties, which is being shown by the French cultivators.

Following the example of her neighbours, Hungary has also applied her scanty resources since the war to the increased culture of the more marketable herbs, and has contributed some items of importance to the slowly accumulating evidence.

Her yield of peppermint is fetching good prices, and the same is reported of the Hungarian chamomile, though in this case it is the wild plant which comes out on top in competition with the cultivated crop elsewhere.

So it goes on; and the challenge cup passes from one country to the next. Medicinal herb-growing is a fascinating branch of agriculture, which is controlled more than any other by the incalculable elements in the vegetable cell. It only remains now to tell the story of the attempts at cultivation and collection made in England since the year 1916.

CHAPTER IX

CULTIVATION IN ENGLAND

THE DRUG PLANTS OF THE BRITISH EMPIRE

PODOPHYLLUM PELTATUM

Drawn from a specimen cultivated in Kew Gardens; the fruit added
from A. Gray
1. A bud.   2. Vertical section of flower.   3. Transverse section of
ovary.   4. Vertical section of fruit.   5. A seed showing the fleshy
arillus.   6. Section of seed.   (5 and 6 enlarged).

From *Medicinal Plants*, Bentley & Trimen

By courtesy of Messrs. Churchill, publishers; reproduced from Stafford Allen's
'Romance of Empire Drugs'

THE POSITION IN ENGLAND IN 1914

IN October 1914 the Board of Agriculture and Fisheries issued their 'Pamphlet 228', dealing with the shortage of medicinal drugs consequent upon the closing of the European markets since the war. No sober and instructive leaflet ever had more dramatic consequences. It stated the bare facts that the bulk of our supplies came from Central Europe, and that owing to their stoppage, the hospitals were being increasingly denuded of such things as atropine, hyoscine and even digitalin, while the cost of drugs had risen from 50 to 500 per cent in some cases over the normal figure. The Board suggested that it might be profitable as well as patriotic to collect the indigenous herbs, and to cultivate certain species which were scarce in Britain. There were, it seemed, a few large manufacturing firms who still grew their own stuff, but this was in no way sufficient to meet the growing demand.

This knowledge fell into a world too preoccupied with urgent matters to give it much attention; but later, early in 1915, the Board of Agriculture very properly acted upon its recommendations and convened a meeting, including delegates from the various drug firms, for discussion. These gentlemen, however, were in a cautious mood. The drug industry, they said, had passed away from England partly because it was a troublesome affair, and also because it was such a small trade that it was scarcely worth while making a stand against foreign competition. The present shortage might at any time be relieved by the end of the war, and prices would return to the normal. The meeting broke up upon a note of prudence and foresight, and there seemed nothing to be done.

Meanwhile Pamphlet 228 went floating about the country; and one day, with Puckish irresponsibility, it fell into the hands of a delicate, cultured lady who was immediately fired with a desire to help. By January, 1916, through her social influence and initiative, she had drawn round her a little committee of women with funds sufficient for the running of a small London office and an embryo organization for collecting and growing medicinal herbs. About the same time, the Central Committee of National Patriotic Organizations, under the Chairmanship of the late Mr. Henry Cust, also began to work on similar lines. Pamphlet 228 might seem dry bones, but out of its substance had arisen a vision which embraced the past and the future. The committees worked like slaves. They went down into the docks and storehouses, and up crazy staircases into the haunts of the drug merchants who were doing so badly that they were glad to welcome any outside suggestions. Both the Herb Growing Association and the Central Committee had for their adviser a man of European reputation, Mr. E. M. Holmes, of Sevenoaks, whose knowledge of medical botany could hardly be surpassed. The response in the country was at first enthusiastic, and many schools organized collection by school children. It was at this stage that troubles arose. School children returned from the foxglove woods bearing in their hot little hands things quite other than foxglove, and the collections took hours to sort. Other very intelligent children, their minds sharpened by war prices, saw no fun in grubbing up male fern unless the labour were remunerative, whereas the associations wished it to be more patriotic than remunerative. And while they were muddling with their foxglove, their elders were muddling with things like the red valerian from the walls, which they sent up to the committees in quantities, taking it to be the medicinal species which of course it was not. The sensation Press as usual added to the confusion by a paragraph one morning headed 'Money in Dandelion Roots', after which the small office was so flooded with inquiries that the staff worked late into the night without being able to answer them. Then the drying shed that had been hired burnt down for no apparent reason, after which the gallant subscribers to the Association began to dry their own herbs in ovens, stables and greenhouses. The amount of work that people undertook was aptly expressed by one lady who had spent the summer in drying. 'It nearly killed me,' she said, 'and I lost exactly five pounds.'

Finally another and excellent drying shed was hired, in which a great deal of excellent work was done. The Board of Agriculture in the meantime expressed themselves as most interested 'that a little group of ladies had taken the matter up', and the Treasury, when approached in the matter, also expressed interest, but gave no hope whatever of financial support. The hospitals themselves were grateful and encouraging. In October 1916 the Secretary of St. Thomas's Hospital wrote to the Herb Growing Association as follows:

The work your association is doing is certainly of national importance. The hospitals undoubtedly benefit by your endeavours. Although the list of drugs which can be grown in Britain is not a large one, it comprises some of the most valuable remedies used in medicine.

The Medical Officer of the Charing Cross Hospital also wrote in similar sense:

I fully appreciate the national importance of your efforts . . . I therefore heartily support an undertaking which will develop a national drug industry, and make us in the near future free from foreign control.

Although this was, in fact, the dream of some of our most ardent workers, it was of course, not to be realized. The Association failed, and badly, partly from lack of capital but also from lack of good organization. It was true that to keep nine sheds working, as for a short time in 1917 we contrived to do, was in face of all the difficulties no mean achievement, but to make them pay was another matter. Finally, when the foreign imports returned in bulk as they naturally did after the war, it became impossible. The work lapsed from much the same reason that it had passed from England into the hands of Central Europe fifty years before: many of the drug plants grew wild in large quantities on the Continent; the labour of harvesting them was undertaken for a small sum, and the distribution was well organized. Japanese competition was another factor. At a time when English belladonna was selling for two shillings a pound the Japanese product could be had for about sixpence.

There are several crops which have always given their maximum yield on English soil: they are dill, liquorice, peppermint, and belladonna: all these remain under steady cultivation, but even these crops have to be augmented from foreign supplies.

If the drug plant industry is ever to any large extent increased in this country, it must share with other branches of agriculture in the application of modern scientific methods. All our food producing is more beset with difficulties in England than elsewhere; but eventually it will probably be removed from the arbitrary control of the weather. If this can be brought about, and agriculture can be further aided by intensive methods and electricity, let us hope that more than ten per cent of our forty millions will be fed from our own soil.

Meanwhile, although our work failed to establish a co-operative system in which the smallholder and the collector of wildings might have worked together for a reasonable profit, yet it had several effects which we could not have anticipated. There is no doubt that from it the herbalist's trade received a new stimulus, even although our chief occupation was with the 'official' crops. Mrs. Grieve's work at Chalfont St. Peter, enlarged since the war, has done much to arouse interest in purely herbal remedies; and although none can recommend an indiscriminate doctoring even with the most innocent looking simples, still, the extension of herbal practice has in many cases brought people back to ancient and effective remedies which had long been overlooked or forgotten. Mr. J. K. Oliver's articles in the *Daily Herald* have aroused a new interest in the subject, and his book, *Common Ailments and How to Treat Them*, has gone into numerous editions. So large is the demand that some of the herbalist firms will purchase good, clean herbs in small quantities from collectors.

HERB DRYING

A 'good, clean herb', root, leaf or bark, is one that has been perfectly dried. Good drying, where drug plants are concerned, is nine-tenths of the law. The process varies: in some cases sun drying is recommended; in others, the plant should be dried in the shade. Generally, a current of hot air maintained by a stove is the desideratum and all methods are aimed at the extraction of the water from the cells, leaving the residue, the alkaloids, etc., uninjured. The green colour must be preserved, and brown or shrivelled leaves are useless. Some leaves are more difficult to dry than others. In the foxglove, for instance, the rather tough and woolly mid-rib is thicker and therefore takes longer to dry than the rest of the leaf. After drying, the crop – which has then shrunk to a quarter, or less, of its weight – must be immediately enclosed in air-tight boxes to prevent the re-absorption of water vapour from the air. The belladonna leaf dries to a uniform grey-green; and the root, which presents the wrinkled appearance of all dried roots, has a characteristic grey-brown colour. Like gentian root, it is slowly dried in artificial heat. During the drying, fermentative changes take place in all these roots: in the gentian, the bitter glycosides become less bitter, and in the valerian rhizome a free acid is gradually formed by enzyme action as the process goes on. Rapid drying is fatal to a thick root, whose external layers will thus become hardened and so prevent the escape of the internal moisture.

Mr. Holmes, in his pamphlet written for the Central Committee in 1916, gave some valuable advice in this important matter. He pointed out that in several cases a rapid deterioration of the dried drug, whether root or leaf, sets in, and that therefore every country keeps its best produce, that is the produce of the current year, for home consumption, exporting the older crop. This is particularly the case with *Cannabis indica*, which changes very quickly. The Bolivians are also said to keep their supplies of Coca for home consumption and to export their second best. Before the war this was recognized in the commercial world, and experts in this country frequently found impurities in the foreign consignments, particularly in the seeds like caraway, etc., which could easily include weed seeds in the collection. The Dutch and the English crops were, in Mr. Holmes's experience, the cleanest on the market. He used these facts in support of his argument for the increase of herb cultivation in this country, and pointed out that a good deal of heat was wasted in the brick-kilns and lime-kilns where native crops could be dried. The boarded floor of an oast-house is, of course, an excellent drying place for many of the lighter things like hops and opium poppy capsules. The latter are easily dried when spread on the floor and turned over occasionally.

In the same pamphlet, Mr. Holmes dealt with the larger issues of herb cultivation in England and the colonies. He said:

> The only hope, so it appears to me, of making the cultivation of medicinal plants profitable in this country is to pay attention to the details which ensure a better dried, better looking, and more reliable product than can be obtained elsewhere. With modern knowledge of enzymes, the analysis of soils and the analysis of ash, and the study of destructive fungi and insects, this desideratum is rendered quite possible. Unfortunately the new British Pharmacopoeia does not give any support to British cultivation, requiring only that a certain percentage of alkaloids should be present without defining what the alkaloids should be, and not requiring the fresh plant for use in galenical preparations. Thus the cheap imported plants from the Continent can be used, and even if the alkaloids, of foreign aconite for instance, consist chiefly of aconitine, there is nothing to prevent their use.

It was with this standard kept steadily in mind that the Herb Growing Association, backed by such counsellors as Mr. Holmes, Professor Greenish, and Mr. Shenstone of the Pharmaceutical Society, set themselves to put on the market only such herbs as were 'better dried, better looking, and more reliable than could be obtained elsewhere', and during the first two years of the work, the prices paid for first-class English stuff were extremely high. Continental belladonna root, normally 40s. per hundredweight, cost 200s. in 1916, while the English root rose to 300s. Foreign henbane, which used to be sold at 30s., went up to 200s., and English to 448s. Similar prices ruled in the case of other drug plants of the Pharmacopoeia, while even the cheaper 'herbalists' herbs', many of which could be collected in the country, commanded a good sale. 'All these have been hitherto obtained from Germany, and elsewhere,' wrote Mr. Holmes, 'and at prices which do not pay the herb gatherers to collect.' He went on to enumerate the wild herbs which were wanted in quantity

through the Continentinal supplies having ceased, and the list is
an interesting and rather surprising one.

Here it is:

Agrimony–*Agrimonia Eupatoria*
Archangel (White Dead nettle)–*Lamium album*
Avens–*Geum urbanum*
Broom–*Cytisus scoparius*
Buckbean–*Menyanthes trifoliata*
Burdock (root)–*Arctium Lappa*
Greater Burnet–*Sanguisorba officinalis*
Greater Celandine–*Chelidonium majus*
Centaury–*Erythroea Centaurium*
Cleavers–*Galium Aparine*
Comfrey–*Symphytum officinale*
Dandelion–*Taraxacum officinale*
Dog Mercury–*Mercurialis perennis*
Eyebright–*Euphrasia officinalis*
Figwort–*Scrophularia nodosa*
Fumitory–*Fumaria officinalis*
Ground Ivy–*Glechoma hederacea*
Hemlock–*Conium maculatum*
Meadow Sweet–*Spiraea Ulmaria*
Mountain Flax–*Linum catharticum*
Mugwort–*Artemesia vulgaris*
Mullein–*Verbascum Thapsus*
Ragwort–*Senecio Jacoboea*
Raspberry–*Rubus Idoeus*
Sanicle–*Sanicula Europoea*
Vervain–*Verbena officinalis*
Wild Carrot–*Daucus Carota*
Wood Betony–*Stachys Betonica*
Woodsage–*Teucrium Scorodonia*
Yarrow–*Achillea Millefolium*

The plants in the above list were wanted by the hundredweight
or the ton, and were all common in many districts, and could be

collected. Except in the few cases where the roots were used in pharmacy, the proper gathering of the flower heads and leafy stems would not lead to extermination of the species.

Mr. Holmes also issued a list of all the culinary or 'pot herbs' which as he said could be grown in any cottage garden, but which we imported before the war in thousands of pots and bottles from Central Europe. One of the schemes which he always had in mind was the reclaiming of waste land for cultivation. He always declared that Poole Harbour, with its fifty miles of estuarine waste, could be converted into a henbane field if the Government would move in the matter!

THE ENGLISH DRUG FARMS

When the war ended, the medicinal plant firms carried on as hitherto, while some increased their acreage of cultivation. The following are all well known: Messrs. Burroughs, Wellcome & Co.; Duncan, Flockart & Co.; Evans, Lescher & Webb; Stafford Allen & Sons, and Messrs. Potter and Clarke. At the end of the war, Messrs. Ryder & Co. started business under the name of Heath and Heather, and have worked up a vigorous industry in purely herbal medicines. One of the older firms, Stafford Allen & Sons, celebrated their centenary in 1933, and the history of the firm, related in their recent booklet, has some interesting features worth quoting.

Until the eighteenth century the cultivation of medicinal plants remained in the hands of small growers, but after 1800 several farms came into existence; one, occupying about 250 acres at Mitcham, and another, started by Charles May or his immediate predecessors, at Ampthill in Bedfordshire. Records were kept showing good crops of peppermint, lavender and henbane. Charles May, who was a druggist as well as herb-grower, was a friend of Stafford Allen, the nephew of William Allen, F.R.S., the senior partner in the firm of Allen and Hanbury, and later the first President of the Pharmaceutical Society of Great Britain. Allen was a member of the Society of Friends, and therefore, like all other members of that honourable and honoured community, set his face against corrupt and dishonourable practice. In those days adulteration in the grinding of drugs was accepted as customary, and there was no Act of Parliament to protect the unlucky purchaser who was palmed off with powder mixed with sawdust. Stafford Allen, then a miller of Amersham, co-operated with Charles May in a strong movement against the vested interests that obtained in the drug trade and tolerated dishonesty. The two men entered into partnership under the style of May & Allen in North Street (now Cowper Street), Finsbury, and later, Charles May's place was taken by Allen's younger brother, George. This was the beginning of the firm whose works are still in Cowper Street, while their farms and factories cover about 250 acres at Long Melford.

Speaking of the early beginnings in 1833, the authors of the Centenary Pamphlet write as follows:

> It is significant that many of the great business houses which are world-famous to-day were cradled in this enterprising period. The Reform Act was passed in 1832; and in the next year a Bill for the Abolition of Slavery was on its way through the Houses of Parliament. It was in 1833 that the firm now known as Stafford Allen came into existence with a view to introducing another much needed reform intimately affecting the life of the community, namely, the removal of drug adulteration. It is of particular interest that one of the men to whom in great part the company owes its inception was a prominent protagonist in the anti-slavery movement.

The manufacture of chemicals for the wholesale trade was begun by May and Allen on an extensive scale; they installed at Ampthill the first steam engine ever seen in Bedfordshire together with a plant for making extracts and other galenicals. The high standard of their produce led to success, and the firm gradually increased its plant and premises. Two celebrated products of the firm are sandalwood oil which they were the first in England to distil, and almond oil, which is first expressed by grinding machinery and filter presses from sweet or bitter almonds, while secondly, the almond cake from the process is distintegrated and sent to the still for the manufacture of essential oil of almonds. Peach and apricot kernels sent direct from Syria are used to produce the cheaper persic oil.

English distilled sandalwood oil is preferred to any other, and was introduced to medical practice in 1865.

'Staff Allen's' oil of cloves is another product long associated with the firm. 'At first,' to quote again from the pamphlet, 'its uses were confined to medicine and perfumery. After a time, the realization of the fact that eugenol, the principal constituent of the oil, was the most convenient starting point for the production of vanillin on a commercial scale, led to a large increase in the demand; and to-day, distillation by the ton is the rule. Iso-eugenol, another derivation of eugenol, has a range of uses in perfumery.'

Other proprietaries sent out by Stafford Allen are the popular pyrethrum insecticide, Pysect, prepared from the pyrethrum crops on the farm, and Erbolin, a physiologically standardized defatted preparation of ergot.

In their Centenary booklet the firm gave some interesting figures showing how prices have altered since the war. A few of these may be quoted:

	1913	1917	1922	1933
Camphor per lb.	2½d.	3/6	4/4	2/3
Castor-oil per lb.	2½d.	9d.	60/- cwt.	55/- cwt.
Menthol	10/-	13/9	35/-	14/6
Quinine	1/- oz.	2/9	2/3	1/9

Essential Oils

	1913	1917	1922	1933
Almond per lb.	16/6	45/-	20/-	38/-
Anise	7/3	3/6	2/4	1/9
English Lavender	54/-	150/-	140/-	80/-
French Lavender	17/-	18/6	18/-	9/-
English Peppermint Oil	32/-	95/-	100/-	50/-

THE DRUGS OF THE BRITISH COMMONWEALTH

The enterprising little book, *The Romance of Empire Drugs*, issued by Stafford Allen Ltd. at 1s., reminds one that this side of the matter should not be overlooked. Many of the most important medicinal substances come from the varied lands of the British Empire. From the British West Indies and Jamaica we import *Sarsaparilla*, logwood, and ginger. Kenya sends us *Pyrethrum*, and East and West Africa *Capsicum*. From South Africa come *Buchu* and aloes. Wintergreen, cascara, *Podophyllum* and *Cimicifuga* are Canadian products; and Catechu, pepper and *Ipecacuanha* come from the Federated Malay States. Australia gives us *Eucalyptus*, and Zanzibar the clove. From India of course we import largely, *Cannabis indica*, cardamom, castor-oil, cinnamon, *Nux-vomica*, senna and opium being among the most important products.

A more detailed reference should be made to the following plants, some of which have not been mentioned in our earlier chapters.

Senega root is obtained from *Polygala senega*, Linn, N.O. *Polygalaceae*. The plant was brought here in 1734 with the tradition that the American Indians used it for snake-bite; and the Indians still gather it in the summer and sell it to travellers for the root. It is used officially as a stimulant expectorant in bronchial affections.

Empire sources of pepper are Ceylon, Singapore, East Africa and Sarawak. The spice, yielded by the dried, unripe fruits of *Piper nigrum* Linn, N.O. *Piperaceae*, was known to the Greeks, and was one of the chief spices in the trade of the Middle Ages, when tribute was levied in 'pepper rents'. The pungent taste of the berry is due to a resin and an aromatic oil, but the spice was also the source of the synthetic perfume called Heliotropin, and a series of uric acid solvents (piperazine) have been derived from the same source.

Haematoxylon campechianum, Linn., N.O. *Leguminoseae*, is the Logwood tree of Central America, now naturalized in the West Indies where it was introduced in 1715. Its principal use was in yielding a dye, but in the London Pharmacopoeia of 1740 it was prescribed as an astringent in phthisis and dysentery. It is still in use and is marketed in the form of chips from the wood.

In the Imperial Institute, where many photographs of medicinal plantations can be seen, there is one showing a Lime plantation in the British West Indies, where the cultivation of the tree, *Citrus aurantifolia*, Swingle, N.O. *Rutaceae*, forms a basic industry.

Lime juice has been used in the treatment of scurvy since the tenth century, and the oil of lime is used in many beverages. This commercial oil is a product of distillation in the evaporation of the juice of the fruit, but the peel yields by expression the golden-coloured oil called oil of limette whose constituent, citrol, gives it a rich aroma and flavour. An aromatic oil is also present in the leaves.

Eucalyptus oil is obtained from distillation of the leaves of *E. Globulus*, N.O. *Myrtaceae*, and several other Australian species. Through its antiseptic properties the oil has come into popular use as an inhalant; and some industrial oils containing terpenes, and obtained from the stems and leaves, are used industrially in flotation processes in mining for the extraction of ores. The oil from *E. citriodora* is utilized in perfumery.

The citronella oil of Ceylon is the base of an old and increasing industry. It is distilled from *Cymbopogon Nardus*, Rendle, N.O. *Gramineae*, the Lanu Bata grass which is indigenous to Ceylon but is now cultivated in the West Indies and the South Seas. The following quotation is taken from *The Romance of Empire Drugs*:

Only well-dried grass is distilled. Care has to be exercised in drying in order to avoid fermentation and decomposition. In general the grass is cut three but occasionally four times a year. About 60 or 70 lb. of oil per acre are obtained as an average yield. Owing to the necessity for the plentiful supply of cool water, the distilleries are usually located at the foot of a range of hills where the desired conditions obtain. Distillation is mainly in the hands of natives who display remarkable aptitude for the work. Direct steam distillation is employed, the oil collecting in a receiver which is locked and carefully safeguarded. Citronella is one of the most important essential oils produced within the Empire, which has supplied increasingly large quantities in recent years. It is extensively used in perfumery — in soaps, hair preparations and skin lotions, and is the raw material from which geraniol is produced.

Capsicum minimum, N.O. *Solanaceae*, bears the long red fruits known as chillies, and is a plant of India and Africa. From this and several allied species the pungent fruits which when ground form

Cayenne pepper, are obtained. The medicine, capsicum, is official in the B.P. as a stomachic, and — externally — as a stimulant. The active principle, capsicin, is used for its pungency in ginger ale and ginger wine.

Vanilla which is the subject of a delightful picture in the Imperial Institute exhibition, though it is universally known as a flavouring agent, is still prepared in a fluid extract used as a carminative. *Vanilla planifolia* Linn., is a climbing orchid of Central America, but several British possessions contribute to the trade demand, chiefly British Honduras, the Seychelles and the West Indies.

Sandalwood, the product of the evergreen tree, *Santalum album*, Linn. N.O. *Santalaceae*, was mentioned in the Vedie records, and was brought — probably by the Arabians — to Europe in the eleventh century.

The tree — which is a partial parasite — forms an important Indian industry in Mysore and Madras. The wood is, as we all know, exquisitely fragrant, and formerly an oil was distilled from the bark and used in medicine, but the use of this 'Santal Oil' is now almost confined to perfumery. A West Australian oil from *Fusanus spicatus* is also used in soaps and face powders.

Until about the fifteenth century, ginger came exclusively from Bengal, and was — as it is still — prescribed in therapeutics as a carminative, but the present source of supply is Jamaica. Commercial Ginger is the scraped root of *Zingiber officinale*, Roscoe, N.O. *Scitaminaceae*. It contains fifty per cent of starch, 1 to 37 per cent of volatile oil, together with proteins and pungent material. In every Pharmacopoeia there are numerous preparations containing the drug which was mentioned in ancient Indian and Chinese literature.

The castor-oil plant, *Ricinus communis*, Linn. (N.O. *Euphorbiaceae*) grows extensively in Southern India, from whence most of the world's present supply is obtained — the seeds, not the oil, being chiefly exported. They are graded and their shells broken between rollers, after which the kernels are pressed hydraulically to obtain the medicinal oil.

'Cubebs' are imported from Java. The name is given to the dried, unripe fruits of *Piper Cubeba*, L., which look like black peppercorn with stalks. The drug which was official in the 1914 B.P. is a diuretic stimulating to the mucous membrane. *Oleum cubeboe* is obtained from the fruit by distillation.

Zanzibar produces ninety per cent of the world's cloves, and the plantations are largely cultivated by Arabs. When the Dutch owned the Molucca Islands they proceeded to destroy the clove trees, thereby setting up a monopoly; but they also incurred the wrath of the natives whose habit it was to plant a clove tree at the birth of a child in order to give a rough indication of its age. In 1770, the French brought the tree to Mauritius, and later it was introduced into the Malay States whence cloves of a superior quality are now exported.

The important drug, *Chaulmoogra* oil given in leprosy was mentioned in Chapter v. It comes from a group of closely allied plants of the N.O. *Flacourtaceae.*

One of the species, *Gynocardia oderata*, figured in the Chinese herbal of Pun-tsaou. Other species that yield the Chaulmoogric acid are *Oncoba echinata* of Sierra Leone, and some kinds of the *Hydnocarpus* trees of South and West India, notably *H. Wightiana* Blume. The *Oleum Chaulmoograe* of the B.P. comes from *Tarakogenos Kurzii*, King, and is exported from Burmah. The chief difficulty in the administration, externally or internally, of the oil is its extremely nauseating quality. In 1915 Martindale introduced a sodium salt by fractionating the Chaulmoogric acids which are then saponified with sodium hydroxide. The British Empire Relief Association has for some time been sending out large quantities of this salt to our Eastern dependencies, and it was estimated that in 1930, 400,000 doses were given. Experiments are still being carried on with the oil from *Oncoba*, and with the ethyl esters of *Hydnocarpus*. A full account of the drug will be found in Martindale's Extra Pharmacopoeia.

From Ceylon, as everyone knows, we import large quantities of tea and coffee. The former was introduced into England in the seventeenth century and was thought to be worth 6os. a pound. The plants from which the Ceylon crops are derived are *Thea sinensis*, Linn. and *T. viridis*, N.O. *Theaceae*. The older name *Camellia Thea*, Linn. was given to commemorate the Dutch Jesuit missionary,

George Joseph Camel or Camelli, whose plant illustrations came into the hands of James Petiver and are now in the British Museum. The alkaloid, theine, in the tea leaf, is identical with that of caffeine, in coffee. The latter is official in the B.P.

There are, however, several other plants, natives of various countries, from whose leaves a 'tea' is prepared. Especially stimulating is the *Maté* tea of Brazil from *Ilex Paraguayensis*. The Brazilians also use the leaf of *Lantana pseudo-thea* in the same way. The Northern Americans make a tea from the native Partridge berry, *Gantheria procumbens*; and in India toolsie tea is infused from a Labiate, *Ocymum album*, related to the basil. Many simple teas are made by our English peasantry from wild plants like agrimony, ground-ivy, and the common speedwell.

Coffee is the ground and roasted seed of the beautiful African plant *Coffea arabica*, Linn., N.O. *Cinchonaceae*. It was said to have been first introduced into this country in the fifteenth century from Abyssinia, but it did not become a common beverage until 1652. The alkaloid caffeine occurs in tea, coffee, guarana, maté tea and kola nuts. The following is a quotation from Bentley and Trimen's *Medical Botany*: 'In moderate quantities coffee stimulates the stomach gently and the nervous system decidedly without much exciting the circulation or producing any narcotic impression on the brain. . . . These are the properties which characterize the nervous stimulants, and to this class it therefore properly belongs.'

Caffeine is also a powerful diuretic, and occasionally useful in migraine, but it is less used than phenacetin.

Although *Oleum Theobromae*, from *Theobroma Cacao*, Linn., the source of cocoa and chocolate, is not an Empire product, its alkaloid so closely resembles that of tea and coffee that it naturally belongs to this group. The plant is a native of South America, and was introduced here in 1759. The seeds are the source from whence cocoa and chocolate are derived. The roasted seeds are the cocoa nibs which make the purest and most nourishing beverage.

The alkaloid theobromine is more powerfully diuretic than caffeine, and there is a derivative, diuretin, which is prescribed to relieve oedema in diseases of the kidneys and the heart.

THE PHYSICK GARDEN

MEDICINAL PLANT GARDENS

In addition to the drug farms there are several smaller gardens in the country, notably at Swansea and Aberystwyth. Other growers who supply the wholesale trade are Mr. Seymour of Halbeach, Messrs. Flemons & Keary of Dunstable and Mr. Alder of Leighton Buzzard.

One of the oldest established instructors in medicinal plant cultivation is Mrs. Grieve, of Chalfont St. Peter in Buckinghamshire, who long before the war had grown drug plants and supplied the manufacturing chemists with her own produce. She also instituted classes for instruction in horticulture, and kept the whole work going with indefatigable industry.

Some of her students took up the work of collecting and drying for the market; and though the work is very exacting — for there are no soft jobs in herb-growing — Mrs. Grieve has been able in one or two notable cases to help the adventurers to make good and earn a sufficient income. During the war the garden at The Whins was enlarged and new enterprises taken up with the assistance of Miss Oswald (Medallist of the Society of Apothecaries). Mrs. Grieve's numerous pamphlets dealing with every branch of the industry, and with practically every native plant used in medical practice and in cooking, are indispensable to any student who desires instruction in the preparation of plants for the trade and for medicine. She has a large collection of medicinal herbs and shrubs in her garden.

The cultivation of semi-tropical and foreign species is naturally dependent upon situation, and it used to be thought impossible to grow such things in England anywhere but in the extreme west. The very interesting experiment in a Scarborough garden has, however, shown us what can be done in the north-east provided that the site is near the seaside. The largest private garden there, known as Ashburn, had been utilized by the tenant, Miss Smart, as a vegetable garden for the British Navy during the war period, and many tons of wholesome vegetables had gone to vary the menu for our own Jack Tars. After the armistice, Miss Smart looked around for some good use that the garden could be put to, and curiously enough, at the same time, a well-known Scarborough botanical chemist, Mr. H. M. Hirst, F.R.H.S., M.P.S., was looking for a plot of ground where he could grow a few medicinal plants for the use of the pharmaceutical students he was training at the local chemistry classes. Miss Smart learning of his wishes, the result was a happy co-operation which has gone on to this day. The story of the garden may be told in Mr. Hirst's own words.

THE ASHBURN (SCARBOROUGH) HERB GARDEN

'After the war had ended, I was asked to conduct the classes in botany and materia medica held for the benefit of Scarborough's pharmaceutical students. The difficulty was to obtain fresh botanical specimens of medicinal interest, and so in the second year (1920), I determined to grow my own. A dear old friend (Miss E. Smart) offered me the free use of her garden, and in addition had a small greenhouse erected without any cost to myself. 1921 was the active start, and then began the worrying task of obtaining roots and seeds. Thanks to several firms and individuals, I gradually got a small collection together, and was bold enough to send an account of my modest work to the *Pharmaceutical Journal*. The article was published, and it led to many inquiries with resulting new and valued friendships formed. Also it gave me much unexpected work through people writing and begging for plants and seeds. I had a whole-time position as chemist's manager, as well as taking the evening classes, but this new work was a labour of love, and for the last twelve years I have spent nearly every minute of half-holidays, evenings, and Sundays either working in the garden or getting away correspondence, plants and seeds. The first person who wrote to me after reading my article was Mr. E. M. Holmes, and I kept his sincere friendship until his death. No one could have been more kind and helpful — he sent roots and seeds, verified my specimens grown from other sources, and constantly wrote offering advice or criticizing my efforts. It would take up too much space to name all the other botanical friends

— sufficient to say that during the past eleven years, I have had correspondence and friendly suggestions from every botanist of note in the United Kingdom, indeed, my post box has held letters from all over the world, and seeds have been sent to Canada, U.S.A., Africa, China, and Australia.

'It was no easy matter at first to obtain seeds or plants of the desired subjects, for growing enthusiasm led me to draw up a list of every plant in the syllabus for the Pharmaceutical Society's examinations, which I thought ought to grow in England, and hundreds of catalogues were carefully scanned, finding one plant here, or seeds there, until by 1923 I had everything on the list. During this time, experimental planting was constantly carried on, for I could not find a textbook which gave the cultural details of many of the plants. What I had to find out was whether they were hardy, or at any rate would stand a normal Scarborough winter with slight protection — what soil they thrived in — what position suited them best — and how to propagate them. From time to time, the *Pharmaceutical Journal* accepted notes from me about my efforts, and after such publication, I had inquiries for specimens or seeds, which led to my offering yearly surplus plants and seeds at a nominal figure to cover expenses. Correspondence came from pharmacy colleges and technical schools asking terms for boxes of cut specimens, and also one got pleading letters from students who were just going up for examination begging seasonal examples of plants they were likely to be asked about. Later, one got inquiries from schools and colleges for help with planning their own gardens and furnishing specimens. I have often wondered how many chemists who have qualified since the war have been helped by learning from botanical specimens sent as seeds, plants, or cut blooms from my garden. In addition to all I have mentioned, I have exchanged specimens with Chelsea Physic Gardens and many similar places, and it can be very few students who have not seen produce from Ashburn, even unknowingly. Research laboratories, makers of microscopical slides, and suppliers of mounted dried specimens have all been helped occasionally when their usual source had run dry. I would venture to say that 90 per cent of post-war chemists have knowingly or unknowingly examined Yorkshire botanical material. Hundreds of pharmacists and their apprentices have visited the Ashburn Garden while on holiday, and on dozens of occasions I have given up meal-times to take newly-made chemist friends through the garden, for as I have said, I had a full working day shop position to attend to. On one memorable Sunday, the chemists of Northumberland and Durham together with the pupils of the Sunderland Technical College made my garden their objective for a special journey outing. On this occasion, they were given a civic reception by the then Mayor (the late Alderman George Whitfield, J.P., PH.C.) who very kindly spoke of the pride that Scarborough took in my efforts.

'Financially, this spare time enterprise has never paid its way — it has always had to be regarded as a "labour of love" done with a desire to give students help as I was helped in other directions in college days. One could not expect nurserymen to give me seeds and plants when I was unknown. The initial expenses were heavy for these, and carriage hefty. Stamps and postages add up tremendously in the course of a year, and owing to my whole-time work, I have had to pay for labour for rough digging and garden path tidying. I mention this as the excuse for not being able to oblige many people who seemed to think that a letter would bring them free plants back per return.

'Commercially, I only made one effort to make a little money, and it showed me how unprofitable herb-growing was if unorganized. Some four or five years ago, the rhizomes of my original patch of *Valeriana officinalis* had spread to such an extent that I had to take the whole bed up and remake it. The result was that I had a heap of Valerian rhizome and roots with encrusted earth which must have weighed several hundredweight. It seemed a pity to throw this on the rubbish heap, so I wrote to the wholesale drug houses who supplied the pharmacy I was connected with, asking if this valerian was of any use to them. Nobody seemed to want it — foreign grown rhizome was plentiful and cheap, but at last one wholesale house said they would have it at their own price if I would wash and rough dry it. It took me nearly a week in my spare time to "swill the muck" off at the garden, using a tub with pails of water. Then I spread it out to dry somewhat, and placed it in two sacks to take home to re-wash it thoroughly. The next result was to clog up the waste pipe in the wash-kitchen with debris and dirt, and I had to get a plumber in to re-model the "trap" with new fittings. However, by this time, the weight had been reduced to about one cwt. and I commenced to rough dry it over the kitchen range much to the disgust of my family, for the odour developed was atrocious. At length the mass was ready for sending away, and the final weight was about 40 lb., for as it dried, much earth came out of crevices of the root system which had withstood the repeated washings. In due course I received £1 1s. for the valerian, and the same week I got a bill from the plumber for 25s. for the damage I had caused. It may be guessed that I have never tried to sell any plant products commercially since; all surplus plants not saleable go on the bonfire.

'Last autumn, I told this tale to a carriageful of chemists when I was up at Aberdeen for the British Pharmaceutical Conference, and when I had finished and the laughter had died down, a voice from the corner said: "What a pity! We have to buy fresh valerian root from the Continent for a special preparation we make." I looked, and saw that a director of a world-famous firm with whom I had not dealt was sitting there. Such is life.

'Successes and failures. The failures have been few. Of hardy plants there are only two which have beaten me. *Glycyrrhiza glabra* was a plant which I was years in obtaining roots of, for the Pontefract growers jealously guard their "sets" and vigorously refuse specimens even for experimental work. How I got a dozen pieces of root at last was by the influence of a friend whom I was able to help in exchange. Duly planted as per directions which he wormed out of the grower, they came up, but very thinly, and died away the second year. It did not like our heavy loamy clay — I learn it must have a deep sandy loam. I cannot get *Arnica montana* to grow, as it is an Alpine plant, needing rockery condition which I could not give it. On the other hand, we have an old garden variety of *Arnica* here (specific name unknown) which thrives like a weed in the heaviest of clay. The other failures have been with "tender plants" which thrive outside all right until we get one of our rare frosts. Most of these

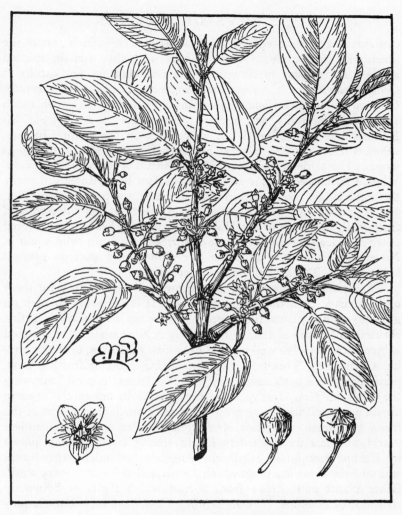

RHAMNUS PURSHIANA
Cascara Sagrada

casualties have been replaced, but are now in eight-inch pots in the greenhouse for safety. Grown in this way, they remain stunted and are not typical specimens. I refer to such foreign shrubs as *Gelsemium nitidum*, *Cinnamonum Camphora*, *Liquidamber orientalis*, *Olea europa*, and *Quillaja Saponaria*. Still, I have met with much success unexpectedly, and in many cases where the late Mr. E. M. Holmes told me he could not grow them in the south. In fact, subjects like *Grindelia robusta* and *Euphorbia pilulifera*, come up as weeds. The pride of the garden is a fine shrub of *Rhamnus Purshiana*. When I purchased this, it was about one foot high. In eleven years, the trunk is now over a foot in circumference, the height is nine feet, and it spreads out with branches for 15 feet. It both flowers and fruits well, and much to Mr. Holmes's surprise, it has always flowered twice in a season, firstly in June with resulting fruits, and again in November, when the following December cold periods prevent fruit setting. The bark bears the typical lichen.

'*Chrysanthemum cinerariaefolium* grows and flowers well for three or four years; then the plants die away. It is necessary to keep on growing young plants from seed. *Hamamelis Virginiana* is a fine shrub in either sun or shade, and flowers in November. Acclimatized subjects which thrive well include *Ecballium Elaterium*, or the Squirting Cucumber. This is a most interesting plant at fruiting time, particularly on a hot autumn day when the fruits "pop off" throwing the seeds for feet. I have taken these home to dry in the oven to obtain seed, and they have given my family much amusement as the fruits got warm. *Angelica Archangelica* forms a massive subject yearly, and is only rivalled in height among Umbelliferous plants by *Conium maculatum*. Still, the Angelica has much larger leaves and umbels. This is a plant which is unequalled for shrubbery work. Other plants and shrubs from abroad which thrive well include *Artemisia Absinthium*, *Berberis aristata*, *Cimicifuga racemosa*, *Coriandrum sativum*, *Crocus sativus*, *Drimys Winteri*, *Delphinium Staphisagria*, *Fabiana Imbricata*, *Fraxinus Ornus* (the prettiest shrub in the garden when in flower), *Gaultheria procumbens*, *Gentiana lutea*, *Hyssopus officinalis*, *Juniperus Sabina*, *Lactuca virosa*, *Laurus nobilis*, *Lobelia inflata*, *Datura Tatula*, *Mentha piperita* (I have the French form as well as the ordinary), *Mentha pulegium*, *Hydrastis Canadensis*, *Phytolacca decandra*, *Podophyllum peltatum et Emodi* (beloved by slugs), *Pyrus Cydonia*, *Rheum palmatum*, *Urginea scilla*, *Trigonella Foenumgraecum*, *Viburnum prunifolium*, and lastly one must mention *Astragalus gummifer*, which I have had in flower but which has a nasty habit of dying away in patches. *Eucalyptus globulus* does well in many Scarborough gardens, and I know of shrubs ten feet high which have lived outside for several years.

'In a friend's hothouse, we have been very successful in growing tropical plants from cuttings or seeds, mainly obtained in exchange from the Chelsea Physic Gardens. We have tamarinds, true castor-oil, cocaine, yams, brazil nuts, indigo, monkey nuts, banana, orange, fig, *Eucalyptus Citriodora*, and have been particularly successful in growing loofahs over tanks of water.

'Such has been the experimental work carried out. Now, owing to the claims of business, I have relinquished this year most of the plants as I am now living some miles from Ashburn. The trees and shrubs will remain there until the ever-encroaching builder comes along and destroys its beauty. May this time be far distant, for I have spent many happy hours in this garden, and in the greenhouse which has housed the aloes and *Cereus grandiflora*. If any reader feels I have been "blowing my own trumpet" too loudly — well, they must blame the authoress of this book who has graciously but firmly demanded a full report of my activities. I do feel that my work however has been unique in the North of England, and I hope has been of some little use in the pharmaceutical world.'

Looking back once more to the war-time activities, we are entitled to claim that the heroic element was not wanting in our work. In one or two cases, growing and drying for the market was carried on by enthusiasts, who had just sufficient private means to hold on until the work brought some return. One of the most gallant attempts at making the industry pay on a small scale was carried out by Edith Hughes, who after a short course of study at the Herb Growing Association's drying shed at Chalfont in 1917, took charge of the Chester shed which, under the auspices of an influential committee, was opened in that same year. It was the most flourishing and well-organized of all our existing groups. An association of collectors and growers was organized all over the county, their herbs being sold to the parent Association, which issued from time to time a list of the herbs most required. These were at that time mainly belladonna, henbane, foxglove, dandelion and opium poppy; but marigold petals, coltsfoot, raspberry leaves, etc., provided for some of the herbalists' demands. The drying-shed was well fitted up, but the drying plant worked by gas proved far too expensive. During the autumn, the staff experimented with the canning of various fruits; and in the winter, roots, vegetables and apple rings were dried. When, in June 1918, the Herb Growing Association was wound up, the Chester group with its strong committee, enthusiastic helpers and good collectors, decided to carry on. They worked for another year, always finding a ready market for the herbs, but the trouble was that the prices paid to the collectors did not really satisfy them, while those paid by the drug firms did not repay the Association. Miss Hughes states that in eleven months the turnover was about £250, but the expenses were greater.

The rest of Miss Hughes's narrative is so graphic that it should be told in her own words:

'In the autumn of 1921, I started a small herb farm in Sussex. I rented some ground and a shed for drying and worked hard for two seasons, selling my produce to wholesale firms. I employed schoolchildren to collect wild herbs. I think my actual profits that year were £11, and I could not have made this without the voluntary help of my brother and a friend. The best paying crop that year was marigold at about 4s. a pound. The second year I obtained definite orders from a few retail chemists and herbalists, and this paid better as it eliminated the middleman. Also it showed me how to limit my range and quantities. That year I cleared about £21. Soon afterwards circumstances compelled me to live in Brighton, where I carried on my work with a large herb garden near the Downs. That winter my storeroom was stocked with about thirty kinds of useful herbs — from five to ten pounds of each — and I looked about for the best markets. I was determined to make my venture pay somehow! If only I could get retail instead of wholesale prices for my produce! With this idea I took a small shop in Brighton and sold my goods there, while I devoted all my spare time for the next two years to the study of materia medica. In the second year, I made a profit of £70, but the work became overwhelming, and at length I sold the business to a very good herbalist who is still carrying it on successfully but without growing her own herbs.

'I then started a postal business in herbs, pitching my tent at Kew. There I made a considerable connection all over England, and beyond, but the expenses of that enterprise were too great, and I moved back to Brighton, carrying on the business which I had named "The Green-Harvest Industry" all the time. At Kew I had discovered the popularity of what may be called the "luxury" herbs, lavender, sweet herbs and potpourri. I was able to take stalls at some of the large Handcraft exhibitions at Westminster, and found that my "Garden Gay Potpourri" was a great favourite, and that the packets of culinary herbs sold "like hot cakes". In Brighton I always had a difficulty in growing and drying enough medicinal produce to supply my customers, and after a time I decided to pass on the medicine part of the work to the lady herbalist who had my shop while I devoted myself to producing the "luxury" herbs and a few other things like bags of hair tonic herbs for which I had a constant market. This phase is a promising one commercially. . . . The whole industry is delightful and interesting on every side, but it is hard work for an amateur.'

The last words can be endorsed by one who knew the writer from the first, and knew the loving perfection in detail and the high conscientiousness which she brought into her work, together with the strenuous life entailed by the undertaking.

Another of the post-war enterprises has resulted in a very flourishing little industry. This has been built up by Miss Hewer, B.SC., of the Herb Farm, Seal, near Sevenoaks. Her work is in medicinal and culinary herbs as well as in special branches of the 'luxury' trade, in potpourri, bath preparations, preserves, etc. Her little pamphlet is delightfully illustrated with pictures of the farm and the harvesting. The dried herbs she sells at her shop at 16 North Audley

Street, where she has some distinguished patrons. She tells me that last season she supplied one customer with 10,000 chamomile plants, and has a second order for 8,000 more. Many people have small herb gardens, and there seems to be a good demand for fresh plants. Her *potpourris* are a speciality. In her pamphlet she says of them: 'The flowers are grown and dried on the farm, and we have tried to combine the natural odours and the beautiful summer colours in such a way that you can keep a bit of real summer through the winter. We recommend potpourri to those who appreciate the perfume of the rose. "Lady Anne" takes her note from Lemon Verbena; Santal is a warm potpourri in which the glow of marigolds is combined with the refreshing odour of santalwood, while the eighteenth-century potpourri is made from a combination of recipes dated about 1750, and has the lasting spiciness of our great-grandmothers' preparations.'

Miss Hewer also says that in the course of her work in the villages and in the Women's Institutes, etc., she has come into contact with a surprising number of people (other than the gipsies who are noted for their herbal lore) who take the simples and herbal drinks.

But is this really so surprising? There are many things in the changing world that drop away quietly and inevitably so that it becomes only a misplaced sentiment to revive them; but the foundation of this old plant lore belongs to the peasant life that is of all things the most unchanging. In an age when the machine is rapidly displacing labour, when the very land itself is shifting in every direction, and the younger men are being drawn away into the grinding jaws of urbanism, the way of a man with his earth still remain as unaltered as his tools, the spade, the pruning hook and the hoe. They who would study racial characteristics in every country must study him, for he is of all classes the most typical. And they will find that in respect to many practical matters folk-knowledge is not infrequently folk-wisdom.

THE CONTENTS OF THE VEGETABLE CELL

ESSENTIAL OILS; RESINS, ETC

BACTERIA

To sum up in a chapter the immense advances made in chemistry, biology, and physics during the nineteenth century and after, would impossible even if the subject did not lie outside the scope of this essay, but as pharmacy rests entirely upon pharmacology, even our small particular quest of 'the plant in medicine' cannot be finished without some excursion into the specialist's world.

We have seen how, for five thousand years, medicine was thought of as curative, but our present-day science has come more and more to consider it as preventive. A deeper knowledge of physiology has shown us that the body, as a matter of fact, elaborates its own mechanism of protection and even of curative substances. Protoplasm, the basic substance of the tissues, has been defined by Dr. Dixon as 'a system of ferments co-ordinated together'. The action of a drug upon the tissues is not yet entirely understood, but as we watch its effect, we judge that it has an affinity for some of the particles or for the ferments themselves, and that it can hasten or retard the vital processes of growth. But all such speculation is based upon knowledge that is comparatively new; knowledge to which all the natural sciences have contributed.

During the eighteenth century the chief concern of scientific men, especially in Italy, had been with physics. It was Grimaldi who discovered the diffraction of light, and the names of Galvani and Volta became household words long before Marconi.

But towards the end of the century interest in biology was furthered through the work of a group of German and English students. In 1774, a Unitarian minister of Birmingham, Joseph Priestley, in his experiments upon the green plant, showed that by an interchange of gases the 'goodness' was restored to the air after it had been vitiated by the breathing of animals, or in his own more precise terms 'after it had been spoiled by mice'. This fundamental discovery that animal and plant are to a great extent complementary was further expanded by Ingenbourg and De Saussure till the work of the chlorophyll was finally established as the fact upon which terrestrial life ultimately depends. The liberation of oxygen by the chlorophyll under the influence of light was later known as photo-synthesis, and a great deal of work was carried on through the nineteenth century with the green cell as its starting-point. The cell contains numerous discs of an exquisite emerald colour: their protoplasm is in fact impregnated with a complex of green pigments termed chlorophyll. This absorbs part of the light falling on to the leaves, and through the energy thus obtained, the carbon dioxide is assimilated, the oxygen released and the carbon retained. The exudation of oxygen can often be observed, as for instance in the bubbles given off by the cut surface of a plant under water. The carbon dioxide taken in by the leaf when combined with the water in the cell yields a series of carbo-hydrates that begin with glucose and end with starch. This photo-synthesis is most active in direct sunlight when the assimilation carried on in the vegetable cells proceeds at a prodigious rate. In the absence of light or in the night hours it becomes apparent that the plant is respiring; that is, evolving carbon dioxide and absorbing oxygen like an animal. Indeed this respiration is actually taking place all the time, but it is so masked in daytime by the more vigorous process of assimilation as to be negligible. This respiration of plants can easily be measured, but the CO_2 given off by them in the dark has no practical importance.

The other process which is carried on in the dark as well as the light depends upon the root action. The salts such as nitrates, phosphates and sulphates absorbed by the root, form, together with the carbo-hydrates, the material for the synthesis of proteins which in turn form the animals' food.

The universal structure of living things was not known much before 1835. Then it was understood, from the work of Schwann, Virchow, and others, that all living organisms arose from a single — usually a nucleated — cell which gave rise to a cell aggregate. The inherent instability of protoplasm, enabling the primal units to use the electro-magnetic waves of solar radiation, may be said to have given life its first opportunity. Of the parting of the ways for plant and animal we have no definite knowledge, but there are certain microscopic organisms which have been termed 'borderland' because they have some characteristics of both. The differentiation of the plant may be looked upon as closely connected with the origin of chlorophyll and the rounding, limiting cell wall. The cellular structure was, at any rate, primordial; it exists in the lowest forms to-day; and it foreshadowed the plant of the future, self-regulating, balancing, intensely responsive, and incapable of movement. Motility was at first characteristic of both unicellular plants and animals, for the cells rotated by means of a lash or cilium projecting through the cell wall. In fact, the *Ginkgo biloba*, the sacred Ginkgo tree of the Chinese, still preserves in its male reproductive cells the cilia which are reminiscent of the remote evolutionary stage when the male swam to the female. The earliest vegetable cells — of the Algae or the Fungi — are as a rule as rounded in outline as the earth that mothered them and the ancestral sun, while the cell wall is their distinctive feature except among some of the polymorphic bacteria which are nevertheless unicellular plants of a differentiated form.

To the substance of this wall which is secreted from the cell contents, Lindley in 1835 gave the name of cellulose. Schwann had already shown that it was very variable; in the Mallows it was soft and mucilaginous, while it was hard and lignified in the 'vessels' of wood. Sometimes it was so impregnated with mineral matter as to lose its original constitution. The walls grow in thickness by successive layers formed from the inside, and at the same time they may grow in surface so that their volume often increases a hundredfold. The cellulose, whose formula is $C_6H_{10}O_5$, turns blue when treated with iodine and sulphuric acid, and is insoluble in water, ether or dilute acids. Cotton is pure cellulose; and indeed the substance of these cell walls, tough and enduring long after the cell contents have perished, forms the basis of a thousand articles of our civilization.

By 1840 this outline of cell structure had been practically worked out, though many details of the structure remained to be filled in. For instance, the intricate and wonderful arrangement of the nuclear substance, or chromatin, upon which the hereditary transmission depends, was still undeciphered. By 1884 this was also known through the independent researches of Strasburger, Weismann and other morphologists; and in the next decade the physiology of plant life was elucidated by many other workers. For the corresponding advances in pharmacy we must go back to an earlier date.

FORERUNNERS IN PHARMACY

An important sign-post had been set up by Valerius Cordus, the son of a German botanist, in the sixteenth century. Making use of steam distillation, he prepared several of the essential oils like oil of aniseed. It was in his time that the word pharmacy came into general use, derived from the Greek *pharmakon*, a drug, which by the way, had been used indifferently for a remedy, a spell or a poison.

In the seventeenth century the French began to experiment with plants on a different scale, using dry distillation after the plants had been reduced to ash, but beyond the discovery of thymol, this did not carry them very far. The most substantial advance came through pure chemistry, and from the labours of Charles William Scheele, the Swede, in the eighteenth century. He showed that the components of plants must be prepared in the form of chemical individuals, and he obtained for the first time the malic, oxalic, tartaric, and citric acids. He also determined the nature of prussic acid, chlorine and manganese. Scheele is properly regarded as the founder of pharmacology.

After the acids came the bases. Early in the nineteenth century, French and German chemists carried on intensive research, in the first place with opium, finding that the substance isolated was a base capable of forming a salt.[1] This vegetable alkaloid they called morphine. After this, the names of the organic alkaloids were regularly formed in ine; and strychnine, solanine, aconitine and hyoscyamine were all found in the early part of the century. In 1821, Magendie, who was the teacher of Claude Bernard, brought strychnine into medical use.

In his *Elementary Chemistry*, Roscoe says: 'The alkaloids act most powerfully in the animal economy: some such as strychnine, nicotine,

[1] Cf p. 96.

etc., form the most violent poisons with which we are acquainted, whilst others like quinine and morphine act as valuable medicines.'

A little later in the nineteenth century, the technique of distillation was improved with marked results upon the manufacture of perfumes and essences. The modern manufacturer, like the pharmacist, uses several methods in dealing with the plant cells whose products are sensitive to high temperatures. The plants may be dried and powdered, and then distilled with steam, when the resulting oil is separated from the distilled water by a Florentine flask. Any portion of the oil that gets into the water may then be separated by common salt. Or, by another method, the cells may be broken up by maceration and the oil extracted with petroleum or with ether. This is the crude oil, and its essence has to be still further refined for the pharmacist. These processes are highly technical; and often the exact properties of an oil have to be determined by its specific gravity and optical reaction. Similarly with the alkaloids. The work of extraction is long and tedious, and it often happens that two or more alkaloids are mingled in the plant cell and have to be separated. Hydrochloric and sulphuric acids are used in extraction alternatively with chloroform.

This extraction of active substances in drugs without admixtures has been the great work of the nineteenth century, for pure drugs can now be isolated and used without adulteration. Upon this work all modern pharmacology has been based.

OILS OF DISTILLATION

The essential or volatile oils are highly important in pharmacy. They are light, mobile, and easily distilled, but extremely complex in character. They usually contain hydrocarbons known as terpenes of which the commonest is pinene, the main constituent of *Oleum terebinthinae* (turpentine), distilled from the oleo-resin of *Pinus sylvestris* and its oxygenated products. The group formula for all the terpenes is $C_{10}H_{16}$.

Some of the most widely used oils are the following: clove, pimento, allspice, lavender, rosemary, sandalwood, sumbul, garlic, juniper, valerian, eucalyptus, cinnamon, lemon, marjoram, thyme, peppermint, and the group of *Umbelliferae* including dill, fennel, caraway, and asafoetida.

The stearoptenes or constituents which solidify on cooling include menthol, thymol and camphor, which are all oxygenated bodies; but the stearoptene of, for example, rose oil, is a mixture of hydrocarbons.

All the essential oils have a poisonous effect on protoplasm, and being easily absorbed by the blood, are germicidal and anti-fermentatives. They increase the secretions of the mucous membranes, promote digestion, and are slightly stimulative to the brain, spinal cord and circulation. Those that relieve colic (such as oil of marjoram and oil of cloves) are the carminatives.

The volatile or essential oils generally occur in special glands; they may be detected, for instance, in the round translucent dots in the side of an orange. The oils of lemon and some others are so quickly acted on by the air after separation from the plant as to undergo oxidation, when they change their characteristic aroma for one that is less pleasant. Air and light has in these cases to be excluded in the process of distillation. All the essential oils are connected with the scent-bearing constituents of plants. Thus, French lavender oil is judged by its proportion of ethereal salts or 'esters' yielded by the particular variety, and the commercial value of the oil depends upon the esters. The oil drops from the glands of the *Labiatae* and other scented plants are a beautiful sight under the microscope, especially when stained with alkannet, a pink colouring matter obtained from *Anchusa*. If a drop of alcohol be added, they remain *in situ* and are not dissolved, but if warmed and treated with a drop of potash, they disappear. The compounds — or chemical groups of substances — in these essential oils are classified in pharmacy. The important 'camphor group' are oxygenated terpenes or sesquiterpenes. Such terpenes exist in the oils of juniper, eucalyptus, coriander, and many other plants: they are mostly liquid hydrocarbons which can be distilled at the ordinary pressure without undergoing decomposition. Geraniol and menthol belong to the group.

In the benzine group we find safrol, from sassafras; thymol from thyme and other related plants; salicylic acid from the oil of wintergreen and birch: and eugenol from the oil of clove. Some substances, such as cymene, belong to both the benzine and terpene classes.

The 'fixed' oils in the plant world are related to the animal fats. They are glycerine esters of various complex organic acids of the fatty series. Since their function is that of reserve materials, they are most frequently stored in the seeds. Examples are linseed oil, palm kernels, sunflower and hemp.

One of the most extensively used from ancient times is olive oil, *Oleum Olivae*, obtained by expression from the pericarp of the ripe fruit of *Olea Europaea*. It is nutrient, emollient and laxative.

Oleum Ricini (Castor-oil) has ricinoleic acid as its base. It is used internally and externally.

Oleum Tiglii comes from the seeds of *Croton Tiglium*; strongly purgative.

Both the bitter and sweet almonds have a large percentage of fixed oil in their seeds.

THE BALSAMS

These are oleo-resins which contain resin and essential oil.

Oil of bitter almonds contains benzaldehyde; oil of gautheria, methyl salicylate which is the methyl ester both of the wintergreen and the sweet birch. The formula for the artificial oil which is identical with the chief constituents of the natural oil is $C_6H_4(OH)COOCH_3$. The properties are those of an ester and a phenol, and the artificial oil is said to be superior to the natural for the purposes of pharmacy. Balsam of Tolu has twelve per cent of cinnamic acid with benzoic acid. Balsam of Peru has thirty per cent of resin and sixty per cent of volatile oil with benzoic acid.

Benzoinum is the balsamic resin from *Styrax benzoin*. It has forty per cent of cinnamic and benzoic acid. The liquid storax of commerce comes from *Liquidamber orientale*, and is called *Styrax praeparatus*. The storax of Dioscorides and Pliny is said to have been that of *Styrax officinale*. These fragrant resins exude in small white tears, but they, like the tannins, exist in structureless masses in the cell sap. A simple laboratory test for a resin is to take a section of a young ivy stem, when the resin drops will show out clearly, stained with alkannet.

The tannins can be extracted with hot water. They are the astringent substances of the pharmacist, as for instance, oak galls and oak bark.

Crystals, of which the commonest are calcium oxalate, are most characteristic objects in the cell. Single crystals occur in groups in mucilaginous cells and are called raphides. Beautiful prismatic crystals of this character occur in the rhubarb stem, in Cinnamon bark, *Cascara Sagrada*, liquorice root, gentian root and many other plants. Sometimes rosettes are formed of the calcium oxalates as in *Stramonium*. In the belladonna the crystals are so minute as to fill up the cell and give it an opaque appearance. These 'sandy' crystals are very common in the *Solanaceae*. They are easily dissolved out by concentrated sulphuric acid.

THE SUGARS

These important and widely distributed substances fall into two groups. The formula for the one group, the hexoses, is $C_6H_{12}O_6$; for the second group, the disaccharids, it is $C_{12}H_{22}O_{11}$. From the first group we get *glucose*, which is the first sugar to be formed in the process of proto-synthesis, and which is the main 'sweet' constituent in ripe fruits. Sometimes the sugar content of a fruit will be more than 50 per cent of the weight.

Allied sugars of the glucose group are maltose (malt sugar), sucrose (cane sugar), and fructose (levilose). Glucose and fructose are the most common constituents of ripe fruits, but to this there are some exceptions; notably the banana and the pineapple, in which sucrose predominates. Nor are fruits the only sugar-producing organs in the vegetable world, for the enlarged stems ('roots') of the beet, carrot and turnip have storage sugars which are also occasionally present in the sap of trees.

CONTENTS OF VEGETABLE CELL

The levilose found in the Jerusalem artichoke seems likely to bring this homely vegetable into the limelight, as its superlative sweetness has given rise to a suggestion that it might be commercially more valuable than beet. Maltose is formed in the process of melting from the starch of the barley grain. The starch so commonly obtained from tubers like the potato, and from seeds or 'grains' like the wheat or the rice, is chemically a poly-saccharid, and is usually derived from glucose. In the case of the Jerusalem artichoke it is derived from fructose, and called inulin.

Two other constituents of the cell sap are iodine and bromine. The latter was isolated by Ballard in 1826; a poisonous substance with a horrid smell. Its derivatives, the bromides of sodium, potassium, etc., are largely used medicinally.

Iodine exists in many plants, e.g. in the watercress; but is most abundant in coastal species, and particularly in a seaweed known commercially as kelp. It was accidentally found by Courtois while experimenting in the extraction of an alkaloid from the brown seaweed (Fucus). The name was given from the Greek *ion*, Violet. The commercial source at the present day is Chile saltpetre.

GLYCOSIDES

If we left the subject here, as it would once have been left, the transmutation of the plant through pharmacy into medicine would have seemed a relatively simple affair; but now that bio-chemistry has revealed more of the vital actions in the vegetable cell, and has in fact taken us into a world of startling and almost fantastic complexity, one feels bound, in justice to the subject, to give some rough idea of the working.

A passage from Armstrong's book on the *Glycosides* will show how this extension of our knowledge may be regarded:

'The field of plant chemistry is urgently in need of further workers. The possibility of advance in agriculture, in horticulture, in the understanding of life itself, largely depends on exact knowledge in regard to the facts of plant life. In an age of organic synthesis in industry, we cannot know too much of the methods of the plant, the great worker of synthetic miracles. Solar energy, carbon dioxide, a catalyst, and the directive forces of nature daily perform the task of creating the living world.'

The name glycoside, obviously derived from glucose, has been given to a very varied group of substances, many of which can be obtained in crystalline form. Often they have a bitter taste. They are condensation products of a sugar and other substances, and when this sugar is glucose, they are called glucosides. When broken down either by an enzyme or by the action of the acid, the sugar and the other substances can be regenerated. One of the earliest known was amygdalin from the bitter almond which yielded glucose, hydro-cyanic acid, and an aromatic substance, benzaldehyde. Mustard oils result from the breaking down of a glucoside. Sinigrin, present in black mustard, yields glucose, potassium bi-sulphate and allyl isothiocyanate (black mustard oil). Apropos of these chemical interactions, it should be appropriate to mention some experiments extending those formerly undertaken by Sir Jagadis Bose, in which Guignard has shown that an anaesthetic applied to a plant cell brings about an interaction between a glucoside and its corresponding enzyme. For instance, mustard oil has been formed in a Crucifer after the action of chloroform, and hydrogen cyanide is said to have resulted from a similar application to a laurel leaf.

Glucosides are responsible for the blue and red colouring matters of fruits and flowers which yield glucose and the colouring residue called anthocyanidin. In pharmacy, most of the purgative drugs, like aloes, senna, cascara, and rhubarb, are glucosides. The yield varies with the species and with the season of the year. In many cases, notably in the foxglove already mentioned, there are several glucosides associated in one cell.

Dr. Armstrong, in the paragraph quoted, mentioned the word catalyst, by which he meant a ferment or enzyme. Two classes of ferments have been recognized in chemistry: the organized agents of fermentation, such as the yeast which is a member of the Fungi, and unorganized or chemical ferments, such as diastase and a host of others which have been more lately discovered, to which the modern name of enzyme has been given. The first enzyme found by Payer and Persog in 1883 was the disatase of malt, and two years later, von Liebig, working with the amygdalin of the bitter almond, found the enzyme called emulsin. It is by the agency of these enzymes that the plant carries on its work in the plant-animal cycle. It is they which bring about all the fermentative changes, lactic, acetous, putrefactive, etc., in organic compounds. In the interior of the vegetable cells they break down starch into the transmissible glucose, and act upon the glucosides to break them down into sugars and other organic substances. They are part of the wonderful specialization of the vegetable world.

The yeast fungus works by means of several enzymes. This interesting microscopic plant is now being used internally and externally in medicine, while its activities in the brewer's vat are too well known to need comment. It is, however, worth while to watch a bowl of yeast bubbling and dividing under your eyes in order to gain some idea of cellular energy. For these Robots of enzymes that it has harnessed to its work act with incredible speed. One of them, the maltase, converts maltose into glucose; another, invertase, converts sucrose into glucose and fructose (the latter name was given by Béchamp). The third enzyme, zymase, was discovered by Büchner in 1894: it converts the products of the sugars into carbon dioxide and alcohol.

Various moral reflections have been drawn from this exuberant organism. One with an obvious bearing upon temperance, points out that the yeast plant while consuming its sugar in the vat, only forms ten per cent of alcohol. A larger percentage of alcohol would, it is said, be detrimental to the process, alcohol in excess being poisonous to the vegetable cell.

The use of enzymes and other bio-chemical products was furthered by the work of Arrenhius in 1887 which followed that of Graham upon the colloids, a name given to the gelatinous substances into which cell tissue is changed in degeneration. The work of Arrenhius was entirely chemical, but it has proved of great significance in modern pharmacy. Chemistry, in fact, has been more and more applied to the specialized methods of the pharmacist, particularly in the standardization of the alkaloidal contents of a drug, and in the newer methods of biological assay which are now adopted by the chief drug-producing countries.

BACTERIA

These earliest forms of life are often only $\frac{1}{20000}$ of an inch in diameter; and though they resemble the higher microscopic plants in having a flexible limiting layer, this is usually devoid of the characteristic cellulose. They are equally adapted to arctic conditions and to hot springs. They float in enormous quantities in the air, especially in the lower atmosphere, and they swarm in water, in the ocean, and on the ground. Their power of deriving energy — or food — directly from inorganic compounds shows them to be the most elementary of living organisms, and they flourish to-day in the same condition as they must have originated in the lifeless world many millions of years ago. By storing nitrogen they become the earliest food supply of the plants and animals that came after them, but on the other hand they gradually acquired parasitic relations with the rest of the organic world. They performed the indispensable function of remoulding the earth's crust just as they break up and prepare the soil to-day for plant life; but they are also closely associated with the infectious diseases that occur in the lower animals, in many vegetable species, and in the human race.

The story of Pasteur and Béchamp's experiments, and of Tyndall's similar work at the Royal Institution, is now well known. It disposed of the theory that putrefactions and sepsis were the result of agencies which had been spontaneously generated, and it was shown that the infections entered from the air. Contemporaneously Robert Koch made his discovery of the tubercle bacillus, and laid the foundation of bacteriology. The problem of disease was thus simplified, and the way was cleared for the work of Joseph Lister. Before his time the relation between dirt and disease had never been understood, and forty-five per cent of the amputations and other operations in the dreaded hospital wards were followed by death, while gangrene, erysipelas and other horrors were the surgeon's despair. The scornful and ungenerous treatment meted out to Lister by his colleagues is one of the oddest and saddest stories in modern medicine. When finally his carbolic spray was adopted, it led the way to the further development of aseptic treatment, wherein the germs are not killed, but merely prevented from entering a wound by an elaborate system of sterilization.

While bacteriology was going ahead, light was thrown upon the constitution of the blood by researches begun by Metchnikoff, which showed how the white corpuscles (phagocytes) of the blood existed to destroy any malignant body that might get into the blood stream. This natural conflict between the bacilli and the phagocytes is the central theme of the story of infection. The sequel to that story belongs to our own century and is still being written, but, even now, it is one of the most exciting and interesting serials in the world. Pasteur and his colleagues naturally thought of the vegetable cell as the unit of life; they knew naught of 'ultra-microbes', the sub-microscopic organisms or corpuscles which might be only two molecules in size and therefore below the limits of microscopic resolution. But we now know that these 'ultra-microbes' exist, that they, like bacteria, are agents of infection; and that their presence can be detected after being passed through a fine-pored filter which ordinary microbes could not negotiate. These viruses, as they are called in England, may be living units of protoplasm, or merely formless agents belonging to the cells, and constantly renewed by the cell in which they act. That is uncertain, but we do know that, like bacteria, they are connected with infection and immunity. For a long time we have observed that the attack of a certain infectious disease will render the animal or person immune from that sickness for a definite period, through the protecting substance formed in the blood. Now we find that prolonged immunity is also given by a virus attack. Such infections have been carefully worked out. In the vegetable world, they are the cause of what are known as the 'mosaic' diseases, potato streak, strawberry yellow, raspberry streak, rosette of wheat, rosette of peach, the sugar-cane disease, spinach blight, and spotted wilt in tomatoes.

All these infections are very 'catching', especially in the tomato crops. They are also selective. One Abutilon has been found to be susceptible to a virus disease which does not attack an allied species. As to immunity, some interesting results have been accumulated. The dock, *Rumus crispus*, has been made immune from an acute virus attack by an inoculation.

Among animals, a system of protection against distemper has also been evolved through a virus injection, the whole evidence pointing to the formation of an anti-body in the tissue of the host, by which resistance to the invader is mobilized in the ordinary way. Among animals, the fatal foot-and-mouth disease, as well as encephalitis, trench fever, measles and other infections are now traced to the virus.

Nor is this the last word. Beyond it again, on the dim threshold of life, the veil is being lifted on a scene of swarming activity where another invisible army advances upon the bacteriological line. The unit in this encounter can only be defined as a corpuscle which unites with a microbe, multiplies in it and destroys its substance. It is, in fact, the natural enemy of the bacterium and is well named bacteriophage, or devourer of the germ. It is the ally of man, inasmuch as it destroys the malignant organisms that invade the body. Therefore we find at the very beginning of organic life a system tending to maintain the wholeness which belongs to health and automatically resists disease. We see now that a perfectly healthy person is one in whom the controlling centres of thought and will are reinforced by an elaborate physical mechanism of protection. The white blood cell — the phagocyte — and the bacteriophage are twin agents in this system. It will be also realized that the bacteriophage is largely the agent in acquired immunity. Add to these considerations the further fact that disease bacteria are killed in direct sunlight, and are favoured by the 'unnatural' agencies of darkness and dirt, and we then realize that, in relying on the inherent 'will to health', Hippocrates pointed forward.

The thrilling serial of the twentieth century will have in its chapters upon radiation some further unexpected sidelights in regard to the vegetable world; for since the work begun by H. G. Muller in 1927, we have been on the track of mutations under a *beta* radiation, with the result that variations have been obtained, especially among tobacco plants. This is primarily a matter affecting genetics, but even so, the co-ordination of knowledge is going on at such a pace that repercussions from any side are liable to be felt in the world of healing.

Finally, in every country synthetics are now being made. In the modern biochemical laboratory the chemical constituents of the vegetable cell are analysed, and the structural formulae discovered. Then the atoms can be put together so perfectly that the artificial product resembles the original. Only light, the revealer of all things, can detect the difference, for the artificial alkaloids have no effect upon polarized light. The commercial effect of the synthetic work, largely developed by German enterprise, has of course been considerable. To take the most obvious case, the natural product of salicylic acid used to cost twelve guineas a pound, but the artificial now costs only a few shillings.

VITAMINS

The progress of medicine has brought us continually nearer to measures of control based upon nature's own methods, and many diseases have thus been eliminated. There remains one disease group which must be mentioned in relation to our food supply from the vegetable world, and this brings us to the accessory food products called vitamins. The importance of these in a dietary was indirectly discovered by Sir John Pringle and Joseph Lind when in the eighteenth century they set to work among the crews and in the camps where men were dying of scurvy. The disease was no new thing. It had been known to the Roman doctors who advised green vegetables for its cure, but no definite clinical treatment had ever been devised, even in Drake's time when half a crew or more frequently died of it. Pringle and Lind discovered that a supply of lemons and green-stuffs in the food could be relied upon to keep the disease at bay; and after this, preventive measures were more successful. Scurvy at the present day occurs in all races where there is malnutrition, and the modern treatment when babies are affected includes the juice of twenty lemons a day.

The vitamins belong to the green plant, and of their origin no more can at present be said. The name was given by Funk, and in 1912 the work of Sir F. Gowland Hopkins greatly extended our knowledge of their chemical composition and paved the way for the future research which is still being carried on, especially by our own physiological school at Cambridge. It is now possible to define the composition of at least two of the vitamins, A and D, with some degree of certainty. Vitamin A is concerned with the growth and preservation of body tissue. It is seen to resist a temperature of 100 degrees, but is destroyed by oxidation. It is obtained from fresh vegetables and fruits; from cod liver oil, butter, milk, and some animal fats. It is associated with the red colouring matter of many vegetables which is called carotin, a complex hydrocarbon which is now taken for the International standard of Vitamin A. The chemical formula has been worked out as $C_{20}H_{29}OH$.

Vitamin B is the anti-neurotic factor, and the disease of beri-beri has been traced to its absence. Brown bread is rich in this substance. So are many vegetables, seeds, nuts, meat and milk. It is not easily oxidized. The preparation of our cereals, notably the whitening of our bread and the destruction of the outer layer of the rice grain by 'polishing', are two instances where civilization has erred and paid the price. The study of these accessory food products has shown us very plainly how easy it has become to be over-fed and under-nourished. The over-milled cereal and the over-heated food in the tin are both deficient in their normal food content, and it is said that white flour contains only about seventy per cent of the original salts and proteid. The deadly skin disease called pellagra, so often fatal in Egypt and the United States, appears to be a deficiency disease arising from the lack of this vitamin. Its formula of $C_{12}H_{17}N_3OS$ shows it to be a sulphur compound, and it is said to have been obtained from some preparations of yeast. Vitamin C has largely justified Evelyn's enthusiasm over his 'sallets'. It is the anti-scorbutic factor, and is present in many fruits such as oranges, lemons, grape-fruit, tomatoes, grapes, and in most green vegetables, as well as in meat and milk. In 1913 some experiments showed that the juice of the raw swede had a high anti-scurvy value, and the treatment was given to children suffering from infantile scurvy as an alternative to orange juice. It is easily oxidized, and some workers have lately identified it with a derivative of glucose to which the name of 'hexuronic acid' has been given.

Vitamin D is concerned in the wonderful discoveries relating to irradiated food. It is the anti-rachitic factor, stable both to heat and oxidation. The success of English physicists in obtaining this vitamin from irradiated ergosterol was reported by the Medical Research Council in 1922, and since then the two powerful anti-rachitic substances, phytosterol and radiostorol have been given in vitamin D deficiency and in general spasmophilia. The vitamin exists in peas, beans and vegetable oils, but many other substances such as dried milk and wheat flour can be made to develop anti-rachitic properties by exposure to sunlight or the Mercury arc lamp. This irradiation of food to obtain the equivalents of vitamin D is a discovery of great importance to the community, and it is being recognized that underfeeding is a social problem, while in many cases sunlight is more important than diet. In the sunny climate of Siam it is said that rickets are unknown. Experiments are being made with irradiated food, especially in regard to the milk supply. We have found for instance that the yeast plant is richer in its vitamin content after irradiation by direct sunlight, and that when given to cows in minute quantities it increased the richness of the milk. Again, the Norwegian cod has long been esteemed as a source of the cod liver oil which is so valuable in deficiency diseases, and it is said that the green plankton (the sea food upon which the fish feed) is particularly abundant round the Norwegian coast. The indispensable health factor in the food-stuffs is incredibly small, only a millionth part of the whole; yet civilized man has undoubtedly erred through ignorance by removing it from natural foods in the process of manufacture.

Some of the European nations have been more intelligent than others in the matter of their food. The English have travelled farther away from the old country lore than their Gallic neighbours who have long cultivated salads unknown in this country. Or they may have been forgotten, for there is an allusion to their use in Chaucer, where he speaks of people 'gadering Pleasaunt Salades which they made hem eat For to refresh their great unkindly heat'.

The use of salads, however, received an enthusiastic advertisement from John Evelyn in 1680. He returned to England after a visit to the Continent, so enthused with the foreign 'sallets' that he took up the subject with the exuberance of a cult. He buttonholed the King's gardener and tried to make him grow about seventy new vegetables, but Mr. London, the principal gardener, and other gentlemen, ultimately persuaded him that thirty-five sallets were enough for an ordinary table. After that (in 1699) Evelyn published his *Acetaria, a book about sallets*, in which he called the world to return to their 'Pristine Diet', or at least 'to a much more wholesome and temperate diet than was then in fashion'. By a salad he meant an uncooked vegetable, and in the *Acetaria* he gave a careful list of plants which could be grown for every month in the year. Nor need all the herbs be cultivated, for 'the hedges would afford a sallet, not unagreeable', which could be seasoned with vinegar, oil, etc. In the first rank he placed the lettuce, as the Romans had done many centuries earlier. Finally, he gave a recipe for a salad-dressing which is worthy to be transcribed:

'Good olive oil, three parts, sharpest vinegar, lemon, or orange juice one part, in which steep some slices of horse-radish with a little salt: add as much mustard as will lie upon a half-crown piece, beat and mingle all these thoroughly together, then add the yolks of two fresh eggs hard-boiled and well-mashed.'

The bio-chemistry of the vitamins is, as we have said, engaging the attention of scientists not only in Cambridge but all over the world, and although at present their therapeutical action cannot be precisely deduced from their chemical elements, yet in the near future this probably will be done, with the result that more light will be shed upon various problems in dietetics.

Through 5000 years we have seen the plant used — and misused — in the service of man. Now in an age which has perfected its appliances for research we have studied the vegetable cell and its activities until the chromosomes and finally the genes have brought the study of creative evolution within the bounds of an exact science. On the other hand, many physicists have begun to regard matter itself as disappearing in a spate of radiations. In every direction science is changing our ideas about the world, and will one day transform the whole quality of life if we can only guard against its misapplication.

That medicine must in many directions be affected by future scientific advances is inevitable, and indeed one strong hope of the race, which is always dragging its lengthening chain of heredity, lies within the ever-enlarging field of radiation which may one day finally conquer disease. Yet this is not to say that the role of the plant as healer will even then be entirely superseded, nor is it even certain that synthetic medicine is destined to be the last word. This subject is occasionally debated among scientists. Only a few years ago, Dr. Grier of Manchester quoted the German chemist, Tschirch, to the effect that 'the use of combinations such as narcophine and omnopen and of the combined *Cinchona* alkaloids in malaria seem to indicate that the active principles of plants in their natural combinations are more efficacious than when isolated'.

The slogan of 'back to the plant' is not impossible. But in any case, even though we shall probably need it less for our food and our healing, never in the nature of things can the race outgrow its ultimate dependence upon the vegetable kingdom. If we were to add 'the plant' to the vision of Menander in 342 B.C., the words might well hold good for both present and future:

> 'I hold him happiest
> Who, before going quickly whence he came,
> Hath looked ungrieving on those majesties —
> The world wide sun, waters and clouds
> And fire. Live Parmeno, a hundred years
> Or a few weeks, these thou wilt always see,
> And never, never, any greater thing.'

APPENDIX

PLANTS OF THE INDIAN MATERIA MEDICA

INDIAN DRUG PLANTS

Alstonia scholaris, R. Br. (*Apocynaceae*), Dita Bark, used as a substitute for *Cinchona* Bark in malaria.

Arachis hypogaea, Linn. (*Leguminosae*), Ground Nut or Pea Nut; yields fixed oil resembling olive oil. Official in B.P. Cultivated in many tropical countries, including India, the chief British source being Gambia. Native of Brazil.

Berberis aristata, DC. (*Berberidaceae*), and allied species containing berberine. Stem used as bitter tonic.

Butea frondosa, Roxb. (*Leguminosae*), yields a resin, Bengal Kino, or Butea Gum, used as an astringent.

Swertia Chirata, Ham. (*Gentianaceae*), Chiretta, used as a substitute for Gentian.

Anamirta Cocculus, W. & A. (*Menispermaceae*), Levant Berries. Contains a very poisonous substance called picrotoxin.

Croton Tiglium, Linn. (*Euphorbiaceae*), yields a fixed oil, Croton Oil, which is a violent cathartic and vesicant.

Caesalpinia Bonducella, Flem. (*Leguminosae*), Nicker Nut. Esteemed in native medicine, but of doubtful utility.

Hemidesmus indicus, R. Br. (*Asclepiadaceae*), Indian Sarsaparilla, used as a blood-purifier.

Ipomoea hederacea, Jacq. (*Convolvulaceae*), Kalandana or Pharbitis Seeds. Resembles Jalap in action.

Podophyllum Emodi, Wall (*Berberidaceae*), Indian Podophyllum, contains a resin similar to that present in American Podophyllum, but, it is said, in greater amount and of a more active character. Official in B.P. as a cathartic.

Piper nigrum, Linn. (*Piperaceae*), Pepper. *Piper longum*, Linn.; Indian Long Pepper; *Piper Betel*, Linn., Betel Leaf. See *Spices and Condiments*, H. S. Redgrove. The last species is cultivated in India, but is not indigenous.

APPENDIX

Picrorhiza Kurroa, Royle (*Scrophulariaceae*), Kitki, used as a bitter.

Ricinus communis, Linn. (*Euphorbiaceae*), Castor Oil Plant. The oil is expressed from the seeds, and is much employed as a purgative. At one time India was the chief source of supply, but the plant is now widely cultivated in tropical and sub-tropical countries. The oil is official in the B.P.

Saussurea Lappa, Clarke (*Compositae*), Costus or Koot. Used mainly as a perfume, but has been found useful for relief of asthma.

Santalum album, Linn. (*Santalaceae*), source of sandalwood oil, an essential oil much used in perfumery. Also employed in medicine as disinfectant of the urinary passages. Official in B.P.

Urginea indica, Kunth. (*Liliaceae*), Indian Squill, resembles Squill.

Zingiber officinale, Rosc. (*Zingiberaceae*), Ginger. Possibly native. Cultivated in India, Sierra Leone, Jamaica, etc. The Jamaica variety is that official in the B.P.

Elletaria Cardamomum, Maton var. *minuscula*, Rurkill (*Zingiberaceae*), Cardamom. See *Spices and Condiments* (H. S. Redgrove). Official in B.P.

Abroma augusta, Linn. (*Sterculiaceae*), Devil's Cotton, uterine astringent, used in native medicine.

Abrus precatorius, Linn. (*Leguminosae*), Jaquerity seeds. Used in native medicine, but very dangerous, owing to presence of abrin, a violent poison. Roots used as (poor) liquorice substitute. Grown in many tropical countries. The scarlet seeds are used in necklaces.

Carum copticum, Bth. & Hk. (*Umbelliferae*), Ajowan seed, source of natural thymol, antiseptic.

Peucedanum Sowa, Kurz. (*Umbelliferae*), Indian Dill.

Adhatoda Vasica, Nees. (*Acanthaceae*), expectorant, insecticide.

Aegle Marmelos, Corr. (*Rutaceae*), Bael fruit, demulcent.

Allium sativum, Linn. (*Liliaceae*), Garlic. Probably not indigenous but much cultivated in India as well as in many other countries.

Andrographis paniculata, Nees. (*Acanthaceae*), Kreat, bitter tonic and stomachic.

Antiaris toxicaria, Lesch. (*Moraceae*), Upas Tree, very poisonous,

APPENDIX

but seeds are sometimes used in native medicines as a febrifuge. Medicinal properties worthy of further investigation.

Areca Catechu, Linn. (*Palmae*), Betel or Areca Nut. Cultivated in India and other tropical countries.

Bassia latifolia, Roxb., and *B. lingifolia*, Linn. (*Sapotaceae*), astringents used in native medicine; flowers used for manufacture of power alcohol.

Boerhäavia repens, Linn. (*Nyctaginaceae*), contains an alkaloid, punarvine and salts of potassium. Promotes diuresis.

Coptis Teeta, Wall. (*Ranunculaceae*), Mishmee Gold Thread, a bitter tonic containing berberine.

Euphorbia pilulifera, Linn. (*Euphorbiaceae*), Queensland Asthma Herb grown in India and other tropical countries, and is locally used in treatment of asthma.

Hedyotis Auricularia, Linn. (*Rubiaceae*), popularly used for treatment of dysentery, etc. Utility doubtful.

Mallotus philippinensis, Muell. Arg. (*Euphorbiaceae*), Kamala, vermifuge.

Melia Azadirachta, Linn. (*Meliaceae*), Neem or Margosa. The bark is used as a simple bitter. It is locally reputed to be a remedy for skin affections, and various parts of the plant are used in native medicine. The oil is used commercially for lighting.

Moringa oleifera, Lam. (*Moringaceae*), Horseradish Tree. A native panacea. Roots used as a condiment. A source of Ben oil.

Pongamia glabra, Vent. (*Leguminosae*), Thinwin, seeds used locally as a cough cure, and oil for skin diseases.

Rauwolfia serpentina, Benth. (*Apocyanaceae*), sedative, also a reputed remedy for snake-bite.

Saraca indica, Linn. (*Leguminosae*), Asoka-tree, one of the sacred trees of the Hindus, used in native medicine as an astringent and uterine sedative, but of little if any value.

Sida cordifolia, Linn. (*Malvaceae*), much valued in the ancient Hindu medical system. Contains ephedrine, but only in small amount.

Synplocus racemosa, Roxb. (*Styraceae*), Lodh Bark, used locally as an astringent.

APPENDIX

Hydnocarpus Wightiana, Blume (*Flacourtiaceae*). The seeds contain a fixed oil, Hydnocarpus Oil, which is used as a specific in the treatment of leprosy. Chaulmoogra oil from *Taraktogenos Kurzii*, King. (*Flacourtiaceae*), is similar, and has been used in Hindu medicine for centuries.

Vernonia anthelmintica, Willd. (*Compositae*), Bukchie, anthelmintic.

Aconitum (*Ranunculaceae*). A number of species of this highly critical genus are native to India, some of which are non-poisonous while others contain active alkaloids and are used locally as drugs. *A. Napellus*, Linn., whose roots are official in the B.P., does not occur in India, though some of the indigenous species are very near to it.

Artemisia maritima, Linn. (*Compositae*), anthelmintic, containing santonin. At the moment, the chief source of this important drug is *A. Cina*, Berg., but the possibility of utilizing the English and Indian *A. maritima* is being investigated.

Curcuma longa, Linn. Turmeric, is cultivated in India and may be native, though more probably the plant came originally from Cochin China.

Grasses (*Graminaceae*) yielding fragrant essential oils used mainly in perfumery (see *Scent and All About It*, by H. S. Redgrove). *Cymbopogon Flexuosus*, Stapf. (Cochin or Malabar grass), as well as *C. citratus*, Stapf. (cultivated in Ceylon and elsewhere in the tropics), yield Lemongrass Oil, locally used in rheumatism. *C. Martini*, Stapf., or Rusa, exists in two forms, of which motia yields palmrose oil and sofia (which is inferior), ginger grass oil.

C. Nardus, Rendle, and *C. Winterianus*, Jowitt, yield citronella oil. These are not Indian grasses, but are included for sake of completeness. The first is grown in Ceylon, the second in Java. *Vetiveria zizanioides*, Nash, Khus-khus yields vetiver oil.

Hydrocotyle asiatica, Linn. (*Umbelliferae*), Asiatic Pennywort, in long repute locally as an alterative, stimulant and tonic.

Datura metel and *D. Fastuosa* (*Atropaceae*) are used in asthma.

Myrica cerifera, the bayberry (*Myricaceae*), is used as a tonic and rubefacient. Its root bark, together with a little cayenne, ginger, hemlock and clove, forms the 'composition powder', frequently given in dysentery and chills.

Jylophora asthmatica, Wight and Arn. (*Asclepiadeceae*), Indian ipecacuanha; diaphoretic and expectorant.

Strychnos Ignatii, Bergino. Used in native practice like *S. Nux-vomica*. Called St. Ignatius' beans.

Acorus calamus, Linn. (*Acoraceae*). A very old remedy for intermittent fever in the East, formerly used in England for ague.

Diospyros Embryopteris, Pers., and *D. Lotus* are remedies used from the time of Theophrastus for chronic dysentery and diarrhoea, O'Shaughnessy mentions them in his *Bengal Dispensary*.

Valerian Wallichii, de C., has long been official in India as a stimulant and anti-spasmodic.

Ocymum basilicum, Linn. (*Labiatae*). Sweet Basil, a plant revered in ancient tradition. It was sacred to Krishna and Vishnu, and it used to be said that every Hindu slept with a Basil leaf on his breast. It has the same mildly stimulating properties as its allied species, and has always been used in Indian medicine.

INDEX

INDEX

INDEX

INDEX

INDEX

INDEX

A CATALOGUE OF
SELECTED DOVER BOOKS
IN ALL FIELDS OF INTEREST

A CATALOGUE OF SELECTED DOVER
BOOKS IN ALL FIELDS OF INTEREST

RACKHAM'S COLOR ILLUSTRATIONS FOR WAGNER'S RING. Rackham's finest mature work—all 64 full-color watercolors in a faithful and lush interpretation of the *Ring*. Full-sized plates on coated stock of the paintings used by opera companies for authentic staging of Wagner. Captions aid in following complete Ring cycle. Introduction. 64 illustrations plus vignettes. 72pp. 8⅝ x 11¼. 23779-6 Pa. $6.00

CONTEMPORARY POLISH POSTERS IN FULL COLOR, edited by Joseph Czestochowski. 46 full-color examples of brilliant school of Polish graphic design, selected from world's first museum (near Warsaw) dedicated to poster art. Posters on circuses, films, plays, concerts all show cosmopolitan influences, free imagination. Introduction. 48pp. 9⅜ x 12¼. 23780-X Pa. $6.00

GRAPHIC WORKS OF EDVARD MUNCH, Edvard Munch. 90 haunting, evocative prints by first major Expressionist artist and one of the greatest graphic artists of his time: *The Scream, Anxiety, Death Chamber, The Kiss, Madonna,* etc. Introduction by Alfred Werner. 90pp. 9 x 12. 23765-6 Pa. $5.00

THE GOLDEN AGE OF THE POSTER, Hayward and Blanche Cirker. 70 extraordinary posters in full colors, from Maitres de l'Affiche, Mucha, Lautrec, Bradley, Cheret, Beardsley, many others. Total of 78pp. 9⅜ x 12¼. 22753-7 Pa. $5.95

THE NOTEBOOKS OF LEONARDO DA VINCI, edited by J. P. Richter. Extracts from manuscripts reveal great genius; on painting, sculpture, anatomy, sciences, geography, etc. Both Italian and English. 186 ms. pages reproduced, plus 500 additional drawings, including studies for *Last Supper*, Sforza monument, etc. 860pp. 7⅞ x 10¾. (Available in U.S. only) 22572-0, 22573-9 Pa., Two-vol. set $15.90

THE CODEX NUTTALL, as first edited by Zelia Nuttall. Only inexpensive edition, in full color, of a pre-Columbian Mexican (Mixtec) book. 88 color plates show kings, gods, heroes, temples, sacrifices. New explanatory, historical introduction by Arthur G. Miller. 96pp. 11⅜ x 8½. (Available in U.S. only) 23168-2 Pa. $7.95

UNE SEMAINE DE BONTÉ, A SURREALISTIC NOVEL IN COLLAGE, Max Ernst. Masterpiece created out of 19th-century periodical illustrations, explores worlds of terror and surprise. Some consider this Ernst's greatest work. 208pp. 8⅛ x 11. 23252-2 Pa. $5.00

DRAWINGS OF WILLIAM BLAKE, William Blake. 92 plates from Book of Job, *Divine Comedy, Paradise Lost,* visionary heads, mythological figures, Laocoon, etc. Selection, introduction, commentary by Sir Geoffrey Keynes. 178pp. 8⅛ x 11.   22303-5 Pa. $4.00

ENGRAVINGS OF HOGARTH, William Hogarth. 101 of Hogarth's greatest works: *Rake's Progress, Harlot's Progress, Illustrations for Hudibras, Before and After, Beer Street and Gin Lane,* many more. Full commentary. 256pp. 11 x 13¾.   22479-1 Pa. $12.95

DAUMIER: 120 GREAT LITHOGRAPHS, Honore Daumier. Wide-ranging collection of lithographs by the greatest caricaturist of the 19th century. Concentrates on eternally popular series on lawyers, on married life, on liberated women, etc. Selection, introduction, and notes on plates by Charles F. Ramus. Total of 158pp. 9⅜ x 12¼.   23512-2 Pa. $5.50

DRAWINGS OF MUCHA, Alphonse Maria Mucha. Work reveals drafts-man of highest caliber: studies for famous posters and paintings, render-ings for book illustrations and ads, etc. 70 works, 9 in color; including 6 items not drawings. Introduction. List of illustrations. 72pp. 9⅜ x 12¼. (Available in U.S. only)   23672-2 Pa. $4.00

GIOVANNI BATTISTA PIRANESI: DRAWINGS IN THE PIERPONT MORGAN LIBRARY, Giovanni Battista Piranesi. For first time ever all of Morgan Library's collection, world's largest. 167 illustrations of rare Piranesi drawings—archeological, architectural, decorative and visionary. Essay, detailed list of drawings, chronology, captions. Edited by Felice Stampfle. 144pp. 9⅜ x 12¼.   23714-1 Pa. $7.50

NEW YORK ETCHINGS (1905-1949), John Sloan. All of important American artist's N.Y. life etchings. 67 works include some of his best art; also lively historical record—Greenwich Village, tenement scenes. Edited by Sloan's widow. Introduction and captions. 79pp. 8⅜ x 11¼.   23651-X Pa. $4.00

CHINESE PAINTING AND CALLIGRAPHY: A PICTORIAL SURVEY, Wan-go Weng. 69 fine examples from John M. Crawford's matchless private collection: landscapes, birds, flowers, human figures, etc., plus calligraphy. Every basic form included: hanging scrolls, handscrolls, album leaves, fans, etc. 109 illustrations. Introduction. Captions. 192pp. 8⅞ x 11¾.   23707-9 Pa. $7.95

DRAWINGS OF REMBRANDT, edited by Seymour Slive. Updated Lipp-mann, Hofstede de Groot edition, with definitive scholarly apparatus. All portraits, biblical sketches, landscapes, nudes, Oriental figures, classical studies, together with selection of work by followers. 550 illustrations. Total of 630pp. 9⅛ x 12¼.   21485-0, 21486-9 Pa., Two-vol. set $15.00

THE DISASTERS OF WAR, Francisco Goya. 83 etchings record horrors of Napoleonic wars in Spain and war in general. Reprint of 1st edition, plus 3 additional plates. Introduction by Philip Hofer. 97pp. 9⅜ x 8¼.   21872-4 Pa. $3.75

THE EARLY WORK OF AUBREY BEARDSLEY, Aubrey Beardsley. 157 plates, 2 in color: *Manon Lescaut, Madame Bovary, Morte Darthur, Salome,* other. Introduction by H. Marillier. 182pp. 8⅛ x 11. 21816-3 Pa. $4.50

THE LATER WORK OF AUBREY BEARDSLEY, Aubrey Beardsley. Exotic masterpieces of full maturity: *Venus and Tannhauser, Lysistrata, Rape of the Lock, Volpone,* Savoy material, etc. 174 plates, 2 in color. 186pp. 8⅛ x 11. 21817-1 Pa. $4.50

THOMAS NAST'S CHRISTMAS DRAWINGS, Thomas Nast. Almost all Christmas drawings by creator of image of Santa Claus as we know it, and one of America's foremost illustrators and political cartoonists. 66 illustrations. 3 illustrations in color on covers. 96pp. 8⅜ x 11¼. 23660-9 Pa. $3.50

THE DORÉ ILLUSTRATIONS FOR DANTE'S DIVINE COMEDY, Gustave Doré. All 135 plates from Inferno, Purgatory, Paradise; fantastic tortures, infernal landscapes, celestial wonders. Each plate with appropriate (translated) verses. 141pp. 9 x 12. 23231-X Pa. $4.50

DORÉ'S ILLUSTRATIONS FOR RABELAIS, Gustave Doré. 252 striking illustrations of *Gargantua and Pantagruel* books by foremost 19th-century illustrator. Including 60 plates, 192 delightful smaller illustrations. 153pp. 9 x 12. 23656-0 Pa. $5.00

LONDON: A PILGRIMAGE, Gustave Doré, Blanchard Jerrold. Squalor, riches, misery, beauty of mid-Victorian metropolis; 55 wonderful plates, 125 other illustrations, full social, cultural text by Jerrold. 191pp. of text. 9⅜ x 12¼. 22306-X Pa. $7.00

THE RIME OF THE ANCIENT MARINER, Gustave Doré, S. T. Coleridge. Dore's finest work, 34 plates capture moods, subtleties of poem. Full text. Introduction by Millicent Rose. 77pp. 9¼ x 12. 22305-1 Pa. $3.50

THE DORE BIBLE ILLUSTRATIONS, Gustave Doré. All wonderful, detailed plates: Adam and Eve, Flood, Babylon, Life of Jesus, etc. Brief King James text with each plate. Introduction by Millicent Rose. 241 plates. 241pp. 9 x 12. 23004-X Pa. $6.00

THE COMPLETE ENGRAVINGS, ETCHINGS AND DRYPOINTS OF ALBRECHT DURER. "Knight, Death and Devil"; "Melencolia," and more—all Dürer's known works in all three media, including 6 works formerly attributed to him. 120 plates. 235pp. 8⅜ x 11¼. 22851-7 Pa. $6.50

MAXIMILIAN'S TRIUMPHAL ARCH, Albrecht Dürer and others. Incredible monument of woodcut art: 8 foot high elaborate arch—heraldic figures, humans, battle scenes, fantastic elements—that you can assemble yourself. Printed on one side, layout for assembly. 143pp. 11 x 16. 21451-6 Pa. $5.00

THE COMPLETE WOODCUTS OF ALBRECHT DURER, edited by Dr. W. Kurth. 346 in all: "Old Testament," "St. Jerome," "Passion," "Life of Virgin," Apocalypse," many others. Introduction by Campbell Dodgson. 285pp. 8½ x 12¼. 21097-9 Pa. $7.50

DRAWINGS OF ALBRECHT DURER, edited by Heinrich Wolfflin. 81 plates show development from youth to full style. Many favorites; many new. Introduction by Alfred Werner. 96pp. 8⅛ x 11. 22352-3 Pa. $5.00

THE HUMAN FIGURE, Albrecht Dürer. Experiments in various techniques—stereometric, progressive proportional, and others. Also life studies that rank among finest ever done. Complete reprinting of *Dresden Sketchbook*. 170 plates. 355pp. 8⅜ x 11¼. 21042-1 Pa. $7.95

OF THE JUST SHAPING OF LETTERS, Albrecht Dürer. Renaissance artist explains design of Roman majuscules by geometry, also Gothic lower and capitals. Grolier Club edition. 43pp. 7⅞ x 10¾ 21306-4 Pa. $3.00

TEN BOOKS ON ARCHITECTURE, Vitruvius. The most important book ever written on architecture. Early Roman aesthetics, technology, classical orders, site selection, all other aspects. Stands behind everything since. Morgan translation. 331pp. 5⅜ x 8½. 20645-9 Pa. $4.50

THE FOUR BOOKS OF ARCHITECTURE, Andrea Palladio. 16th-century classic responsible for Palladian movement and style. Covers classical architectural remains, Renaissance revivals, classical orders, etc. 1738 Ware English edition. Introduction by A. Placzek. 216 plates. 110pp. of text. 9½ x 12¾. 21308-0 Pa. $10.00

HORIZONS, Norman Bel Geddes. Great industrialist stage designer, "father of streamlining," on application of aesthetics to transportation, amusement, architecture, etc. 1932 prophetic account; function, theory, specific projects. 222 illustrations. 312pp. 7⅞ x 10¾. 23514-9 Pa. $6.95

FRANK LLOYD WRIGHT'S FALLINGWATER, Donald Hoffmann. Full, illustrated story of conception and building of Wright's masterwork at Bear Run, Pa. 100 photographs of site, construction, and details of completed structure. 112pp. 9¼ x 10. 23671-4 Pa. $5.50

THE ELEMENTS OF DRAWING, John Ruskin. Timeless classic by great Viltorian; starts with basic ideas, works through more difficult. Many practical exercises. 48 illustrations. Introduction by Lawrence Campbell. 228pp. 5⅜ x 8½. 22730-8 Pa. $3.75

GIST OF ART, John Sloan. Greatest modern American teacher, Art Students League, offers innumerable hints, instructions, guided comments to help you in painting. Not a formal course. 46 illustrations. Introduction by Helen Sloan. 200pp. 5⅜ x 8½. 23435-5 Pa. $4.00

THE ANATOMY OF THE HORSE, George Stubbs. Often considered the great masterpiece of animal anatomy. Full reproduction of 1766 edition, plus prospectus; original text and modernized text. 36 plates. Introduction by Eleanor Garvey. 121pp. 11 x 14¾. 23402-9 Pa. $6.00

BRIDGMAN'S LIFE DRAWING, George B. Bridgman. More than 500 illustrative drawings and text teach you to abstract the body into its major masses, use light and shade, proportion; as well as specific areas of anatomy, of which Bridgman is master. 192pp. 6½ x 9¼. (Available in U.S. only) 22710-3 Pa. $3.50

ART NOUVEAU DESIGNS IN COLOR, Alphonse Mucha, Maurice Verneuil, Georges Auriol. Full-color reproduction of *Combinaisons ornementales* (c. 1900) by Art Nouveau masters. Floral, animal, geometric, interlacings, swashes—borders, frames, spots—all incredibly beautiful. 60 plates, hundreds of designs. 9⅜ x 8-1/16. 22885-1 Pa. $4.00

FULL-COLOR FLORAL DESIGNS IN THE ART NOUVEAU STYLE, E. A. Seguy. 166 motifs, on 40 plates, from *Les fleurs et leurs applications decoratives* (1902): borders, circular designs, repeats, allovers, "spots." All in authentic Art Nouveau colors. 48pp. 9⅜ x 12¼.
23439-8 Pa. $5.00

A DIDEROT PICTORIAL ENCYCLOPEDIA OF TRADES AND IN-DUSTRY, edited by Charles C. Gillispie. 485 most interesting plates from the great French Encyclopedia of the 18th century show hundreds of working figures, artifacts, process, land and cityscapes; glassmaking, papermaking, metal extraction, construction, weaving, making furniture, clothing, wigs, dozens of other activities. Plates fully explained. 920pp. 9 x 12.
22284-5, 22285-3 Clothbd., Two-vol. set $40.00

HANDBOOK OF EARLY ADVERTISING ART, Clarence P. Hornung. Largest collection of copyright-free early and antique advertising art ever compiled. Over 6,000 illustrations, from Franklin's time to the 1890's for special effects, novelty. Valuable source, almost inexhaustible.
Pictorial Volume. Agriculture, the zodiac, animals, autos, birds, Christmas, fire engines, flowers, trees, musical instruments, ships, games and sports, much more. Arranged by subject matter and use. 237 plates. 288pp. 9 x 12.
20122-8 Clothbd. $14..50

Typographical Volume. Roman and Gothic faces ranging from 10 point to 300 point, "Barnum," German and Old English faces, script, logotypes, scrolls and flourishes, 1115 ornamental initials, 67 complete alphabets, more. 310 plates. 320pp. 9 x 12. 20123-6 Clothbd. $15.00

CALLIGRAPHY (CALLIGRAPHIA LATINA), J. G. Schwandner. High point of 18th-century ornamental calligraphy. Very ornate initials, scrolls, borders, cherubs, birds, lettered examples. 172pp. 9 x 13.
20475-8 Pa. $7.00

ART FORMS IN NATURE, Ernst Haeckel. Multitude of strangely beautiful natural forms: Radiolaria, Foraminifera, jellyfishes, fungi, turtles, bats, etc. All 100 plates of the 19th-century evolutionist's *Kunstformen der Natur* (1904). 100pp. 9⅜ x 12¼. 22987-4 Pa. $5.00

CHILDREN: A PICTORIAL ARCHIVE FROM NINETEENTH-CENTURY SOURCES, edited by Carol Belanger Grafton. 242 rare, copyright-free wood engravings for artists and designers. Widest such selection available. All illustrations in line. 119pp. 8⅜ x 11¼.
23694-3 Pa. $3.50

WOMEN: A PICTORIAL ARCHIVE FROM NINETEENTH-CENTURY SOURCES, edited by Jim Harter. 391 copyright-free wood engravings for artists and designers selected from rare periodicals. Most extensive such collection available. All illustrations in line. 128pp. 9 x 12.
23703-6 Pa. $4.50

ARABIC ART IN COLOR, Prisse d'Avennes. From the greatest ornamentalists of all time—50 plates in color, rarely seen outside the Near East, rich in suggestion and stimulus. Includes 4 plates on covers. 46pp. 9⅜ x 12¼. 23658-7 Pa. $6.00

AUTHENTIC ALGERIAN CARPET DESIGNS AND MOTIFS, edited by June Beveridge. Algerian carpets are world famous. Dozens of geometrical motifs are charted on grids, color-coded, for weavers, needleworkers, craftsmen, designers. 53 illustrations plus 4 in color. 48pp. 8¼ x 11. (Available in U.S. only) 23650-1 Pa. $1.75

DICTIONARY OF AMERICAN PORTRAITS, edited by Hayward and Blanche Cirker. 4000 important Americans, earliest times to 1905, mostly in clear line. Politicians, writers, soldiers, scientists, inventors, industrialists, Indians, Blacks, women, outlaws, etc. Identificatory information. 756pp. 9¼ x 12¾. 21823-6 Clothbd. $40.00

HOW THE OTHER HALF LIVES, Jacob A. Riis. Journalistic record of filth, degradation, upward drive in New York immigrant slums, shops, around 1900. New edition includes 100 original Riis photos, monuments of early photography. 233pp. 10 x 7⅞. 22012-5 Pa. $7.00

NEW YORK IN THE THIRTIES, Berenice Abbott. Noted photographer's fascinating study of city shows new buildings that have become famous and old sights that have disappeared forever. Insightful commentary. 97 photographs. 97pp. 11⅜ x 10. 22967-X Pa. $5.00

MEN AT WORK, Lewis W. Hine. Famous photographic studies of construction workers, railroad men, factory workers and coal miners. New supplement of 18 photos on Empire State building construction. New introduction by Jonathan L. Doherty. Total of 69 photos. 63pp. 8 x 10¾. 23475-4 Pa. $3.00

THE DEPRESSION YEARS AS PHOTOGRAPHED BY ARTHUR ROTH-STEIN, Arthur Rothstein. First collection devoted entirely to the work of outstanding 1930s photographer: famous dust storm photo, ragged children, unemployed, etc. 120 photographs. Captions. 119pp. 9¼ x 10¾.
23590-4 Pa. $5.00

CAMERA WORK: A PICTORIAL GUIDE, Alfred Stieglitz. All 559 illustrations and plates from the most important periodical in the history of art photography, Camera Work (1903-17). Presented four to a page, reduced in size but still clear, in strict chronological order, with complete captions. Three indexes. Glossary. Bibliography. 176pp. 8⅜ x 11¼.
23591-2 Pa. $6.95

ALVIN LANGDON COBURN, PHOTOGRAPHER, Alvin L. Coburn. Revealing autobiography by one of greatest photographers of 20th century gives insider's version of Photo-Secession, plus comments on his own work. 77 photographs by Coburn. Edited by Helmut and Alison Gernsheim. 160pp. 8⅛ x 11.
23685-4 Pa. $6.00

NEW YORK IN THE FORTIES, Andreas Feininger. 162 brilliant photographs by the well-known photographer, formerly with Life magazine, show commuters, shoppers, Times Square at night, Harlem nightclub, Lower East Side, etc. Introduction and full captions by John von Hartz. 181pp. 9¼ x 10¾.
23585-8 Pa. $6.00

GREAT NEWS PHOTOS AND THE STORIES BEHIND THEM, John Faber. Dramatic volume of 140 great news photos, 1855 through 1976, and revealing stories behind them, with both historical and technical information. Hindenburg disaster, shooting of Oswald, nomination of Jimmy Carter, etc. 160pp. 8¼ x 11.
23667-6 Pa. $5.00

THE ART OF THE CINEMATOGRAPHER, Leonard Maltin. Survey of American cinematography history and anecdotal interviews with 5 masters—Arthur Miller, Hal Mohr, Hal Rosson, Lucien Ballard, and Conrad Hall. Very large selection of behind-the-scenes production photos. 105 photographs. Filmographies. Index. Originally Behind the Camera. 144pp. 8¼ x 11.
23686-2 Pa. $5.00

DESIGNS FOR THE THREE-CORNERED HAT (LE TRICORNE), Pablo Picasso. 32 fabulously rare drawings—including 31 color illustrations of costumes and accessories—for 1919 production of famous ballet. Edited by Parmenia Migel, who has written new introduction. 48pp. 9⅜ x 12¼. (Available in U.S. only)
23709-5 Pa. $5.00

NOTES OF A FILM DIRECTOR, Sergei Eisenstein. Greatest Russian filmmaker explains montage, making of Alexander Nevsky, aesthetics; comments on self, associates, great rivals (Chaplin), similar material. 78 illustrations. 240pp. 5⅜ x 8½.
22392-2 Pa. $4.50

HOLLYWOOD GLAMOUR PORTRAITS, edited by John Kobal. 145 photos capture the stars from 1926-49, the high point in portrait photography. Gable, Harlow, Bogart, Bacall, Hedy Lamarr, Marlene Dietrich, Robert Montgomery, Marlon Brando, Veronica Lake; 94 stars in all. Full background on photographers, technical aspects, much more. Total of 160pp. 8⅜ x 11¼. 23352-9 Pa. $6.00

THE NEW YORK STAGE: FAMOUS PRODUCTIONS IN PHOTO-GRAPHS, edited by Stanley Appelbaum. 148 photographs from Museum of City of New York show 142 plays, 1883-1939. *Peter Pan, The Front Page, Dead End, Our Town,* O'Neill, hundreds of actors and actresses, etc. Full indexes. 154pp. 9½ x 10. 23241-7 Pa. $6.00

DIALOGUES CONCERNING TWO NEW SCIENCES, Galileo Galilei. Encompassing 30 years of experiment and thought, these dialogues deal with geometric demonstrations of fracture of solid bodies, cohesion, leverage, speed of light and sound, pendulums, falling bodies, accelerated motion, etc. 300pp. 5⅜ x 8½. 60099-8 Pa. $4.00

THE GREAT OPERA STARS IN HISTORIC PHOTOGRAPHS, edited by James Camner. 343 portraits from the 1850s to the 1940s: Tamburini, Mario, Caliapin, Jeritza, Melchior, Melba, Patti, Pinza, Schipa, Caruso, Farrar, Steber, Gobbi, and many more—270 performers in all. Index. 199pp. 8⅜ x 11¼. 23575-0 Pa. $6.50

J. S. BACH, Albert Schweitzer. Great full-length study of Bach, life, background to music, music, by foremost modern scholar. Ernest Newman translation. 650 musical examples. Total of 928pp. 5⅜ x 8½. (Available in U.S. only) 21631-4, 21632-2 Pa., Two-vol. set $11.00

COMPLETE PIANO SONATAS, Ludwig van Beethoven. All sonatas in the fine Schenker edition, with fingering, analytical material. One of best modern editions. Total of 615pp. 9 x 12. (Available in U.S. only) 23134-8, 23135-6 Pa., Two-vol. set $15.00

KEYBOARD MUSIC, J. S. Bach. Bach-Gesellschaft edition. For harpsichord, piano, other keyboard instruments. English Suites, French Suites, Six Partitas, Goldberg Variations, Two-Part Inventions, Three-Part Sinfonias. 312pp. 8⅛ x 11. (Available in U.S. only) 22360-4 Pa. $6.95

FOUR SYMPHONIES IN FULL SCORE, Franz Schubert. Schubert's four most popular symphonies: No. 4 in C Minor ("Tragic"); No. 5 in B-flat Major; No. 8 in B Minor ("Unfinished"); No. 9 in C Major ("Great"). Breitkopf & Hartel edition. Study score. 261pp. 9⅜ x 12¼. 23681-1 Pa. $6.50

THE AUTHENTIC GILBERT & SULLIVAN SONGBOOK, W. S. Gilbert, A. S. Sullivan. Largest selection available; 92 songs, uncut, original keys, in piano rendering approved by Sullivan. Favorites and lesser-known fine numbers. Edited with plot synopses by James Spero. 3 illustrations. 399pp. 9 x 12. 23482-7 Pa. $9.95

PRINCIPLES OF ORCHESTRATION, Nikolay Rimsky-Korsakov. Great classical orchestrator provides fundamentals of tonal resonance, progression of parts, voice and orchestra, tutti effects, much else in major document. 330pp. of musical excerpts. 489pp. 6½ x 9¼. 21266-1 Pa. $7.50

TRISTAN UND ISOLDE, Richard Wagner. Full orchestral score with complete instrumentation. Do not confuse with piano reduction. Commentary by Felix Mottl, great Wagnerian conductor and scholar. Study score. 655pp. 8⅛ x 11. 22915-7 Pa. $13.95

REQUIEM IN FULL SCORE, Giuseppe Verdi. Immensely popular with choral groups and music lovers. Republication of edition published by C. F. Peters, Leipzig, n. d. German frontmaker in English translation. Glossary. Text in Latin. Study score. 204pp. 9⅜ x 12¼. 23682-X Pa. $6.00

COMPLETE CHAMBER MUSIC FOR STRINGS, Felix Mendelssohn. All of Mendelssohn's chamber music: Octet, 2 Quintets, 6 Quartets, and Four Pieces for String Quartet. (Nothing with piano is included). Complete works edition (1874-7). Study score. 283 pp. 9⅜ x 12¼. 23679-X Pa. $7.50

POPULAR SONGS OF NINETEENTH-CENTURY AMERICA, edited by Richard Jackson. 64 most important songs: "Old Oaken Bucket," "Arkansas Traveler," "Yellow Rose of Texas," etc. Authentic original sheet music, full introduction and commentaries. 290pp. 9 x 12. 23270-0 Pa. $7.95

COLLECTED PIANO WORKS, Scott Joplin. Edited by Vera Brodsky Lawrence. Practically all of Joplin's piano works—rags, two-steps, marches, waltzes, etc., 51 works in all. Extensive introduction by Rudi Blesh. Total of 345pp. 9 x 12. 23106-2 Pa. $14.95

BASIC PRINCIPLES OF CLASSICAL BALLET, Agrippina Vaganova. Great Russian theoretician, teacher explains methods for teaching classical ballet; incorporates best from French, Italian, Russian schools. 118 illustrations. 175pp. 5⅜ x 8½. 22036-2 Pa. $2.50

CHINESE CHARACTERS, L. Wieger. Rich analysis of 2300 characters according to traditional systems into primitives. Historical-semantic analysis to phonetics (Classical Mandarin) and radicals. 820pp. 6⅛ x 9¼. 21321-8 Pa. $10.00

EGYPTIAN LANGUAGE: EASY LESSONS IN EGYPTIAN HIERO-GLYPHICS, E. A. Wallis Budge. Foremost Egyptologist offers Egyptian grammar, explanation of hieroglyphics, many reading texts, dictionary of symbols. 246pp. 5 x 7½. (Available in U.S. only) 21394-3 Clothbd. $7.50

AN ETYMOLOGICAL DICTIONARY OF MODERN ENGLISH, Ernest Weekley. Richest, fullest work, by foremost British lexicographer. Detailed word histories. Inexhaustible. Do not confuse this with *Concise Etymological Dictionary*, which is abridged. Total of 856pp. 6½ x 9¼. 21873-2, 21874-0 Pa., Two-vol. set $12.00

A MAYA GRAMMAR, Alfred M. Tozzer. Practical, useful English-language grammar by the Harvard anthropologist who was one of the three greatest American scholars in the area of Maya culture. Phonetics, grammatical processes, syntax, more. 301pp. 5⅜ x 8½.   23465-7 Pa. $4.00

THE JOURNAL OF HENRY D. THOREAU, edited by Bradford Torrey, F. H. Allen. Complete reprinting of 14 volumes, 1837-61, over two million words; the sourcebooks for *Walden*, etc. Definitive. All original sketches, plus 75 photographs. Introduction by Walter Harding. Total of 1804pp. 8½ x 12¼.   20312-3, 20313-1 Clothbd., Two-vol. set $50.00

CLASSIC GHOST STORIES, Charles Dickens and others. 18 wonderful stories you've wanted to reread: "The Monkey's Paw," "The House and the Brain," "The Upper Berth," "The Signalman," "Dracula's Guest," "The Tapestried Chamber," etc. Dickens, Scott, Mary Shelley, Stoker, etc. 330pp. 5⅜ x 8½.   20735-8 Pa. $4.50

SEVEN SCIENCE FICTION NOVELS, H. G. Wells. Full novels. *First Men in the Moon, Island of Dr. Moreau, War of the Worlds, Food of the Gods, Invisible Man, Time Machine, In the Days of the Comet.* A basic science-fiction library. 1015pp. 5⅜ x 8½. (Available in U.S. only)
20264-X Clothbd. $8.95

ARMADALE, Wilkie Collins. Third great mystery novel by the author of *The Woman in White* and *The Moonstone*. Ingeniously plotted narrative shows an exceptional command of character, incident and mood. Original magazine version with 40 illustrations. 597pp. 5⅜ x 8½.
23429-0 Pa. $6.00

MASTERS OF MYSTERY, H. Douglas Thomson. The first book in English (1931) devoted to history and aesthetics of detective story. Poe, Doyle, LeFanu, Dickens, many others, up to 1930. New introduction and notes by E. F. Bleiler. 288pp. 5⅜ x 8½. (Available in U.S. only)
23606-4 Pa. $4.00

FLATLAND, E. A. Abbott. Science-fiction classic explores life of 2-D being in 3-D world. Read also as introduction to thought about hyperspace. Introduction by Banesh Hoffmann. 16 illustrations. 103pp. 5⅜ x 8½.
20001-9 Pa. $2.00

THREE SUPERNATURAL NOVELS OF THE VICTORIAN PERIOD, edited, with an introduction, by E. F. Bleiler. Reprinted complete and unabridged, three great classics of the supernatural: *The Haunted Hotel* by Wilkie Collins, *The Haunted House at Latchford* by Mrs. J. H. Riddell, and *The Lost Stradivarious* by J. Meade Falkner. 325pp. 5⅜ x 8½.
22571-2 Pa. $4.00

AYESHA: THE RETURN OF "SHE," H. Rider Haggard. Virtuoso sequel featuring the great mythic creation, Ayesha, in an adventure that is fully as good as the first book, *She*. Original magazine version, with 47 original illustrations by Maurice Greiffenhagen. 189pp. 6½ x 9¼.
23649-8 Pa. $3.50

UNCLE SILAS, J. Sheridan LeFanu. Victorian Gothic mystery novel, considered by many best of period, even better than Collins or Dickens. Wonderful psychological terror. Introduction by Frederick Shroyer. 436pp. 5⅜ x 8½.   21715-9 Pa. $6.00

JURGEN, James Branch Cabell. The great erotic fantasy of the 1920's that delighted thousands, shocked thousands more. Full final text, Lane edition with 13 plates by Frank Pape. 346pp. 5⅜ x 8½.
23507-6 Pa. $4.50

THE CLAVERINGS, Anthony Trollope. Major novel, chronicling aspects of British Victorian society, personalities. Reprint of Cornhill serialization, 16 plates by M. Edwards; first reprint of full text. Introduction by Norman Donaldson. 412pp. 5⅜ x 8½.   23464-9 Pa. $5.00

KEPT IN THE DARK, Anthony Trollope. Unusual short novel about Victorian morality and abnormal psychology by the great English author. Probably the first American publication. Frontispiece by Sir John Millais. 92pp. 6½ x 9¼.   23609-9 Pa. $2.50

RALPH THE HEIR, Anthony Trollope. Forgotten tale of illegitimacy, inheritance. Master novel of Trollope's later years. Victorian country estates, clubs, Parliament, fox hunting, world of fully realized characters. Reprint of 1871 edition. 12 illustrations by F. A. Faser. 434pp. of text. 5⅜ x 8½.   23642-0 Pa. $5.00

YEKL and THE IMPORTED BRIDEGROOM AND OTHER STORIES OF THE NEW YORK GHETTO, Abraham Cahan. Film *Hester Street* based on *Yekl* (1896). Novel, other stories among first about Jewish immigrants of N.Y.'s East Side. Highly praised by W. D. Howells—Cahan "a new star of realism." New introduction by Bernard G. Richards. 240pp. 5⅜ x 8½.   22427-9 Pa. $3.50

THE HIGH PLACE, James Branch Cabell. Great fantasy writer's enchanting comedy of disenchantment set in 18th-century France. Considered by some critics to be even better than his famous *Jurgen*. 10 illustrations and numerous vignettes by noted fantasy artist Frank C. Pape. 320pp. 5⅜ x 8½.   23670-6 Pa. $4.00

ALICE'S ADVENTURES UNDER GROUND, Lewis Carroll. Facsimile of ms. Carroll gave Alice Liddell in 1864. Different in many ways from final Alice. Handlettered, illustrated by Carroll. Introduction by Martin Gardner. 128pp. 5⅜ x 8½.   21482-6 Pa. $2.00

FAVORITE ANDREW LANG FAIRY TALE BOOKS IN MANY COLORS, Andrew Lang. The four Lang favorites in a boxed set—the complete *Red, Green, Yellow* and *Blue* Fairy Books. 164 stories; 439 illustrations by Lancelot Speed, Henry Ford and G. P. Jacomb Hood. Total of about 1500pp. 5⅜ x 8½.   23407-X Boxed set, Pa. $14.95

HOUSEHOLD STORIES BY THE BROTHERS GRIMM. All the great Grimm stories: "Rumpelstiltskin," "Snow White," "Hansel and Gretel," etc., with 114 illustrations by Walter Crane. 269pp. 5⅜ x 8½.
21080-4 Pa. $3.50

SLEEPING BEAUTY, illustrated by Arthur Rackham. Perhaps the fullest, most delightful version ever, told by C. S. Evans. Rackham's best work. 49 illustrations. 110pp. 7⅞ x 10¾.   22756-1 Pa. $2.50

AMERICAN FAIRY TALES, L. Frank Baum. Young cowboy lassoes Father Time; dummy in Mr. Floman's department store window comes to life; and 10 other fairy tales. 41 illustrations by N. P. Hall, Harry Kennedy, Ike Morgan, and Ralph Gardner. 209pp. 5⅜ x 8½.   23643-9 Pa. $3.00

THE WONDERFUL WIZARD OF OZ, L. Frank Baum. Facsimile in full color of America's finest children's classic. Introduction by Martin Gardner. 143 illustrations by W. W. Denslow. 267pp. 5⅜ x 8½.
20691-2 Pa. $3.50

THE TALE OF PETER RABBIT, Beatrix Potter. The inimitable Peter's terrifying adventure in Mr. McGregor's garden, with all 27 wonderful, full-color Potter illustrations. 55pp. 4¼ x 5½. (Available in U.S. only)
22827-4 Pa. $1.25

THE STORY OF KING ARTHUR AND HIS KNIGHTS, Howard Pyle. Finest children's version of life of King Arthur. 48 illustrations by Pyle. 131pp. 6⅛ x 9¼.   21445-1 Pa. $4.95

CARUSO'S CARICATURES, Enrico Caruso. Great tenor's remarkable caricatures of self, fellow musicians, composers, others. Toscanini, Puccini, Farrar, etc. Impish, cutting, insightful. 473 illustrations. Preface by M. Sisca. 217pp. 8⅜ x 11¼.   23528-9 Pa. $6.95

PERSONAL NARRATIVE OF A PILGRIMAGE TO ALMADINAH AND MECCAH, Richard Burton. Great travel classic by remarkably colorful personality. Burton, disguised as a Moroccan, visited sacred shrines of Islam, narrowly escaping death. Wonderful observations of Islamic life, customs, personalities. 47 illustrations. Total of 959pp. 5⅜ x 8½.
21217-3, 21218-1 Pa., Two-vol. set $12.00

INCIDENTS OF TRAVEL IN YUCATAN, John L. Stephens. Classic (1843) exploration of jungles of Yucatan, looking for evidences of Maya civilization. Travel adventures, Mexican and Indian culture, etc. Total of 669pp. 5⅜ x 8½.   20926-1, 20927-X Pa., Two-vol. set $7.90

AMERICAN LITERARY AUTOGRAPHS FROM WASHINGTON IRVING TO HENRY JAMES, Herbert Cahoon, et al. Letters, poems, manuscripts of Hawthorne, Thoreau, Twain, Alcott, Whitman, 67 other prominent American authors. Reproductions, full transcripts and commentary. Plus checklist of all American Literary Autographs in The Pierpont Morgan Library. Printed on exceptionally high-quality paper. 136 illustrations. 212pp. 9⅛ x 12¼.   23548-3 Pa. $12.50

AN AUTOBIOGRAPHY, Margaret Sanger. Exciting personal account of hard-fought battle for woman's right to birth control, against prejudice, church, law. Foremost feminist document. 504pp. 5⅜ x 8½.
20470-7 Pa. $5.50

MY BONDAGE AND MY FREEDOM, Frederick Douglass. Born as a slave, Douglass became outspoken force in antislavery movement. The best of Douglass's autobiographies. Graphic description of slave life. Introduction by P. Foner. 464pp. 5⅜ x 8½. 22457-0 Pa. $5.50

LIVING MY LIFE, Emma Goldman. Candid, no holds barred account by foremost American anarchist: her own life, anarchist movement, famous contemporaries, ideas and their impact. Struggles and confrontations in America, plus deportation to U.S.S.R. Shocking inside account of persecution of anarchists under Lenin. 13 plates. Total of 944pp. 5⅜ x 8½.
22543-7, 22544-5 Pa., Two-vol. set $12.00

LETTERS AND NOTES ON THE MANNERS, CUSTOMS AND CONDITIONS OF THE NORTH AMERICAN INDIANS, George Catlin. Classic account of life among Plains Indians: ceremonies, hunt, warfare, etc. Dover edition reproduces for first time all original paintings. 312 plates. 572pp. of text. 6⅛ x 9¼. 22118-0, 22119-9 Pa.. Two-vol. set $12.00

THE MAYA AND THEIR NEIGHBORS, edited by Clarence L. Hay, others. Synoptic view of Maya civilization in broadest sense, together with Northern, Southern neighbors. Integrates much background, valuable detail not elsewhere. Prepared by greatest scholars: Kroeber, Morley, Thompson, Spinden, Vaillant, many others. Sometimes called Tozzer Memorial Volume. 60 illustrations, linguistic map. 634pp. 5⅜ x 8½.
23510-6 Pa. $7.50

HANDBOOK OF THE INDIANS OF CALIFORNIA, A. L. Kroeber. Foremost American anthropologist offers complete ethnographic study of each group. Monumental classic. 459 illustrations, maps. 995pp. 5⅜ x 8½.
23368-5 Pa. $13.00

SHAKTI AND SHAKTA, Arthur Avalon. First book to give clear, cohesive analysis of Shakta doctrine, Shakta ritual and Kundalini Shakti (yoga). Important work by one of world's foremost students of Shaktic and Tantric thought. 732pp. 5⅜ x 8½. (Available in U.S. only)
23645-5 Pa. $7.95

AN INTRODUCTION TO THE STUDY OF THE MAYA HIEROGLYPHS, Syvanus Griswold Morley. Classic study by one of the truly great figures in hieroglyph research. Still the best introduction for the student for reading Maya hieroglyphs. New introduction by J. Eric S. Thompson. 117 illustrations. 284pp. 5⅜ x 8½. 23108-9 Pa. $4.00

A STUDY OF MAYA ART, Herbert J. Spinden. Landmark classic interprets Maya symbolism, estimates styles, covers ceramics, architecture, murals, stone carvings as artforms. Still a basic book in area. New introduction by J. Eric Thompson. Over 750 illustrations. 341pp. 8⅜ x 11¼.
21235-1 Pa. $6.95

GEOMETRY, RELATIVITY AND THE FOURTH DIMENSION, Rudolf Rucker. Exposition of fourth dimension, means of visualization, concepts of relativity as Flatland characters continue adventures. Popular, easily followed yet accurate, profound. 141 illustrations. 133pp. 5⅜ x 8½.
23400-2 Pa. $2.75

THE ORIGIN OF LIFE, A. I. Oparin. Modern classic in biochemistry, the first rigorous examination of possible evolution of life from nitrocarbon compounds. Non-technical, easily followed. Total of 295pp. 5⅜ x 8½.
60213-3 Pa. $4.00

PLANETS, STARS AND GALAXIES, A. E. Fanning. Comprehensive introductory survey: the sun, solar system, stars, galaxies, universe, cosmology; quasars, radio stars, etc. 24pp. of photographs. 189pp. 5⅜ x 8½. (Available in U.S. only)
21680-2 Pa. $3.75

THE THIRTEEN BOOKS OF EUCLID'S ELEMENTS, translated with introduction and commentary by Sir Thomas L. Heath. Definitive edition. Textual and linguistic notes, mathematical analysis, 2500 years of critical commentary. Do not confuse with abridged school editions. Total of 1414pp. 5⅜ x 8½.　　60088-2, 60089-0, 60090-4 Pa., Three-vol. set $18.50

Prices subject to change without notice.

Available at your book dealer or write for free catalogue to Dept. GI, Dover Publications, Inc., 180 Varick St., N.Y., N.Y. 10014. Dover publishes more than 175 books each year on science, elementary and advanced mathematics, biology, music, art, literary history, social sciences and other areas.